George R. Anthonisen

Meditations on the Human Condition

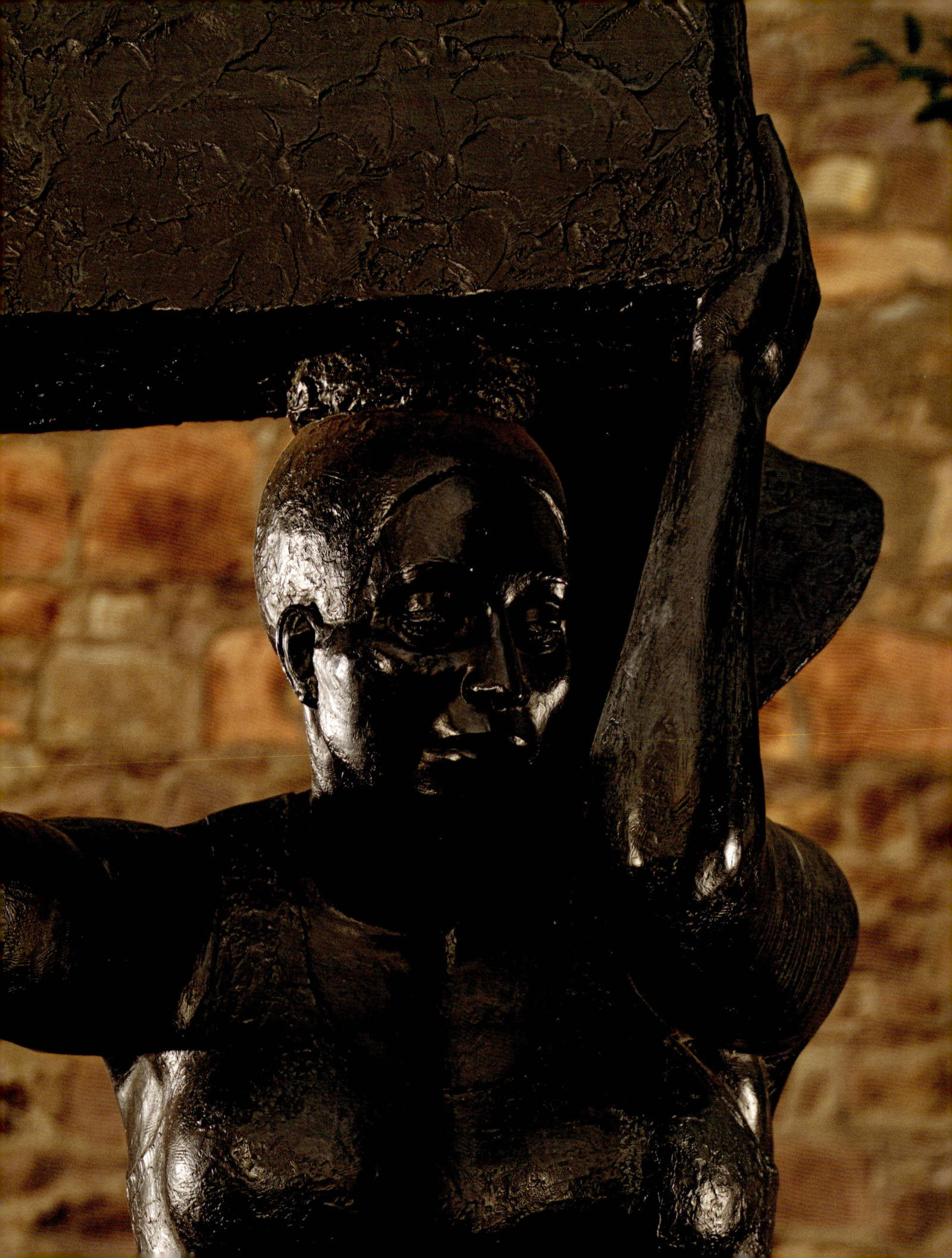

George R. Anthonisen
Meditations on the Human Condition

EDITED BY
Lisa Tremper Hanover

WITH CONTRIBUTIONS BY
Clarisse Fava-Piz AND
Laura Turner Igoe

JAMES A. MICHENER ART MUSEUM
UNIVERSITY OF PENNSYLVANIA PRESS

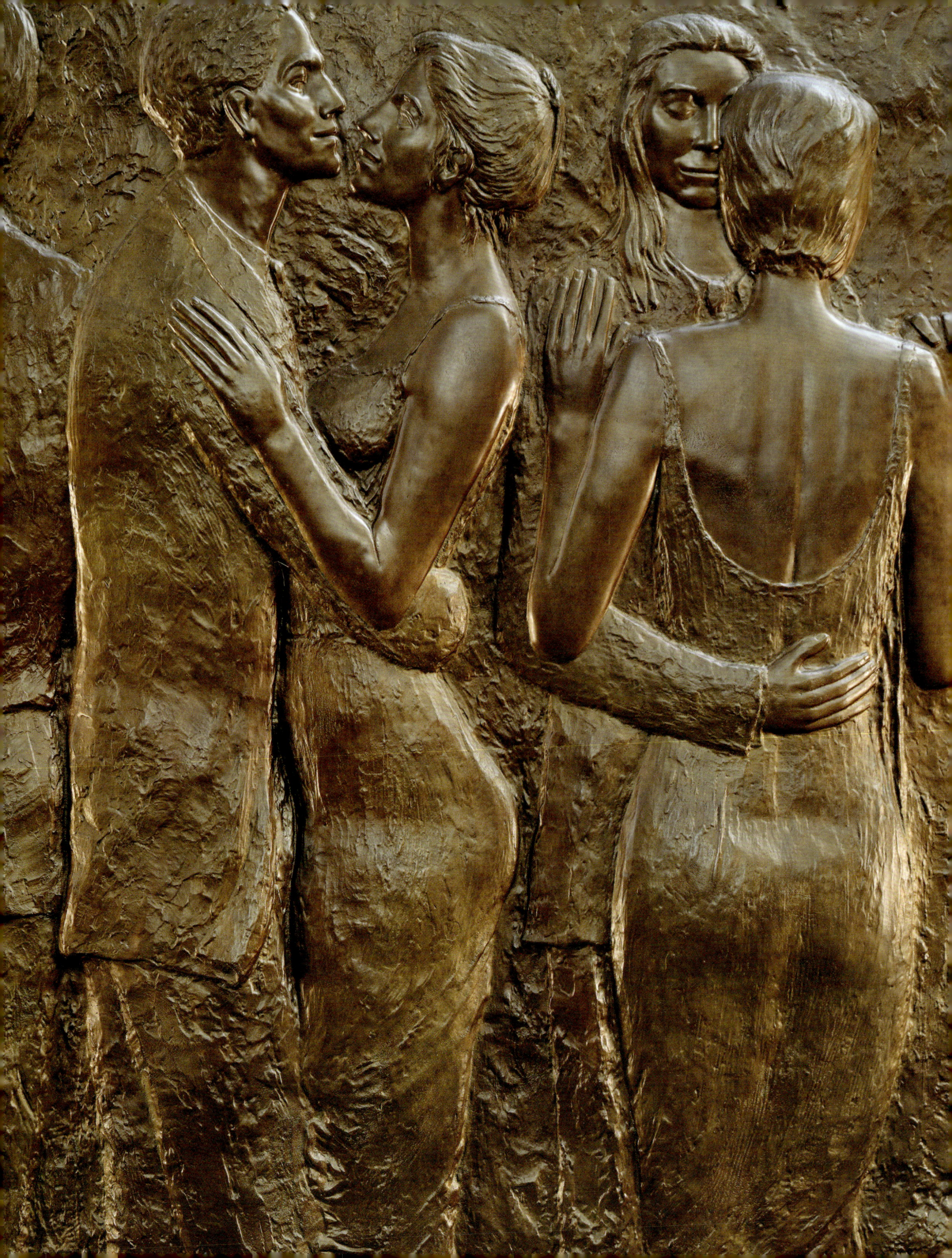

Contents

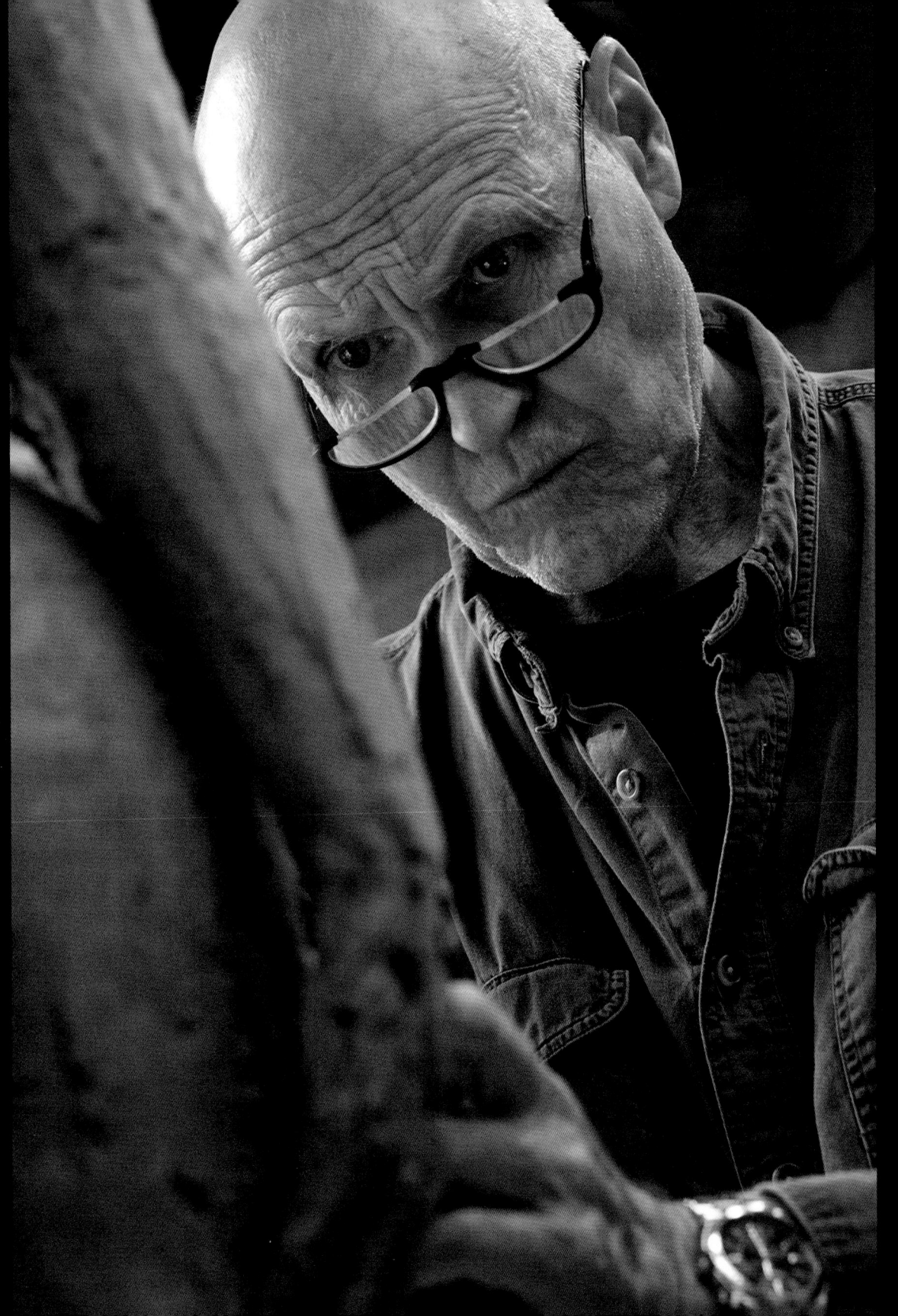

Director's Foreword

It has been my pleasure to know George Anthonisen for more than twenty years, so it is thrilling to see this publication and major exhibition of his work at the James A. Michener Art Museum come to fruition.

George R. Anthonisen: Meditations on the Human Condition explores and celebrates the work and career of a renowned sculptor who calls Bucks County home. His work is beautiful, thought provoking, and inspiring. Thank you to guest curator Lisa Tremper Hanover, who is dually versed in George's work and that of the Michener Art Museum. Her history with the artist, thoughtful insights, and skilled curation are so appreciated and evident in the exhibition and catalogue.

Thank you to the many generous donors who have made *George R. Anthonisen: Meditations on the Human Condition* possible, including Carol and Louis Della Penna, the Byers family, Ann and Daniel Bernstein, and Kathy and Ted Fernberger. Many thanks to Eddie and Cherry Robinson, who reached out to the Anthonisens more than two years ago to fully support this beautiful book. Finally, much gratitude is due to the late Henry W. Pfeiffer, whose support and contributions have been critical to George's legacy.

In addition, we are grateful to the team at Marquand Books, including Gina Broze, Adrian Lucia, Kestrel Rundle, Tom Eykemans, and Kristin Kearns, for their outstanding work on this publication.

They say that behind every successful man is a woman. Ellen Anthonisen's incredible support, determination, and talent for the business of art allowed George to focus on the art itself—and with such success! Finally, I wish to thank our Gerry and Marguerite Lenfest Chief Curator, Dr. Laura Turner Igoe, and my Michener colleagues for their support and commitment to this exciting project.

Dr. Vail P. Garvin
Executive Director, James A. Michener Art Museum

George R. Anthonisen, 2009.

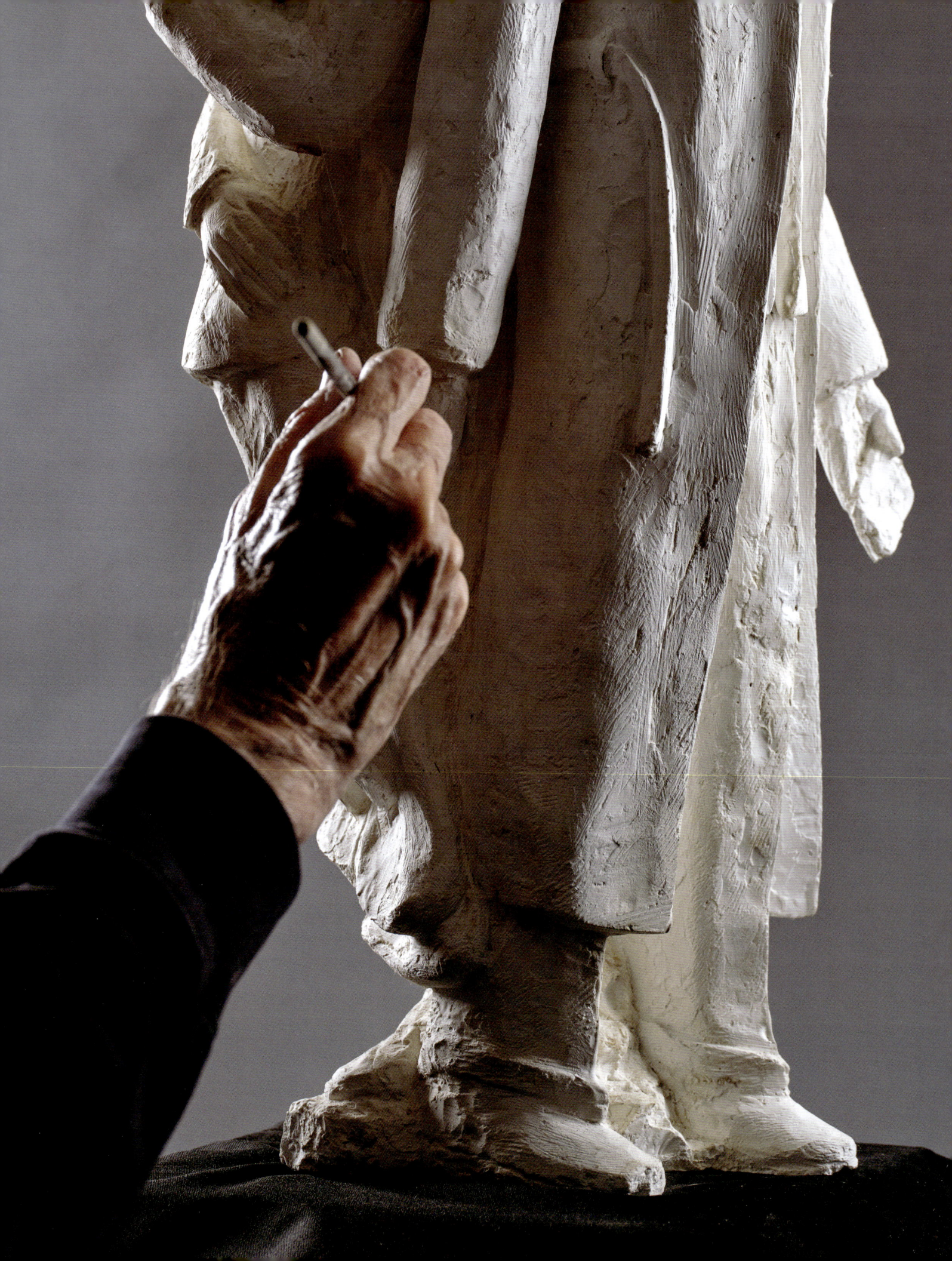

Artist Acknowledgments

Iᴛ ɪs ᴀ ᴘʟᴇᴀsᴜʀᴇ ᴛᴏ ᴄᴏɴᴠᴇʏ ᴍʏ ᴀᴘᴘʀᴇᴄɪᴀᴛɪᴏɴ ᴛᴏ ᴛʜᴏsᴇ ᴡʜᴏ ʜᴀᴠᴇ helped in preparing this exhibition and book, and to lenders who have allowed others to enjoy my works for a time.

I am particularly grateful to Gerry and Marguerite Lenfest Chief Curator Dr. Laura Turner Igoe, not only for mounting this exhibition but also for having the vision to link my work to that of Daniel Chester French and Augustus Saint-Gaudens, whose work is being shown concurrently with mine in the exhibition *Monuments and Myths: The America of Sculptors Augustus Saint-Gaudens and Daniel Chester French* (on view at the Michener Art Museum June 29, 2024, through January 5, 2025). French and Saint-Gaudens were my heroes, mentors, and teachers when I began working and remain so today. Thanks also to Dr. Clarisse Fava-Piz, whose interview questions and curatorial comments assist readers in understanding my work. Special thanks to project manager Evie Kalfaian, whose organizational expertise helped us all to stay on track.

I can never express enough gratitude to Lisa Tremper Hanover, guest curator of this exhibition. I cherish her unfailing support, involvement, enthusiasm, humor, advice, insight, and sense of fun, as I do our thirty-plus years of friendship. She and her husband, Stephen Hanover, are friends who go above and beyond the call of duty.

My appreciation and thanks to the Michener Art Museum's director of exhibitions, Joshua Lessard, for his vision in how to view my work. I am grateful to Mary Byrne, chief advancement officer, and the staff of the Michener for providing help whenever it was needed, and to interim executive director Dr. Vail Garvin for her relentless facility to connect people to one another.

I would be remiss if I neglected to acknowledge Rosa Giletti, art representative, who in 1992 with her quietly demanding demeanor introduced Lisa Tremper Hanover to my work.

My gratitude extends to Eddie and Cherry Robinson, whose belief in my work and generous contribution made it possible to engage Marquand Books to produce this book. Eddie's extraordinary ability to analyze and ask questions has fortified me for nearly forty years. His mentoring and friendship bring me constant joy.

George R. Anthonisen touching up *Raoul Wallenberg I* (1998–99), 2023.

I am forever thankful for the largest collectors of my work, Carol and Lou Della Penna, for their support and friendship; their steadfast belief in my work bolstered me during lean times and hopefully made them proud during successes. My gratitude to collectors of my work throughout my career of nearly sixty years cannot be overstated.

I would like to thank Daniel Bernstein and Walter (Nick) Waits for their constant support and encouragement. They have been there for me since the beginning, and I will hold them in my heart always.

Thanks to my teachers: Betty Gunther, my remedial reading teacher, who taught me the value of expressing my ideas and thoughts regardless of errors in spelling, grammar, and punctuation; Paul Aschenbach at the University of Vermont; Douglas Gorsline at the National Academy of Design; John Hovannes and José de Creeft of the Art Students League; art representative Peter Aaronson, who connected us to Gary Haller, headmaster of Jonathan Edwards College, Yale University; Dr. Donald Martin Reynolds, for his support, insight, and understanding of my work; Henry (Hank) W. Pfeiffer, who inspired me with his support for education and art and his love for life; and Hudson (Pete) Scattergood, whose knowledge about how institutions work gives me confidence to continue to follow my dreams.

I am grateful to Herman Silverman, Robert Byers, Ted and Kathy Fernberger, Helene and Mark Hankin, and others for their vision of enriching our community with the presence of a museum; Lauren Travis and Frank Bianco, art dealers of my work in the Delaware Valley; Charles (Chuck) and Barbara Gale, who introduced my work to those in the broader Philadelphia area; Tom Spain, who graciously came out of retirement to create, direct, and edit the documentary *Anthonisen Sculptor: George and Ellen Stories*; interior designer Miriam Ansell, whose business acumen enabled me to feed my family without anxiety; former congressman Peter H. Kostmayer, whose belief in my work introduced *I Set Before You This Day* to a national audience; and James Alperin, Thomas Alperin, Lucille and Jimmy Amadie, Ann Bernstein, Terry Bird, Robert Bresler, Sybil Costello, Dennis Haggerty, Joan Kahn, Susan Yacubian Klein, Lydia and Ben Kukoff, Susan and Stephen Leeds, Seena and David Levy, Richard Levy, Jon Palmer, Lynne and Alison Simpson, Claudia Waits, and Richard Weil Jr., all of whom were present from the start of my career, bolstering Ellen and me through highs and lows.

I want to express gratitude to my parents, Drs. Margaret and Niels Anthonisen, who gave me constant emotional, psychological, and financial support to pursue my passion, followed by my in-laws, Maxine and Sylvan Friedman, and my brothers, Dr. Nicholas Anthonisen and Theodore (Ted) Anthonisen, whose support for what I was doing never wavered.

I am also grateful to photographers Christian Giannelli and Michael E. Myers for the exceptional quality of their images in this book. My thanks to John Hoenstine, Stephen Barth, Carla M. Klouda, Robin Johnstone, and Stephen Perloff for the long hours they have spent unselfishly photographing my work throughout my career. Special thanks to Ted Nichols (New Hope Photo) and to lifelong friend Charles W. Haney, who hired me to supplement my income and spent years photographing my work. Thank you to Marquand Books for their painstaking attention to quality and visualizing how to present my work.

Thank you to my children, Rachel Anthonisen Gates and Daniel Anthonisen; son-in-law, Michael A. Gates; and granddaughter, Ursula Gates, whose loving criticism made me look more carefully at my work. Their understanding, tolerance, laughter, and belief in my work are a continual source of pleasure. Above all, to Ellen Anthonisen, my full partner in everything, who is equally involved in all the triumphs and joys of our life and work: My deepest thanks for a lifetime of unimaginable encouragement and support.

George R. Anthonisen

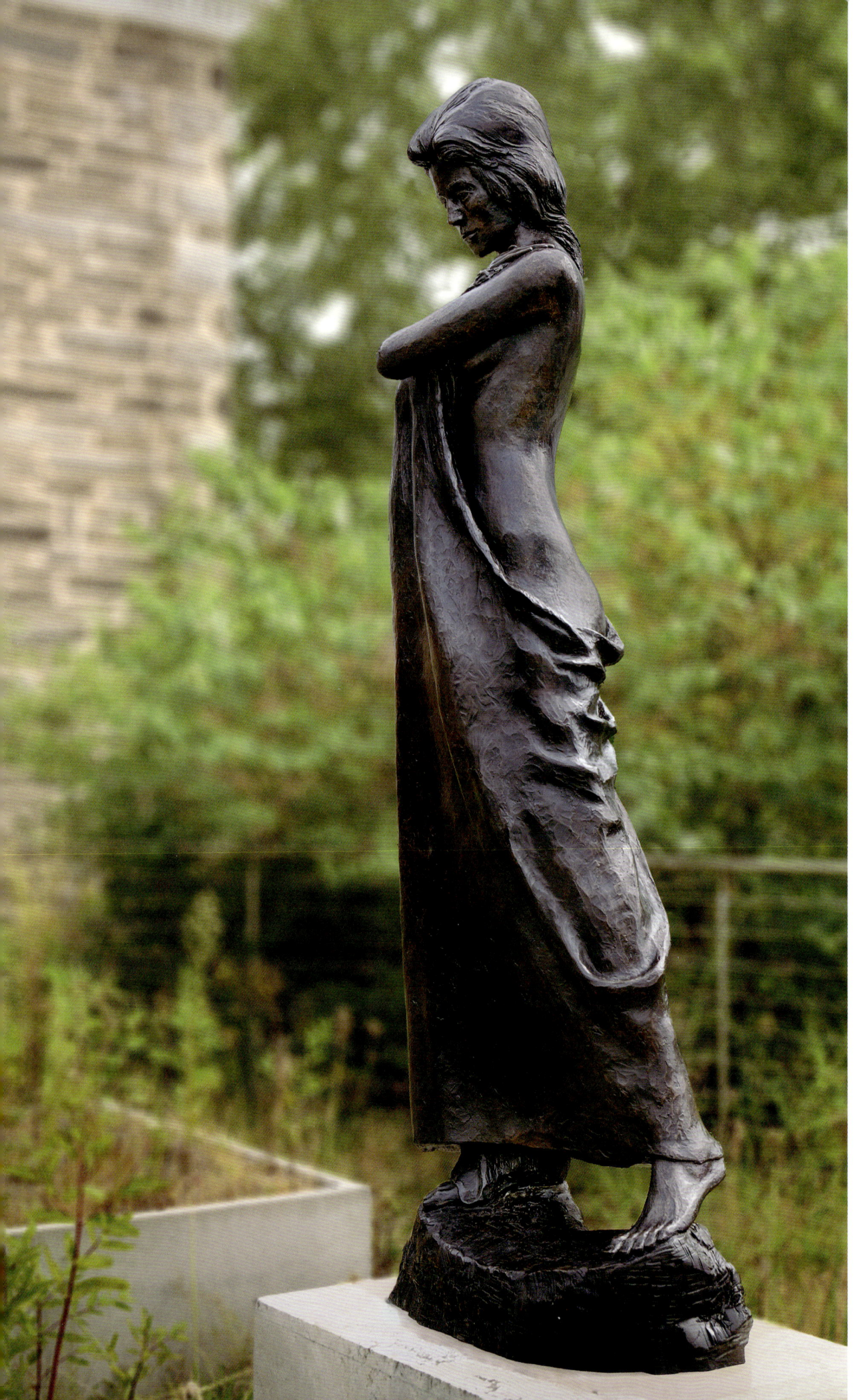

Introduction

Anthonisen's [sculptures] both engage and express the totality of the human person—body, mind, and spirit. While they are vehicles of cultural, social, and moral commentary, they are marvels of formal conception and design. Moreover, in celebrating humanity and life, Anthonisen's images ennoble anew the venerable traditions throughout the history of art in which conception and execution, art and craft, are inseparable.

—DONALD MARTIN REYNOLDS, PHD,
"THE HUMANIZING IMAGES OF GEORGE R. ANTHONISEN"

SINCE ESTABLISHING HIS STUDIO IN SOLEBURY, BUCKS COUNTY, Pennsylvania, in 1971, sculptor George R. Anthonisen (b. 1936) has composed and executed figurative work that is evocative, challenging, expressive, and courageous. The arc of his career includes major commissions, service as sculptor in residence at the Saint-Gaudens National Historical Park, and museum exhibitions. His sculptures have been the subject of symposia and academic and artistic gatherings, as well as numerous essays and articles.

Born and educated in Vermont, Anthonisen knew early on that his primary mode of expression was creating visual dialogues. Well versed in history and current events, the artist thinks critically about the human condition and people's capacity to destroy, to create, to question, and to make noble choices.

This book and the exhibition it accompanies are a tribute to Anthonisen's long career as a figurative sculptor, known for his thoughtful and sometimes haunting content and for championing the elegance and strength of the female form. The James A. Michener Art Museum holds his most important triumvirate of sculptures—*I Set Before You This Day* (Pls. 13–15), *Give Us Grace* (Pls. 42–43), and *Caryatid* (Pls. 47–48)—along with several more works that address important topics in myth and history. George Anthonisen and his wife,

Detail of Plate 41.

Ellen Anthonisen (b. 1934), are a formidable team who have worked hard to establish this artist in the canon of twentieth- and twenty-first-century figurative expression. Major commissions and placements of work in important sites around the world, and notably with several Bucks County–based collectors, point to a distinguished career.

The curatorial team at the Michener Art Museum, especially Gerry and Marguerite Lenfest Chief Curator Dr. Laura Turner Igoe and director of exhibitions Joshua T. Lessard, embraced and executed this significant installation and accompanying publication and provided a collegial infrastructure for my work on behalf of the artist and the museum.

In my capacity as a museum director and curator, I have been a stalwart champion of the Anthonisens since the early 1990s and have had the pleasure of exhibiting, writing about, and lecturing on George Anthonisen's work. This book and exhibition represent the pinnacle of recognition, and the book will serve as a lasting testimonial to a remarkable man and career.

Lisa Tremper Hanover
Guest Curator

EPIGRAPH

Donald Martin Reynolds, "The Humanizing Images of George R. Anthonisen," in *The Compassionate Spirit: Sculpture and Fresco by George R. Anthonisen* (Collegeville, PA: Philip and Muriel Berman Museum of Art, Ursinus College, 1996), 8.

George R. Anthonisen working on *Mother and Child*, ca. 1967.

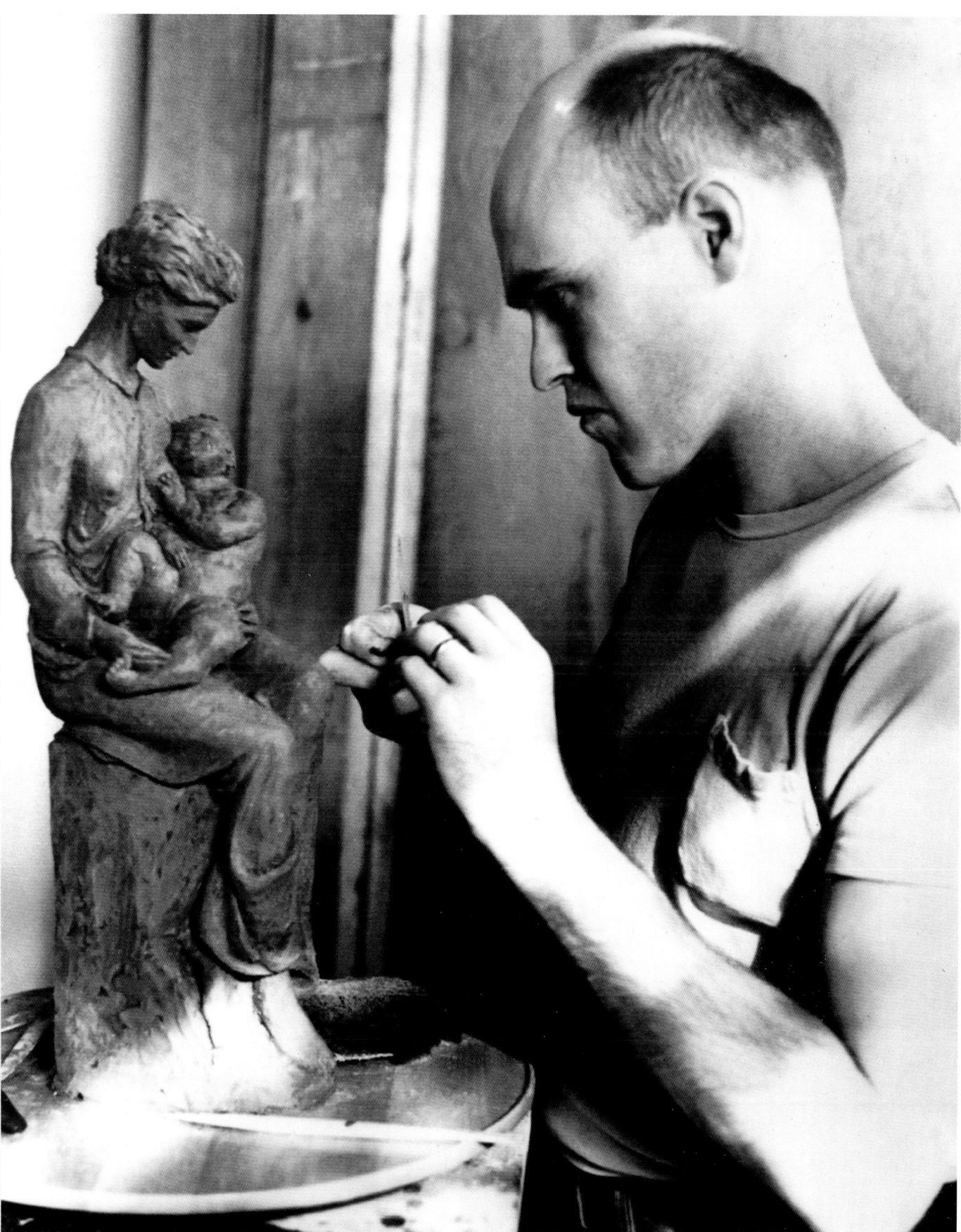

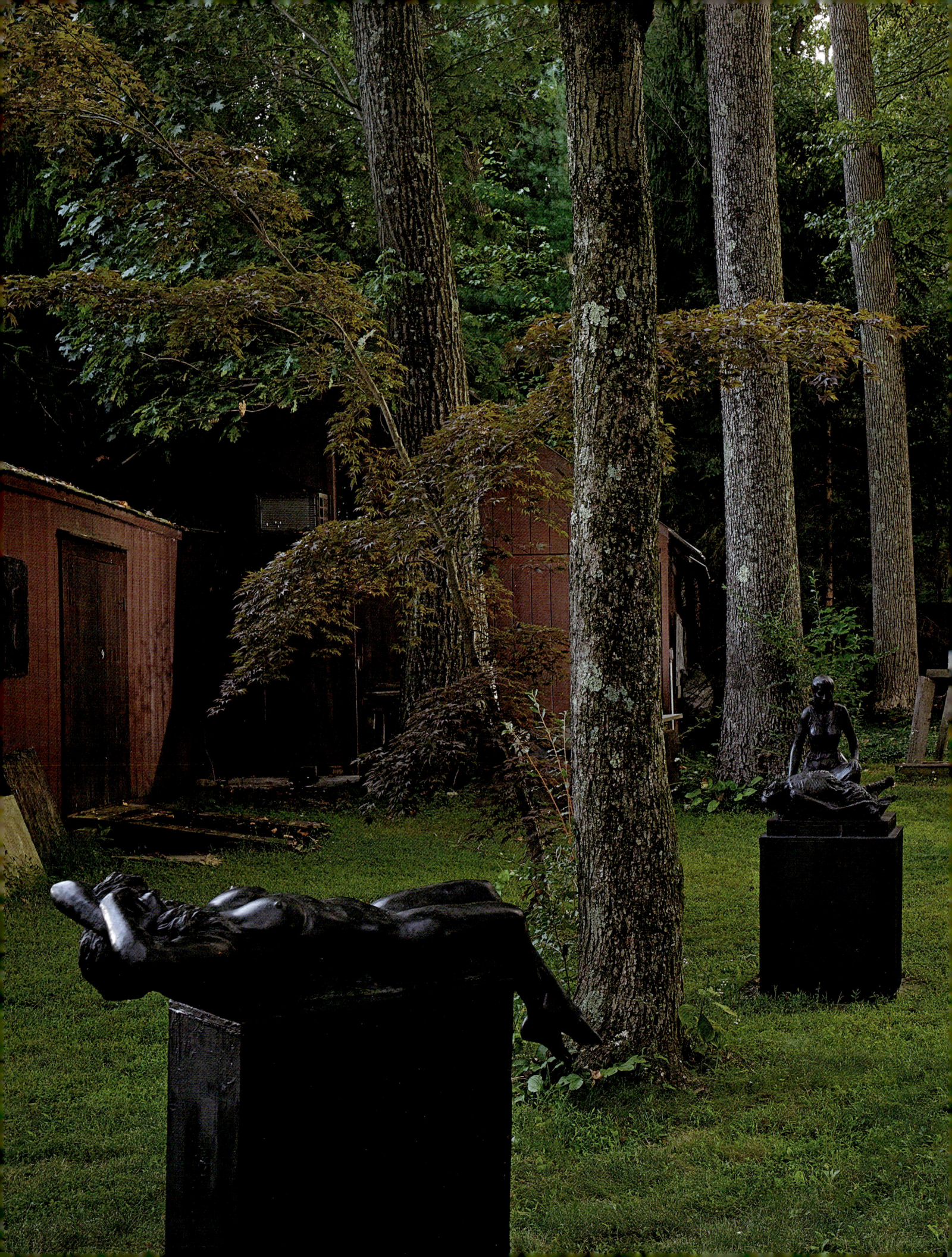

Challenges, Triumphs, and Resilience: A Biography of George R. Anthonisen

LISA TREMPER HANOVER

STEP INTO THE FOYER OF GEORGE AND ELLEN ANTHONISEN'S HOME of over fifty years in Solebury, Bucks County, Pennsylvania, and you are met with a wide range of sculptures, bas-reliefs, frescoes, and drawings representative of the artist's long career. Works by their equally talented son and daughter mingle with examples by other favored artists from the region. An enormous library occupies an expansive, twelve-foot-high wall, bursting with books on art history, mythology, philosophy, poetry, and biography, as well as classical music CDs and pottery. In the backyard, numerous bronzes, editioned for the artist, lead to George's studio, forming an outdoor gallery (Fig. 1). The studio itself is filled with fifty years' worth of clay remnants, maquettes, and unfinished sculptures; a well-worn chair; and the tools necessary for crafting the three-dimensional and bas-relief figures that define the artist's practice (Fig. 2).

At the respective ages of eighty-eight and ninety, George and Ellen, lovingly depicted in a painting by their son, Daniel (Fig. 3), have built a robust and synergetic life, using their individual strengths to grow a family and a livelihood of longevity and substance. Theirs is a remarkable story that continues to flourish.

THE EARLY YEARS

George Rioch Anthonisen was born in 1936 in Boston, Massachusetts, to first-generation immigrant parents. His father, Niels, was from Norway, and his mother, Margaret Rioch, from Canada; they met at Johns Hopkins University, in Baltimore, Maryland, each studying psychiatry. George was the middle of three sons; Nicholas was the oldest and Theodore, the youngest (Fig. 4). The family shared a love of the outdoors, including hiking, picnicking, and fishing, enjoyments George has embraced throughout his life.

The Anthonisens moved to Brattleboro, Vermont, in 1941, when George was five. As immigrants, they wanted to ensure that their children learned the important history of the United States and appreciated music and literature. They read together each evening—*Little House on the Prairie*, *The Deerslayer*, *Treasure Island*, and other classics. *Life* magazine was an influential weekly, and its episodic series of articles and photographs during World War II stuck with

Figure 1. The Anthonisens' backyard sculpture installation, 2023.

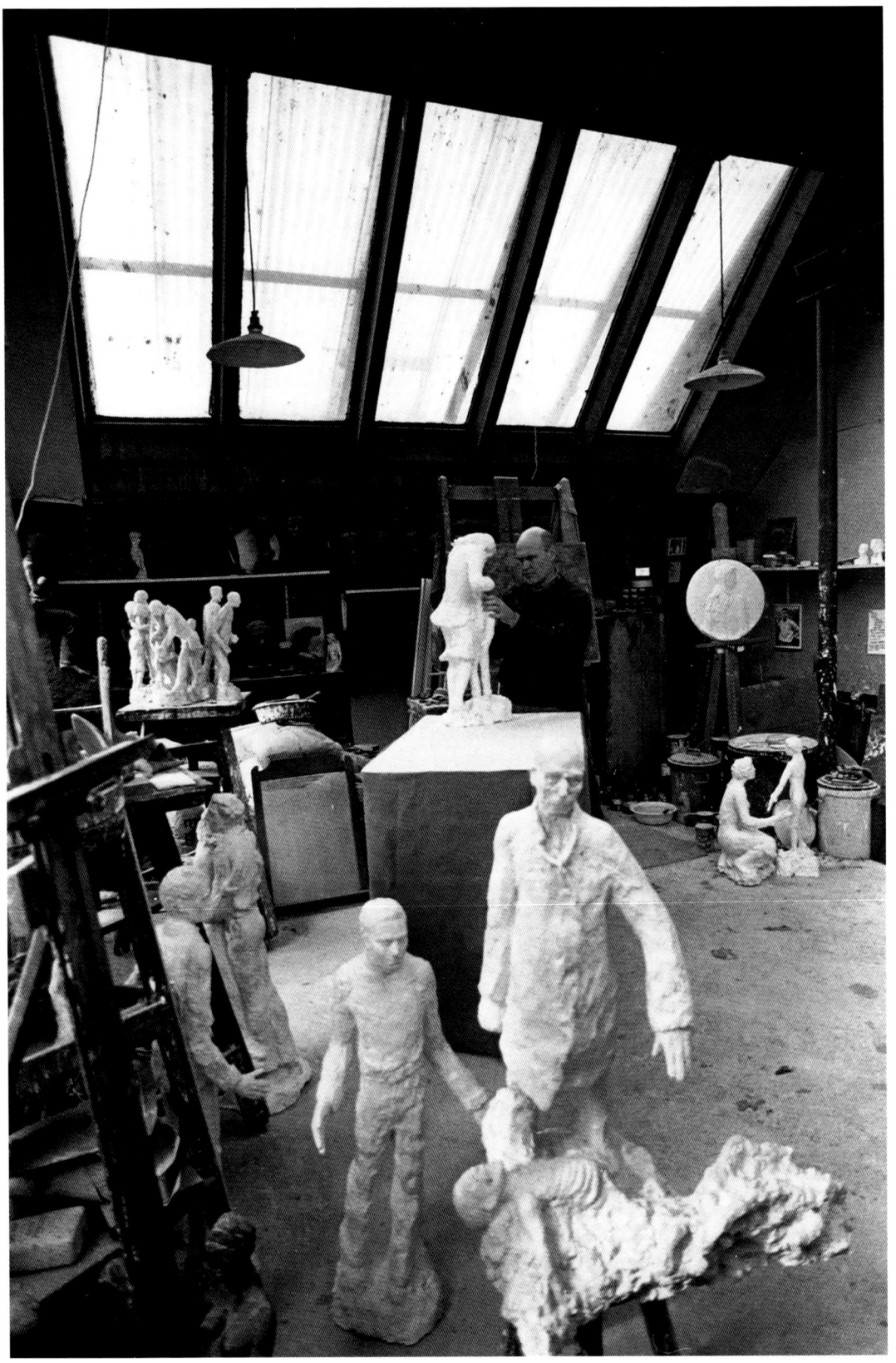

Figure 2. George Anthonisen in his studio, 1985.

GEORGE R. ANTHONISEN: MEDITATIONS ON THE HUMAN CONDITION

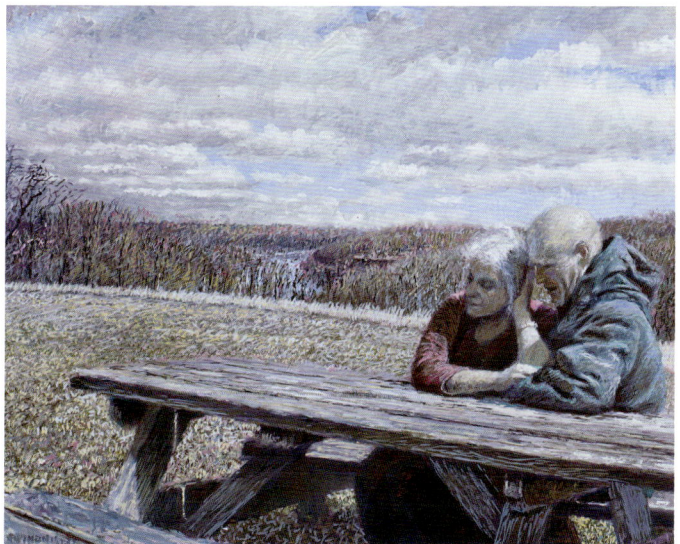

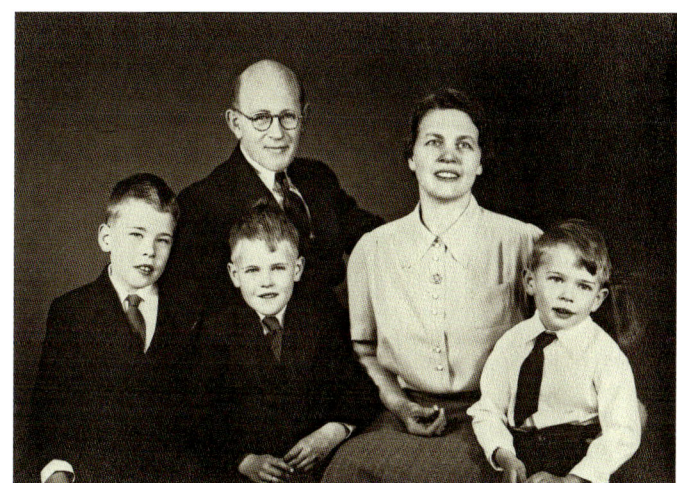

Figure 3. Daniel Anthonisen (b. 1970), *Union*, 2015. Casein on gesso panel, 8 × 10 inches. Collection of George and Ellen Anthonisen.

Figure 4. Nicholas R. Anthonisen, Niels L. Anthonisen, George R. Anthonisen, Margaret R. Anthonisen, and Theodore R. Anthonisen, Brattleboro, Vermont, 1943.

George as an uncensored look at war. All three brothers were athletic, playing football, ice hockey, and baseball, and remained mutually supportive of each other throughout their lives.

George was diagnosed with dyslexia at age five, an unusually early diagnosis, but given his parents' base of knowledge, they were able to act on it and shape how he learned. He spent two summers in Hancock, Vermont, with a family friend, Elizabeth (Betty) Gunther, who tutored him for an hour a day. Gunther understood how dyslexia alters perceptual abilities, and she focused on a tactile and three-dimensional visual language of learning. Her father had been the head of the American Academy in Rome when she was young, and their home was filled with art objects, books, and musical instruments and records; these items did not go unnoticed by George. Gunther's triplet teenage daughters also made an impression and gave him early exposure to the female form. Gunther introduced him to the books of Lynd Ward (1905–1985), who used elaborate woodcuts to tell his stories without words, and these resonated with George, too. Yet it was also essential that he learn how to write, and Gunther guided this process, reinforcing the importance of slow and deliberate concentration.

Because of his parents' interests and wide circle of colleagues, George was exposed to a cadre of interesting, educated people: female pilots, scholars of psychoanalysis, musicians, and adventurers. He would talk with them about their pursuits, and the experiences they shared fed his curiosity about the world. Attentive and intuitive, he learned from what they told him and went on to explore those experiences extensively in his work.

This chronicle of Anthonisen's early life is important in defining how this artist interacted with and absorbed, learned, and modeled from his sphere of relatives, friends, teachers, and colleagues. The strength, confidence, and nurturing personality of George's mother, echoed in his wife, Ellen, and other formidable women in his life, are personified in numerous sculptures and bas-reliefs, including *Generations* (Fig. 5) and *Dialogue* (Pl. 58).

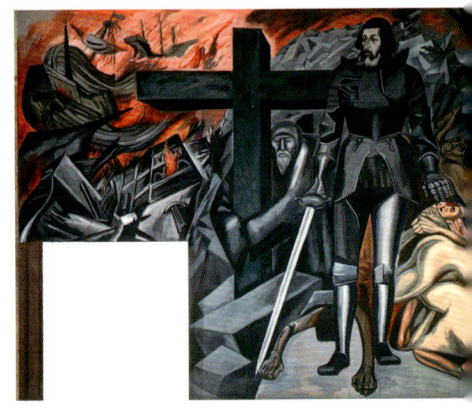

Even with knowledge of his dyslexia, the educational system was not equipped to adapt to his style of learning, so school became more difficult for George. At sixteen, he was given the opportunity to attend Sidwell Friends School, a Quaker school in Washington, DC, through friends of his parents. He had a high IQ but not the grades; his football prowess, however, was a needed talent and gained him acceptance to the school. George modeled his brother Nick's gregarious personality and, living away from home, had no boundaries or constructs, so his academics suffered further. After that first year, he moved in with the football coach; tutors were engaged, and he learned to apply himself with discipline and hard work. Over fifty years later, in 2009, Ursinus College, a liberal arts institution that houses a large collection of the artist's sculpture, bestowed upon him an honorary doctor of humane letters, in recognition of his reflective and insightful contributions to the history of figurative sculpture.

His experience at Sidwell Friends was a transformative one because at the time of his attendance, the school was segregated. Its physical location drew white applicants from the North and the South, and this mixture of progressive and conservative students from diverse backgrounds led to tensions and turmoil. These interactions were not lost on George, who had a deep, ethical sense of justice and fairness, and further shaped his vision.

Another defining moment came with an assignment that required him to research a topic at the Library of Congress. Daunted by this task, George wrote a short, yet insightful, paper with few footnotes based on his observations of José Clemente Orozco's (1883–1949) mural *The Epic of American Civilization* in Dartmouth College's Baker Library (Fig. 6). His mother took him several times to see the Orozco mural, a salient anthropological study of Mexican politics and economics. George's power of observation, in spite of the essay's lack of formal structure, struck his teacher.

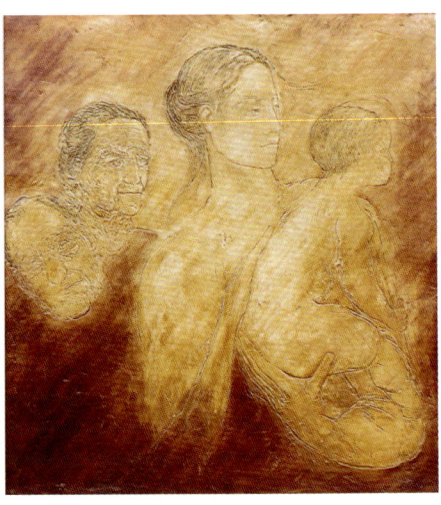

He later had a powerful encounter with the Edward Steichen–curated exhibition *The Family of Man*, mounted in 1955 at the Museum of Modern Art, in New York. Steichen (1879–1973), then the director of MoMA's department of photography, brought together work that showcased a global expression of the universal aspects of the human experience from birth to death. Hundreds of photographers contributed images pertaining to themes including relationships (lovers, couples, marriage), the birth cycle, family dynamics, classical music, dance, religious expression, loneliness, compassion, aspiration, famine, inhumanity, and "man's judgment," to name a few. Every one of these themes became a touchstone in George's work.

George graduated from Sidwell Friends but was not ready to take on the rigors of college, so he volunteered for the draft in 1955 and served in the army for two years. He trained at Fort Knox, Kentucky, with airborne units converted to infantry and artillery support and experienced the integration of the army,

Figure 5. George R. Anthonisen (b. 1936), *Generations*, 1979. Mineral colors on cast Hydrocal, 30 × 31 inches. Collection of Charles W. Haney.

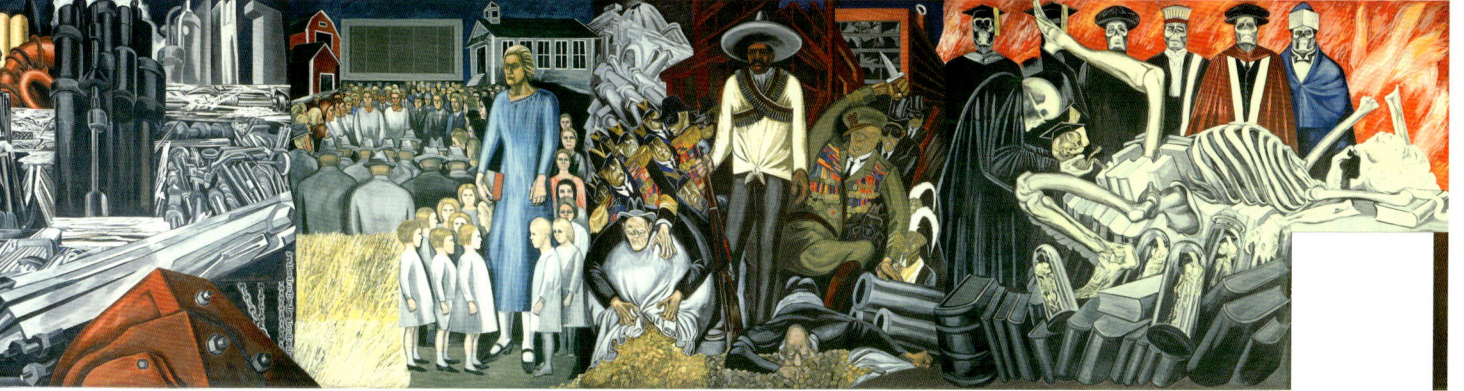

initiated by President Harry S. Truman. He gained new perspectives on history and American culture from the Black soldiers he served with. He was eventually stationed in Germany. This was only ten years after the end of World War II, and George experienced the Germans' continued adherence to Nazi philosophy during his tenure there.

While the concepts and realities of wartime made an impact, it was the classical sculptures the Winged Victory of Samothrace and the Venus de Milo that most impressed George. On leave in Paris, George toured the Louvre with no expectations yet was altered by these powerful and intricate expressions of beauty. Likewise, Michelangelo's (1475–1564) *Rebellious Slave* (Fig. 7), a heroic and muscular figure emerging from raw and textured marble, was a marvel of articulation, almost abstract in nature. These sculptures later inspired several of George's own explorations of the human figure, including *Heroic Torso* (Pl. 1) and *Torso III Drape* (Fig. 8).

Service in the army brought maturity and provided opportunities to attend college, and George enrolled at the University of Vermont in 1958. He majored in English, an ironic choice given his dyslexia. As a junior, he took a painting course, but the medium did not offer the dimensionality he craved, so he enrolled in a sculpture course. As soon as he touched the clay, he was transformed. The university library was a font of information on the great masters of sculpture, and he was motivated. In his determination to make art a career, he had the great support of his parents, who provided financial resources for George to study art and establish a studio.

THE NEW YORK CITY YEARS

University of Vermont professor Paul Aschenbach (1921–1994), a stone and metal sculptor and advocate for public art placements, was a mentor to Anthonisen. Aschenbach, who created abstract, welded monuments, appreciated Anthonisen's evocative figurative work and encouraged him to go to school in New York City. In 1961, Aschenbach took Anthonisen to the National Academy

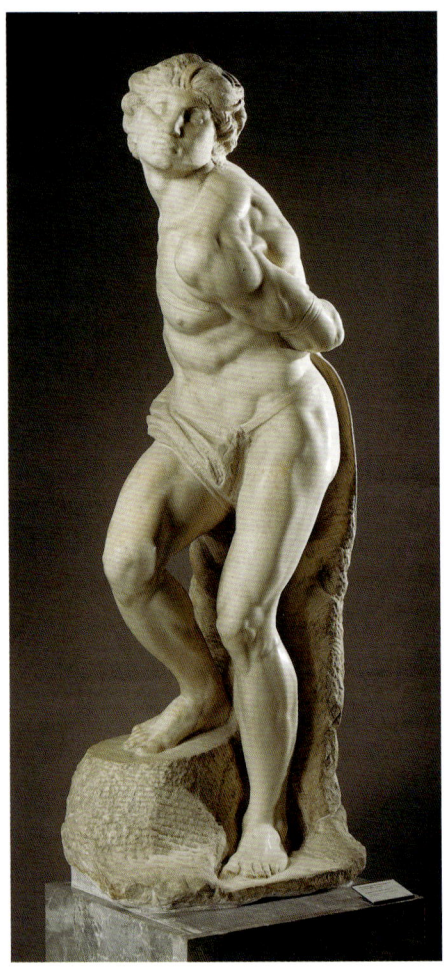

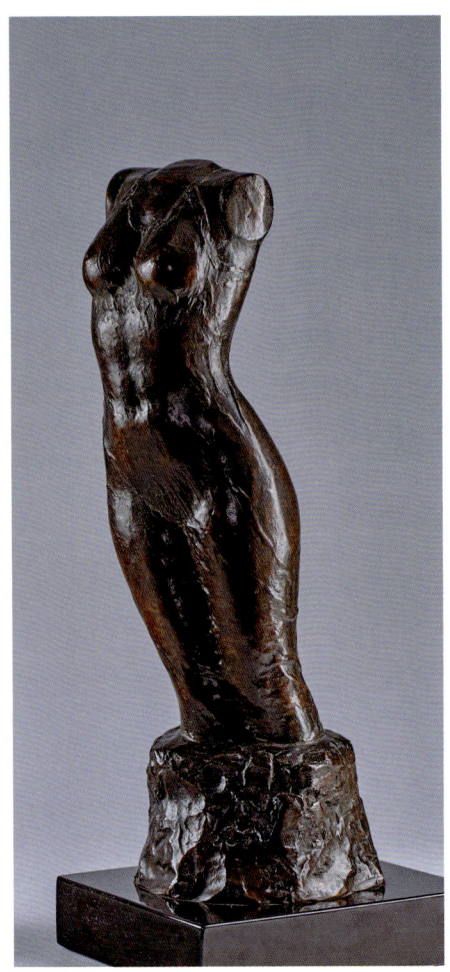

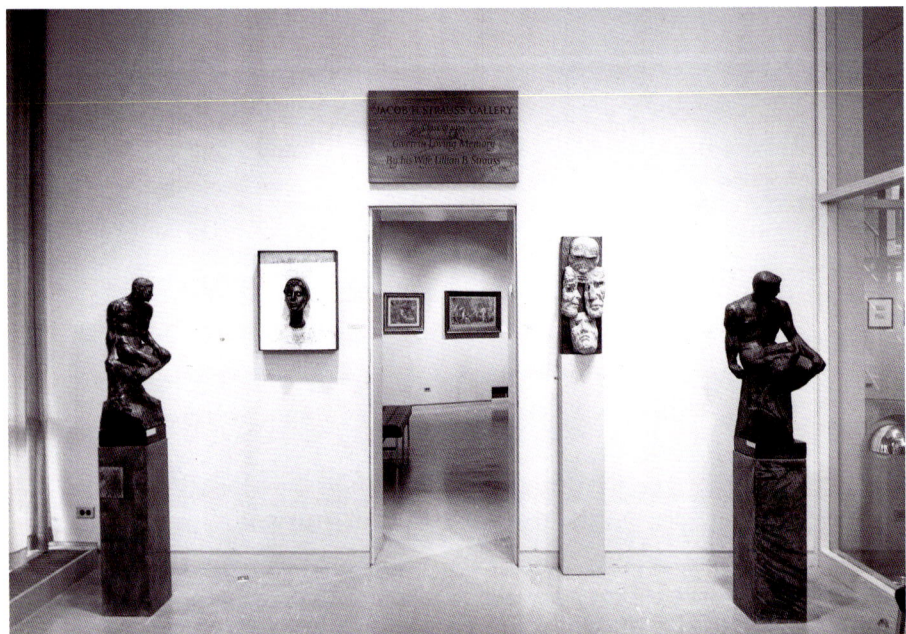

Figure 7. Michelangelo Buonarroti (1475–1564), *Rebellious Slave*, 1513–15. Marble, 85 inches high. Musée du Louvre.

Figure 8. George R. Anthonisen (b. 1936), *Torso III Drape*, 2001. Bronze, 15 × 5 × 4 inches. Edition 2/9. Collection of the artist.

Figure 9. Installation photograph of the exhibition at the Hopkins Center, Dartmouth College, 1966.

of Design, one of the only academies still teaching the figure. This was Anthonisen's first time working with live models. He immediately understood the power of the figure in telling a story.

Through the connections of his parents, Anthonisen spent a semester at Dartmouth Medical School, where he dissected a cadaver alongside medical students. Experiencing the incredible engineering of the layers of muscle and bone and veins and organs was a powerful lesson that, as it had for the nineteenth-century painter Thomas Eakins (1844–1916), informed his understanding of the vocabulary of the figure. The intricate interplay of limbs, hands, feet, and fingers has delicacy and power. Thanks to this training in anatomy, Anthonisen understood the importance of movement and gesture, his expression of which became more nuanced over time.

Anthonisen's exposure to the great classical sculptures and close study of the human form led him to excel in the execution of the female nude, of which *Aspiration* is a prime example (Pl. 61). These nudes are not sinewy; they are robust and strong, dynamic and intelligent, yet elegant, like a dancer's stretches. A series dedicated to movement—arching backs, sensual draped torsos, arms elevated and reaching—reveals muscular tension coupled with a kind of ecstasy and passion reflected in the faces. "My work with the female figures has become a symbol for humankind at its finest. Not just a physical interpretation, I try to imbue the female figure, face, and texture with intelligence, vigor, and all of the qualities that I believe make up a fulfilled human being," says the artist.[1]

New York City was exciting and full of energy. Museum and gallery visits, classes, one year at the National Academy of Design, and two years at the Art Students League further informed Anthonisen's approach to his work—technically and in its content. He learned that there were important organizations that recognized, honored, and provided opportunities to artists, such as Allied Artists of America, Audubon Artists, and the National Sculpture Society, and he pursued these affiliations while enjoying all that New York had to offer.

Anthonisen received his first professional exhibition at the Hopkins Center at Dartmouth College in 1966 (Fig. 9). In preparation for the show, he needed to build a body of work, so he rented a studio in a posh area of the city, near a bar called Chips. This hangout for professionals ranging from newscasters to female impersonators provided a great social balance to solitary studio work. It was here that he met Ellen Friedman (b. 1934), a dynamic personality who continues to provide the emotional and organizational support that frees the artist to focus and create.

George and Ellen married in 1966, and both worked as educators, with George teaching sculpture at Fairleigh Dickinson University, in New Jersey, and drawing at the Fashion Institute of Technology, in New York. He recognized talent and energy in his students and motivated them by example rather than through a prescribed curriculum.

The Civil Rights Movement, which was gathering strength in 1967, influenced Anthonisen's sense of social justice, as reflected in his choice of subject matter. He sculpted *Standing Nude* (Pl. 2), depicting an elegant and elongated Black female, and *Heroic Torso*, reminiscent of the Michelangelo sculptures he viewed in the late 1950s. *Standing Nude* was eventually purchased through the United Negro College Fund and donated to Clark Atlanta University, a historically Black college, in 1975.

The Anthonisens' children, Rachel (b. 1967) and Daniel (b. 1970), were both born in New York, but it was becoming increasingly difficult to make a living and raise a family in an urban environment. They were motivated to consider other locales that inspired artistic practice. With the encouragement of Gene LePere (b. 1926), daughter of entrepreneur and art collector Joseph Hirshhorn (1899–1981), they explored Bucks County, renowned locus of the Pennsylvania Impressionists, who painted in the region in the early twentieth century. In May 1971, the Anthonisens bought the Solebury home they live in today.

THE AUGUSTUS SAINT-GAUDENS RESIDENCY

Also in 1971, Anthonisen applied for and was awarded a sculptor-in-residence fellowship by the US Department of the Interior at the Augustus Saint-Gaudens (1848–1907) home and studio in Cornish, New Hampshire. Anthonisen's mother had passed in December 1970, and the family stayed with his father in his home in Hanover. The residency, which ran through the summer of 1971 and into October, affirmed Anthonisen's focus on the figure as the core of the stories he needed to tell.

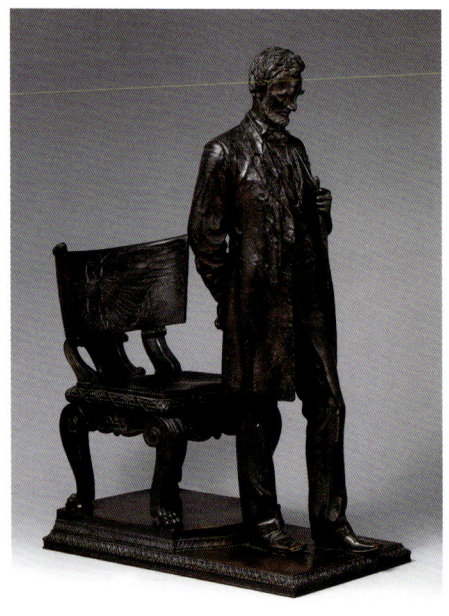
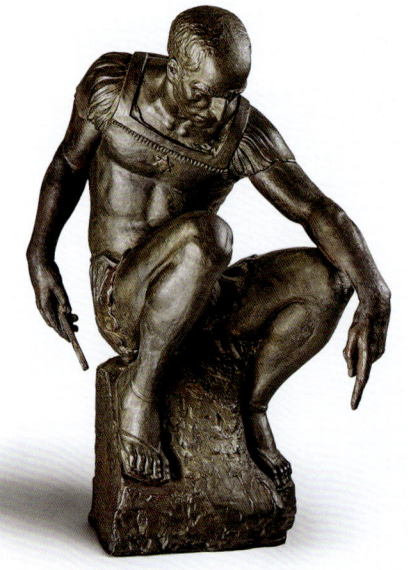

Figure 10. Augustus Saint-Gaudens (1848–1907), *Abraham Lincoln: The Man (Standing Lincoln)*, 1884–87, reduced 1910, cast 1911. Bronze, 40½ × 16½ × 30¼ inches. The Metropolitan Museum of Art.

Figure 11. George R. Anthonisen (b. 1936), *Solomon*, 1972–74. Plaster, 26 × 21 × 12 inches. The Philip and Muriel Berman Museum of Art at Ursinus College.

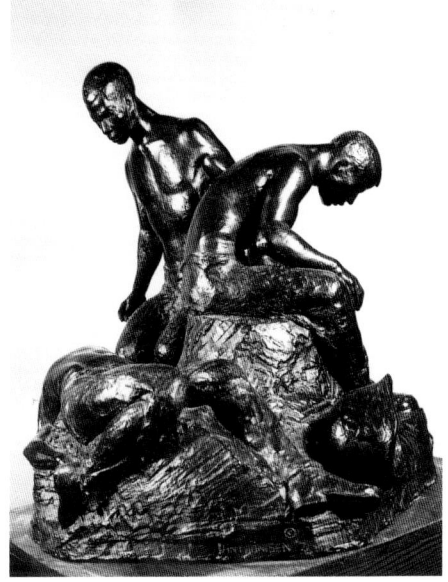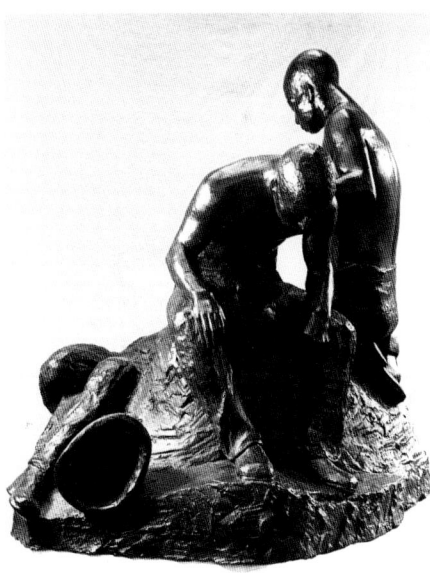

Figures 12–13. George R. Anthonisen (b. 1936), *Memorial: Three Soldiers*, 1971. Plaster, 26 × 26 inches. Collection of Rachel Anthonisen Gates.

The Augustus Saint-Gaudens home and studio was at the time a relatively new site and is now a National Historic Site operated by the National Park Service. Anthonisen recalls that the site was in disarray, with little in the way of organization, catalogued objects, or interpretive content. Yet the magic of Saint-Gaudens's sculptures and bas-reliefs resonated with him, and he felt like he had direction for the kind of work he wanted to execute. Saint-Gaudens understood the concept of the monumental—in scale and in content (Fig. 10). His work made statements about people and events that Anthonisen felt strongly about, and his sculptures inspired Anthonisen's *Solomon* (Fig. 11). In particular, Anthonisen was struck by Saint-Gaudens's plaster sculpture of Abraham Lincoln, which was housed on the grounds, and he learned that Saint-Gaudens was a mentor and teacher to Daniel Chester French (1850–1931), who executed the statue of Lincoln in the Lincoln Memorial in Washington, DC, in 1920.

Anthonisen had a studio on the edge of the property, where visitors could drop in and see how a sculptor worked. Studying Saint-Gaudens's work in sculpture and bas-relief taught him the processes involved in moving from clay to plaster to bronze and in carving and incising stone. These lessons eventually informed the fresco "paintings" Anthonisen conceived and executed beginning in the late 1970s. He completed two pieces during this time: a reclining nude bas-relief and a sculpture titled *Memorial: Three Soldiers* (Figs. 12–13), a statement about death and the Vietnam War.

This residency gave Anthonisen discipline, direction, and a mindset that served as a springboard for his career and sustained him for years to come. In other words, it gave him an artistic identity.

THE GERSHWIN PORTRAIT BUST AND
THE NATIONAL SCULPTURE SOCIETY

The Center Art Gallery on 57th Street, New York, run by Evelyn Marks, represented Anthonisen following the Saint-Gaudens residency. Marks, a former companion to George Gershwin (1898–1937), encouraged him to model a head of Gershwin and use it as part of his portfolio for consideration by the National Sculpture Society. Professors from the National Academy of Design and fellow artists endorsed Anthonisen's application, and he was elected to the society in 1973.

The following year, Gershwin's sister, the musician and performer Frances Gershwin Godowsky (1906–1999), offered Anthonisen's portrait bust (Pl. 4) to Carnegie Hall, which accepted with great fanfare and publicity. The endorsement of the Gershwin family and a desire to revive Gershwin's music motivated both the donation and the acceptance. Daniel Bernstein, a high school friend of the Anthonisens, officially became the Anthonisens' attorney and advised them on this and other negotiations throughout his career.

Portrait busts comprise an important part of George Anthonisen's canon, and his remarkable ability to imbue his bronzes with nuances of personality matches his skill in achieving likeness. He has executed at least sixteen bas-reliefs and over thirty busts, including ones of his patron Robert L. Byers (1938–2020) and neuroscientist David McKenzie Rioch (1900–1985) (Fig. 14), as well as a brilliant interpretation of Pablo Picasso (1881–1973) as a man and cubist construction (Pls. 26–28), referencing the artistic style for which Picasso is best known.

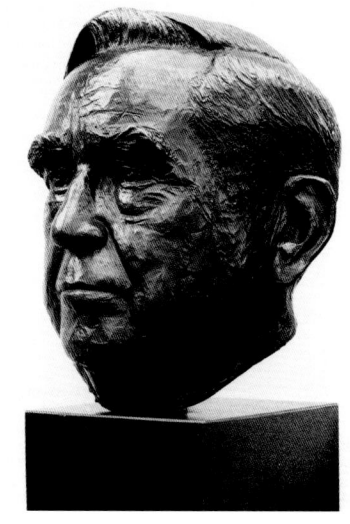

Figure 14. George R. Anthonisen (b. 1936), *David McKenzie Rioch, MD*, 1974. Bronze, life-size. Edition 1/1. Walter Reed Army Institute of Research.

THE SENATOR ERNEST GRUENING COMMISSION

The National Sculpture Society (NSS) controlled many of the monument commissions throughout the country. The director of the NSS, Claire Stein, recognized Anthonisen's work ethic and talent, although he didn't fit the conservative mold that predominated among the society's membership. In 1976, the NSS submitted a list of artists to take part in a competition to execute a life-size sculpture of Ernest Gruening, senator from Alaska from 1959 to 1969. The list did not include Anthonisen's name, but Stein encouraged him to compete individually without the endorsement of the NSS.

Anthonisen traveled to Washington, DC, to see the commemorative sculpted portraits on view in the US Capitol and determine how he would present his vision of Gruening. His original bust was executed in plaster. Maquettes submitted to the competition were judged blindly by the senator's widow and other family members, along with the Alaska State Council on the Arts. Anthonisen won the commission, a validation of his work and direction. While this initially caused a rift with the NSS because Anthonisen did not win under its auspices, the organization nevertheless named him a fellow, its highest honor, that same year.

BUCKS COUNTY AND BEYOND

The success of the Gershwin bust led to recognition of Anthonisen in the *Doylestown Intelligencer*. Katharine Steele Renninger (1925–2004), a respected artist and a powerhouse in Bucks County, played a role in introducing the Anthonisens to patrons and collectors. Anthonisen's first Bucks County exhibition was at Stover Mill in 1974 with the painter Paul Matthews (1933–2019). While abstraction, op art, and pop art were the predominant artistic expressions during this time, Matthews and Anthonisen spoke a similar language about realism in art, and no one else was executing the figure. Matthews was good friends with Anthonisen and later painted a portrait of him (Fig. 15).

In 1985, Anthonisen again exhibited with Matthews, as well as sculptor Charles Wells (1935–2017), in an exhibition at Rodman House, a precursor to the James A. Michener Art Museum. Titled *Artists Three*, the installation brought the artists recognition beyond the region, further establishing their reputations.

Also in 1985, a serendipitous meeting resulted in the acquisition of *Death and Starvation* (Pl. 8) by the World Health Organization (WHO), which was forming a conference in Geneva, Switzerland, to focus on global poverty. President Jimmy Carter was the honorary chairman of the conference, a powerful endorsement for the organization. Anthonisen had made *Death and Starvation* in 1976 in response to the famine in Biafra, now part of Nigeria. A collector saw the sculpture in his studio and shared information about it with Japanese businessman Ryoichi Sasakawa, a philanthropist and sponsor of the WHO's anti-hunger campaign. Sasakawa acquired the work and donated it to the conference site.

In this raw and powerful sculpture, a maternal warrior envisioned in the guise of death cradles a frail, starving figure, a symbol of those affected by famine all over the world. Conceived out of Anthonisen's deep interest in social justice and equity, this signature composition remains relevant today.

In 1997, the Ursinus College classes of the World War II years (1942–1949) commissioned Anthonisen to create a monumental bronze bas-relief diptych documenting the idyllic life on campus, the call to arms, and the heat of battle. *Promise/Anthem* (Pls. 53–54) was dedicated and sited in a central building on campus in 1998.

THE TRIUMVIRATE

George Anthonisen's sculptural triumvirate of *I Set Before You This Day* (Pls. 13–15), *Give Us Grace* (Pls. 42–43), and *Caryatid* (Pls. 47–48) comprises

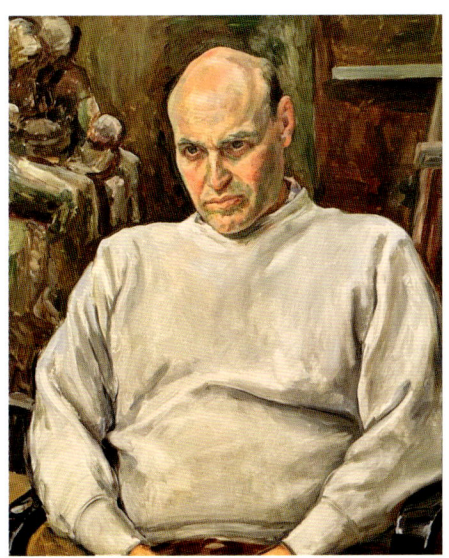

Figure 15. Paul Matthews (1933–2019), *Portrait of George Anthonisen*, 1985. Oil on canvas, 31 × 26 inches. From the home of Brent and Janet Anthonisen.

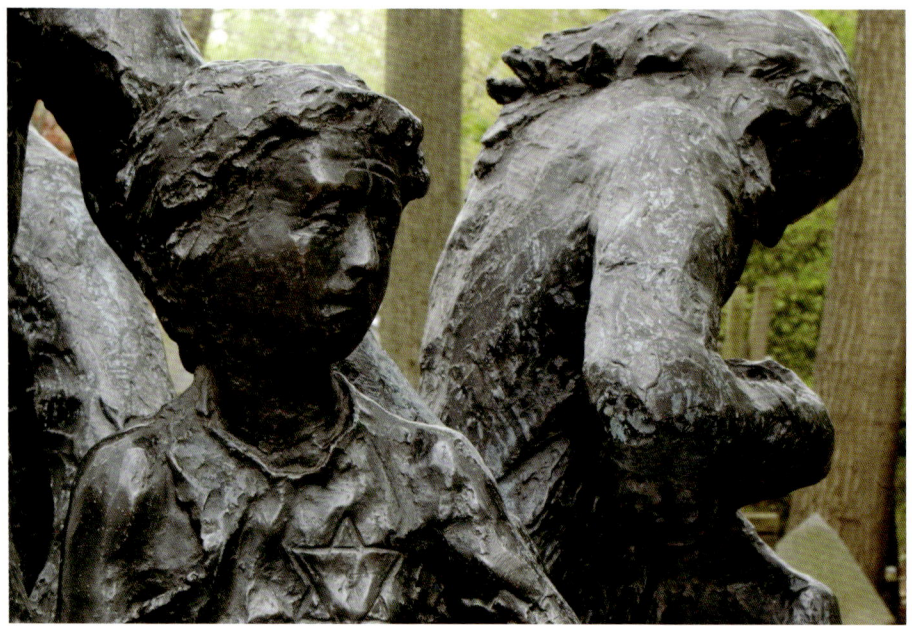

Figure 16. George R. Anthonisen (b. 1936), *I Set Before You This Day* (detail), 1979–87. Bronze, 37 × 29 × 28 inches. Edition 1/9. Collection of Helene and Mark Hankin.

individual artistic statements that were executed sequentially and are philosophically informed by and connected to each other. These works comment on diversity, making choices, and individual responsibility.

Alfred Ronald, a Holocaust survivor, saw *Murder: Cain and Abel* (Pl. 5), a powerful and spare interpretation of sibling brutality, and *Death and Starvation* and requested a meeting with Anthonisen. Haunted by what he could have done to help others during that horrific time, Ronald was interested in how the artist would interpret the trauma of the Holocaust and the deliberate actions taken to save Jews from extermination. The concept of sacrifice versus self-preservation resonated with Anthonisen, who studied Holocaust history and executed different versions of a sculptural grouping between 1979 and 1987. *I Set Before You This Day*, whose title is inspired by Deuteronomy 30:19, features a cadaver as the central, explicit focus of attention. The attitudes of the surrounding figures, depicted in various states of denial, distress, and action, remind us of the risks taken and choices made (Fig. 16). This is man divided. Anthonisen has acknowledged Auguste Rodin's (1840–1917) *The Burghers of Calais* (1884–95) (see Fig. 3 on p. 44), documenting the surrender of the citizens (burghers) of the French city of Calais to England during the Hundred Years' War, as a source of inspiration for *I Set Before You This Day*. Rodin's monumental sculpture portrays six leaders who are prepared to sacrifice themselves to spare the rest of the city's residents.

I Set Before You This Day has been showcased in exhibitions, including as part of major symposia,[2] and shown in the Capitol Rotunda in Washington, DC. It also inspired a series of maquettes, made in 1998–2000, focused on

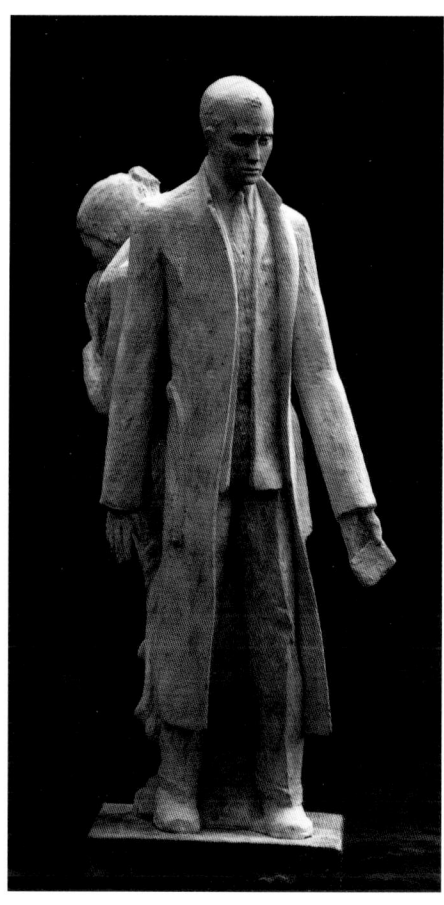

Figure 17. George R. Anthonisen (b. 1936),
Raoul Wallenberg I, 1998–99. Plaster, 27 × 12 ×
12 inches. Collection of the artist.

the humanitarian work of Raoul Wallenberg (1912–1947) (Fig. 17), who saved thousands of Hungarian Jews from the Nazi and fascist regimes.

Give Us Grace started as a three-dimensional grouping of various couples embraced in dance, but Anthonisen changed the concept to a two-sided, convex bas-relief that echoes the circular motion of a dance floor. This depiction of couples of various genders, ethnicities, and generations represents a dance of tolerance and joy. The piece promotes harmonious inclusion, portraying a universal "family" that reflects contemporary society and encourages us to have courage and confidence in our relationships.

Caryatid evolved from a 1984 commission to create an award for Bucks County Volunteer of the Year. Inspired by the John Donne poem "For Whom the Bell Tolls," the Ernest Hemingway novel of the same name, and the symbol of the Liberty Bell, the sculpture embodies the weight of responsibility to our fellow humans, and references the internal struggles and strengths of the individual. The caryatid, a weight-bearing female figure that appears in Greek architecture, is a traditional symbol of carrying a burden. Anthonisen's large, intelligent, sublime figure is unyielding as she balances a lintel and bell.

Bucks County galleries and collectors have sustained Anthonisen's career, and his legacy is cemented by permanent installations of his work at the James A. Michener Art Museum, in Doylestown, Pennsylvania, and the Philip and Muriel Berman Museum of Art at Ursinus College, in Collegeville, Pennsylvania. The Pennsylvania galleries Gentle Winds Gallery in Doylestown, Fred Clark Gallery in Carversville, Bianco Gallery in Buckingham, Travis Gallery in New Hope, and Joy Berman Gallery in Philadelphia, along with Bjorn Lindgren Gallery in New York, were also instrumental in presenting and placing his sculptures and frescoes.

The artist maintains a daily schedule in the studio and reflects on his erudite approach to his artistic practice. "I have worked at defining love, grace, beauty, dignity, serenity, meditation, and constructive action as well as hatred, jealousy, anger, discord, deprivation, and destructive action."[3] The arc of consistency in his focus on the human condition, in all of its manifestations, continues to motivate George Anthonisen.

NOTES

This essay was informed by conversations with George and Ellen Anthonisen between January and May 2023.

1. Cited in Lisa Tremper Hanover, "A Life in Sculpture," *USA Today* magazine, November 2019, 43.

2. *Images of Courage and Compassion*, Millersville University, PA, 1991; *Caring:*

Humanity's Hope for Survival, the Samuel Dorsky Symposium on Public Monuments, Monuments Conservancy, New York, 1997.

3. George Anthonisen, interview by the author, June 2019. Also cited in Hanover, "A Life in Sculpture," 44.

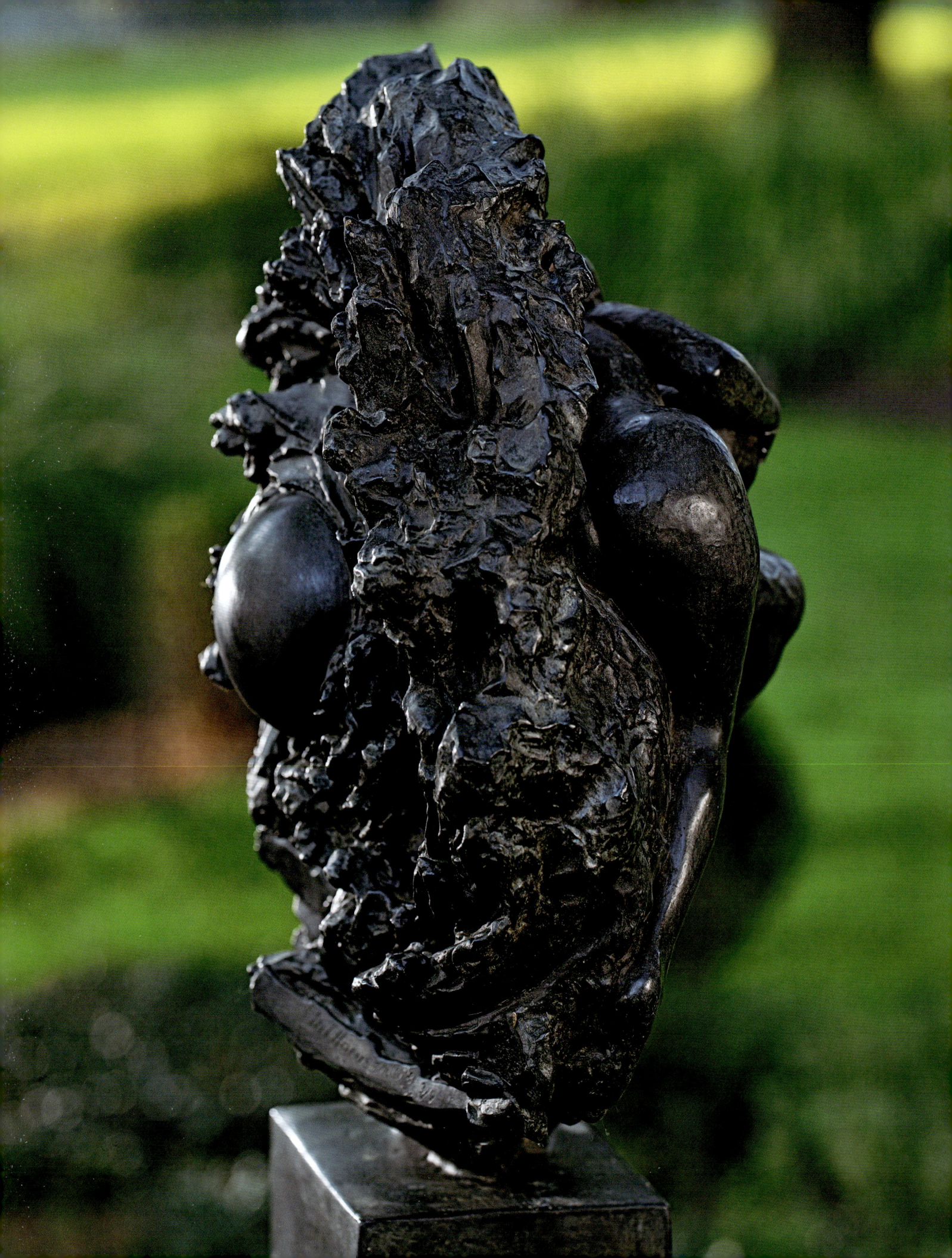

A Birth in Bronze: *Creation* in Context

LAURA TURNER IGOE

CREATION, BY GEORGE R. ANTHONISEN (B. 1936), IS A SUSTAINED sculptural meditation on the many meanings and interpretations of its title: It explores the birth of a child and the birth of humankind, a cosmic birth and the gestation of an idea birthed into three-dimensionality by an artist through the transformative processes of sculpting and casting. Described by the artist as two-sided, it encourages multiple viewpoints to be seen and understood fully. On one side (Pl. 21), a nude man and woman entangled in a passionate embrace emerge and dissolve into a swirling vortex of cast bronze. The focal point is the kiss at the center, where the two figures join, their coming together also suggestive of an act of creation. On the opposite side (Pl. 22), a spiraling maelstrom converges at a surfacing sphere. This smooth, crowning head or cresting planet stands in stark contrast to the active, roughly shaped material that surrounds it. It is a promise of new life born from darkness. Viewed from the side, elements of the figure emerge and dissolve into the roughly shaped bronze, forming compelling, abstract, and amorphous shapes (Fig. 1)

Created early in the 1980s, when postmodernist sculptors were questioning ideas of artistic originality and agency, Anthonisen's *Creation* insisted upon the significance of the artist's intellectual and physical manipulation of his chosen material. Anthonisen was investigating his own definition of modern art at the time and determined that it resided at the intersection of abstraction and realism. *Creation* is the culmination of that sustained exploration. Like many of Anthonisen's works, *Creation* is an homage to the sculptor's artistic heroes, in particular Auguste Rodin (1840–1917) and Michelangelo (1475–1564), and it draws connections between the act of sculpting and divine creation. It is also entangled with popular scientific imagery, as new theories about the creation of our universe circulated in popular media and the press. In total, *Creation* is directly engaged with the artistic and cultural debates of its time, as Anthonisen explored what it meant to be a modern artist.

Figure 1. George R. Anthonisen (b. 1936), *Creation* (side), 1981–82. Bronze, 24 × 24 × 14 inches. Edition 3/9. Collection of Carol and Louis Della Penna.

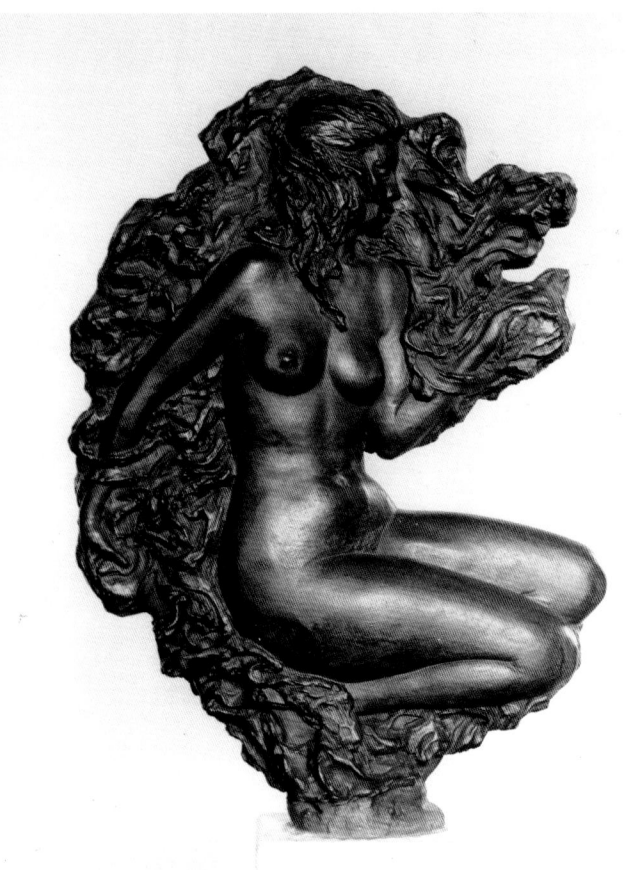
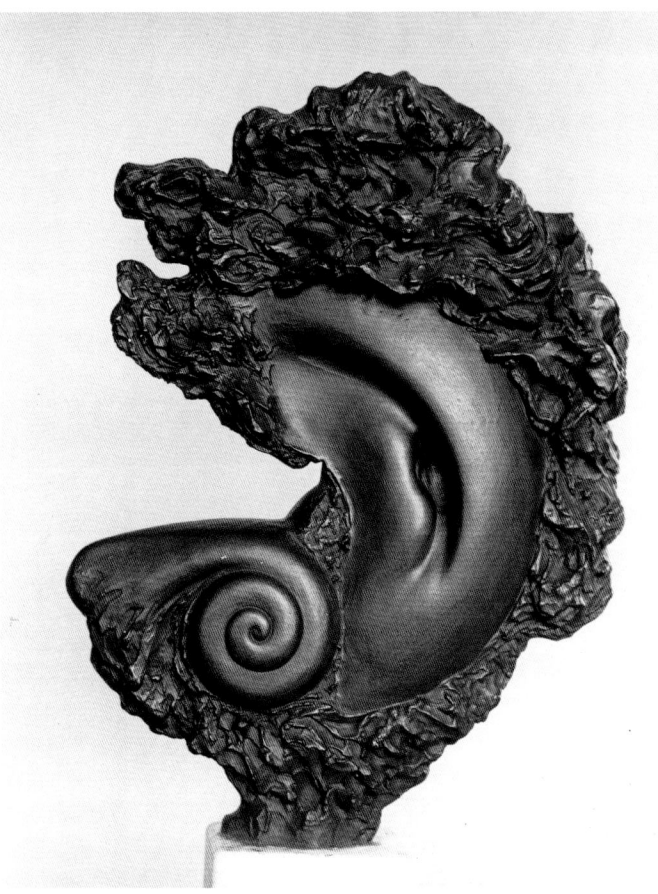

COMBINING REALISM AND ABSTRACTION

Completed in 1982, *Creation* is a part of a series of sculptures by Anthonisen that evocatively combine abstraction and realism, which the artist identified as a potential new direction for modern art. Intentionally double-sided, these works conflate the human body with abstract symbols and shapes and dissolving forms. In *Crouching Nude* (Figs. 2–3), the shape of the female form on one side is echoed by an enlarged ear and coiled spiral on the reverse, visually conjuring echoes and auditory reverberations. *Guitarist* (Figs. 4–5), made around the same time as *Creation*, similarly investigates ideas of the transformation and evolution of form. While the front of the sculpture faithfully represents a seated woman playing a guitar, the reverse of the figure and instrument is abstracted into a cubist construction. Anthonisen was undoubtedly inspired by the guitar sculptures of Pablo Picasso (1881–1973) (Fig. 6), in which the artist reduced the stringed instrument to a planar arrangement of shapes, lines, and shadows to denote volume. Picasso's guitar sculptures—both the original cardboard-and-paper assemblage and the final steel version—were displayed in the Spanish artist's wildly popular retrospective at the Museum of Modern

Figures 2–3. George R. Anthonisen (b. 1936), *Crouching Nude* (front and back), 1981. Bronze, 22 × 16 × 4 inches. Edition 2/9. Collection of the artist.

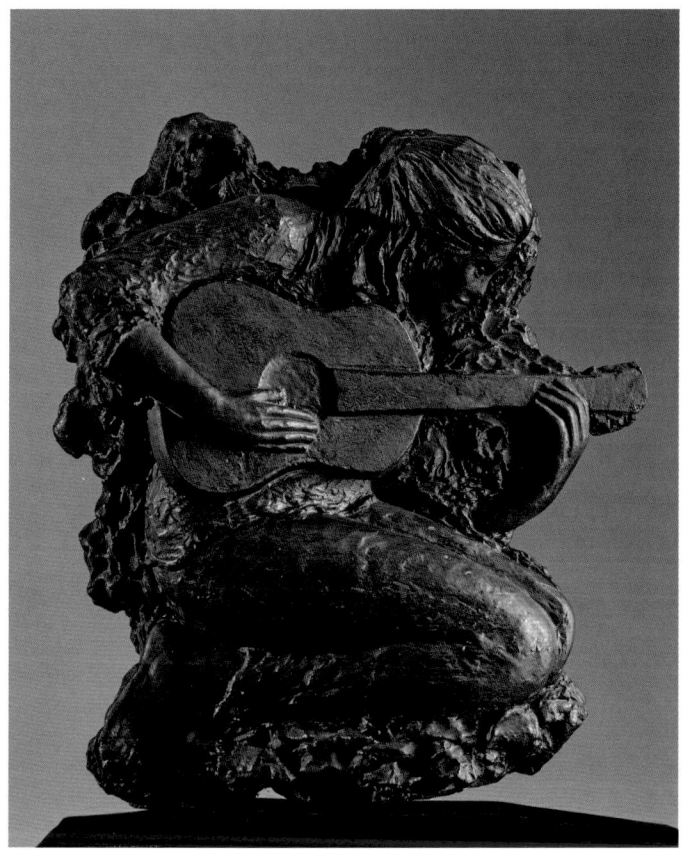
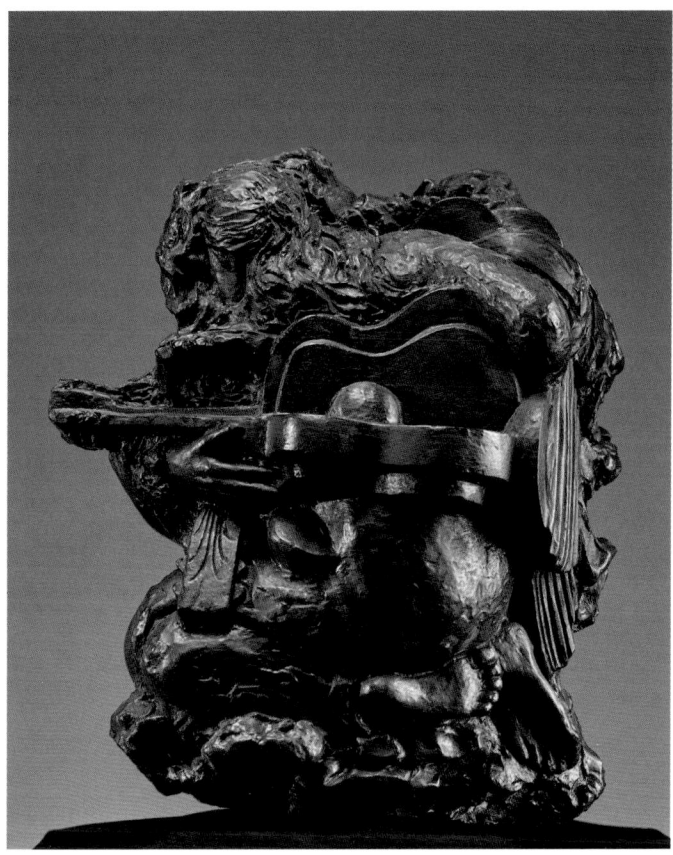

Figures 4–5. George R. Anthonisen (b. 1936),
Guitarist (front and back), 1981–82. Hydrostone,
15 × 12½ × 9½ inches. Edition 8/9. Collection of
the artist.

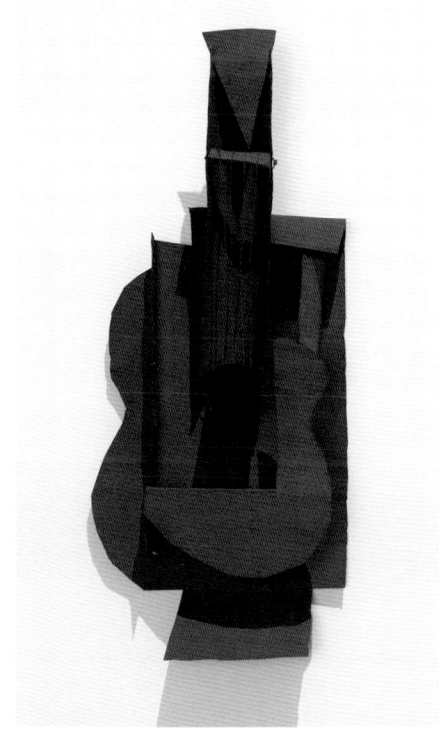

Figure 6. Pablo Picasso (1881–1973), *Guitar*, 1914.
Sheet metal and wire, 30½ × 13¾ × 7⅝ inches.
The Museum of Modern Art, Gift of the artist.

Art in 1980, which drew more than a million visitors and heralded a renewed appreciation of the artist at the time.[1]

Anthonisen sculpted a portrait of Picasso (Pls. 26–28) in 1982, the same year *Creation* was completed, expressing his admiration for the artist and his deconstruction of space. Much like *Crouching Nude*, *Guitar Player*, and *Creation*, the Picasso portrait features a conventional depiction of the artist on one side, while the other side separates into shifting planes, abstracting the artist's visage in the style of one of his cubist compositions. A copulating minotaur and female figure seem to be emerging from Picasso's brain, alluding to the images of sexual violence that dominated the artist's work.[2] These explorations of form and space, especially as they relate to the human figure, were all on Anthonisen's mind when he embarked upon *Creation* in 1981.

When sculpting *Creation*, Anthonisen conceived first of the sphere emerging from the swirling void, in order to confront his hesitancy around abstraction at the outset.[3] According to the artist, he envisioned a woman's hips and the crowning head of a newborn and tried to capture that vision in the sculpture. The smooth, round sphere relates to other circular forms in Anthonisen's work. In *Crucifixion I: Christ and Mary Magdalene* (Pls. 23–24), also completed in 1982, a round circle on the reverse of the piece features a crucified Christ embraced by a kneeling Mary Magdalene. Similar to *Creation*, the circle appears

Figures 7–8. Auguste Rodin (1840–1917), *Hand of God* (front and back), original model before 1895, carved ca. 1907. Marble, 29 × 23¾ × 25½ inches. The Metropolitan Museum of Art, Gift of Edward D. Adams, 1908.

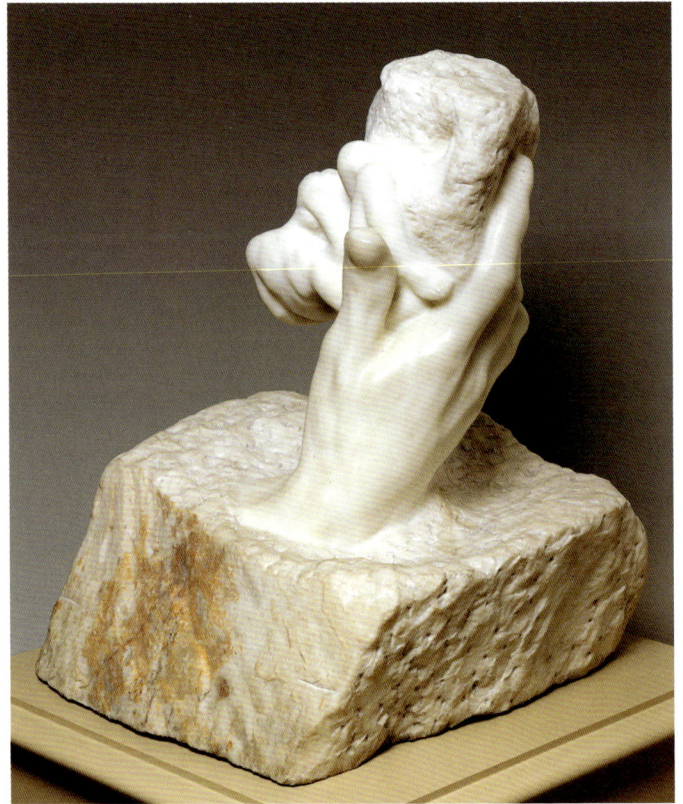
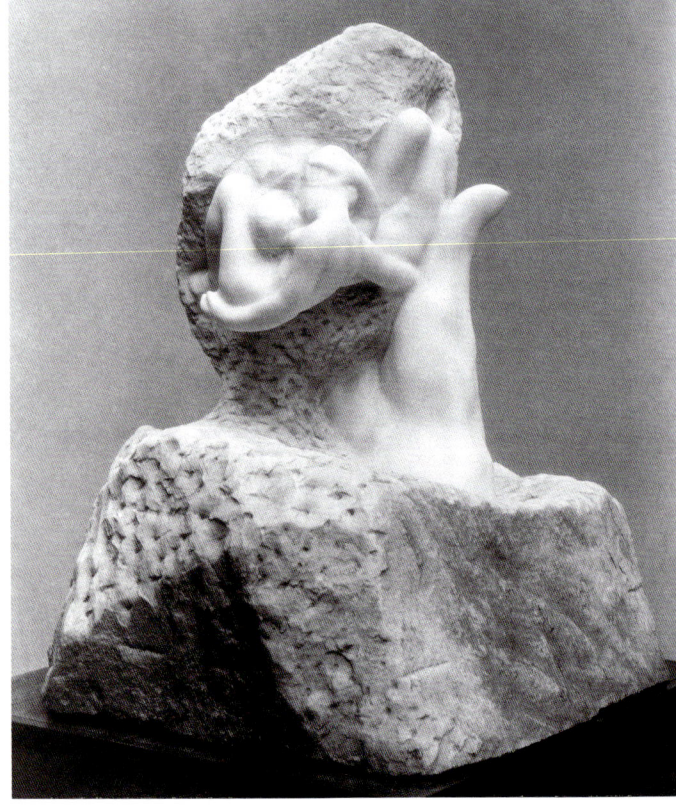

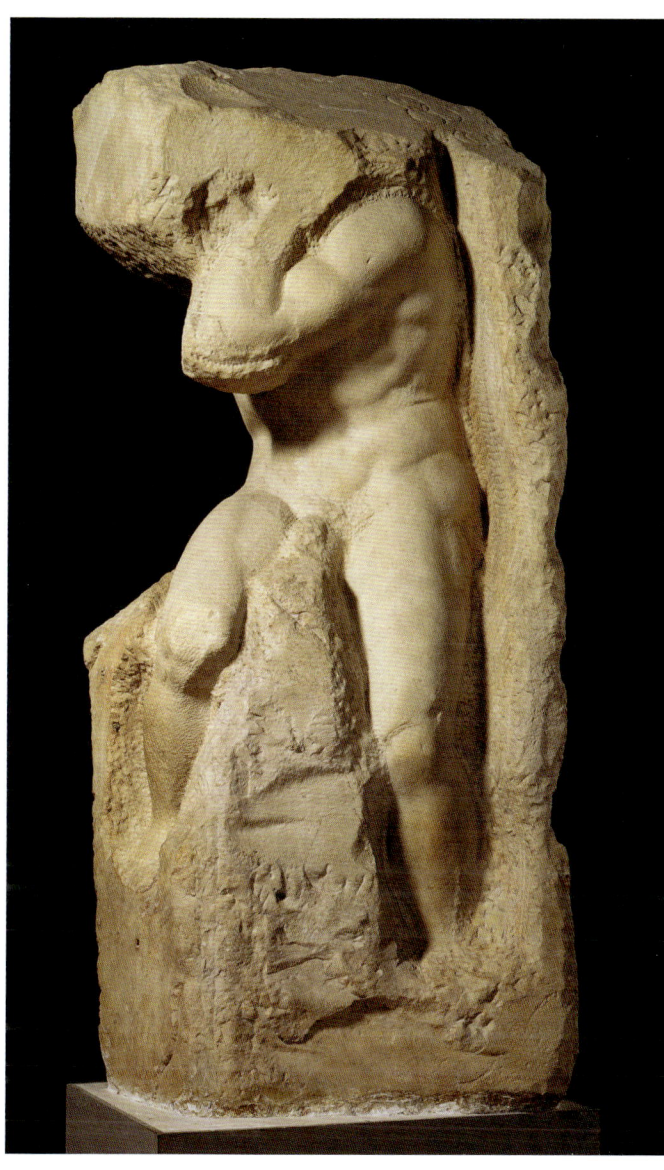

Figure 9. Michelangelo Buonarroti (1475–1564), *Atlas*, 1525–30. Marble, 109 inches high. Galleria dell'Accademia di Firenze.

amid a swirling atmosphere of billowing clouds, a symbol of divine perfection in darkness and chaos.

SCULPTOR AS DIVINE CREATOR

While *Guitarist* was informed by Picasso's investigation of the spatial properties of a musical instrument, Anthonisen turned to a different sculptor as his inspiration for the embracing figures in *Creation*: Auguste Rodin, who was experiencing new attention in the early 1980s.[4] Anthonisen's intertwined figures directly reference Rodin's *Hand of God* (Figs. 7–8), in which embracing male and female figures are suspended in an unfinished sculptural material cradled in a large hand. Rodin's marble versions of this subject serve as a tribute to Michelangelo and the Renaissance sculptor's series of unfinished works in which torqued, muscular figures materialize out of rough stone as if escaping capture (Fig. 9). As the title *Hand of God* suggests, Rodin's figures represent God's creation of humankind through his making of Adam and Eve. Rodin drew a direct comparison between divine creation and his own sculptural practice, declaring, "When God created the world, it is of modeling he must have thought first of all. Isn't it amusing to make God a sculptor before all else?"[5] Rodin's *Hand of God* positions the sculptor as creator of life through the manipulation of his chosen materials.

Through this sculptural homage to Rodin, Anthonisen's *Creation* similarly asserts the sculptor's capability to produce figures and forms from clay, stone, and metals as comparable to divine creation. The work celebrates the creation of mankind and new birth, but it also references the artist's own sculptural process. According to Anthonisen, although he struggled with painting while in school, sculpture came naturally to him. He loved the feeling and simplicity of clay, which was always accessible and easy to work with. Sculpting in clay requires tactile manipulation and is less reliant on tools than painting. In the words of the artist, "finger sensitivity goes beyond the eye."[6] Anthonisen usually sculpts his initial compositions with plasteline, a type of clay mixed with oil or wax to prevent hardening. Plasteline does not set or dry and can become more malleable when warmed by touch. It is difficult to view *Creation* and not imagine the artist's own hand in its construction, stretching and twisting the plasteline to create the roughly textured background and then shaping and smoothing the rounded sphere to evoke the head of a crowning newborn.

This clay sculpture underwent several additional material transformations through the bronze casting process. First, a plaster model was made using small, sectional molds; that plaster model, further reshaped and refined by the artist, was then used to create an additional mold, into which molten bronze was poured to produce the completed sculpture. *Creation* visually evokes this casting process through its roughly formed background, which recalls the formation of the sculpture through the setting of liquid bronze. The embracing figures materialize from their support similarly to the way the sculpture takes on its shape through the mold.

This assertive celebration of the artist's hand and material transformation runs counter to the tenets of postmodernism that dominated contemporary art in the 1980s, when *Creation* was cast. In his widely read essay "The Death of the Author," French philosopher Roland Barthes (1915–1980) challenged the mythology of the artist as an innovative genius and instead embraced appropriation as integral to artistic creation. He declared literature, for example, to be "a multi-dimensional space in which a variety of writings, none of them original, blend and clash. The text is a tissue of quotations drawn from the innumerable centers of culture."[7] While Anthonisen's work, and *Creation* in particular, draws from sculptural references across history and therefore in some ways exemplifies Barthes's interest in appropriation, Anthonisen still insists upon the significance of the artist's hand and mind in the act of creation. In that way, *Creation* acts as a foil to postmodernist sculpture, like the work of Anthonisen's contemporary Jeff Koons (b. 1955). Koons introduced a series of sculptures in 1980 called *The New*, which featured vacuum cleaners seductively displayed in lighted Plexiglas cases (Fig. 10). These assemblages negated the hand of the artist, as Koons selected ready-made objects to comment on the place of mass-produced commodities within our fantasies and desires. Like Anthonisen's *Creation*, Koons's vacuum cleaners expressed ideas about the female form and birth, albeit in a very different way. Koons has explained that he chose the vacuums for their anthropomorphic qualities; he said, "I had this idea of encasing the pieces and letting them just display their integrity of birth, their newness, and treating them like eternal virgins."[8] Even though Anthonisen explored abstraction in his work, he never strayed from the human figure. As curator John Zarobell has argued, Anthonisen is a humanist sculptor who maintains the human figure as "a central and timeless element in the sculptural enterprise."[9]

In Koons's *The New* series, the act of artistic creation and the human figure are not integral to the idea of birth. In many ways, Koons's readymade sculptures

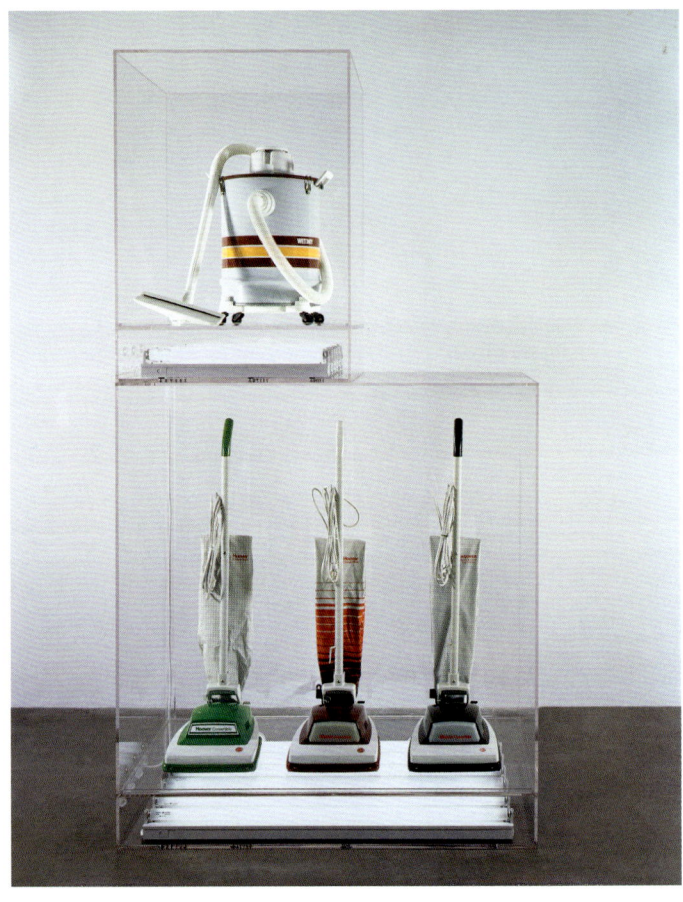

Figure 10. Jeff Koons (b. 1955), *New Hoover Convertibles, Green, Red, Brown, New Shelton Wet/ Dry 10 Gallon Displaced Doubledecker*, 1981–87. Four vacuum cleaners, acrylic, and fluorescent lights, 99 × 54 × 28 inches. Tate Modern, London, Acquired jointly with the National Galleries of Scotland through The d'Offay Donation with assistance from the National Heritage Memorial Fund and the Art Fund 2008. © Jeff Koons.

remove the hand of the artist entirely. Anthonisen's *Creation*, however, through its multiple references to birth, divine creation, and its own material production, argues for the significance of the artist, creative genius, technical skill, and the figure within contemporary art.

THE BIG BANG

The birth abstractly represented in *Creation*, with its swirling vortex delineated by rough, tumultuous clay, plaster, and then bronze, additionally relates to popular imagery and theories of space and black holes, including the big bang theory of creation, that percolated in media and the popular press in the late 1970s and early 1980s. Fred Hoyle (1915–2001) is credited with coining the term "big bang" in 1949 to describe the theory, which he did not agree with, that an exploding microscopic ball of hot and dense material created our expanding universe. The theory did not catch on until the 1960s and 1970s, however, when scientists observed new evidence of its occurrence.[10] In 1965, the *New York Times* published a front-page article, "Signals Imply a 'Big Bang' Universe," sharing that Princeton University scientists had discovered "remnants of an explosion that gave birth to the universe."[11] In 1982, the year *Creation* was completed, the *Philadelphia Inquirer* published an article about an expanded view of the universe proposed by physicists at the University of Pennsylvania. Their new models of a universe much larger and vaster than initially known built upon the big bang theory of creation, "for which now there is supporting evidence," as the *Inquirer* explained.[12] Between 1980 and 1982, the *Philadelphia Inquirer* published nearly forty articles that investigated or referenced the big bang theory, demonstrating the appeal of this cosmological event to a wide public audience.

Visualizations of black holes were also popular in the scientific community and mass media at this time. In 1979, forty-three years before the Event Horizon Telescope captured an image of the supermassive black hole at the center of the

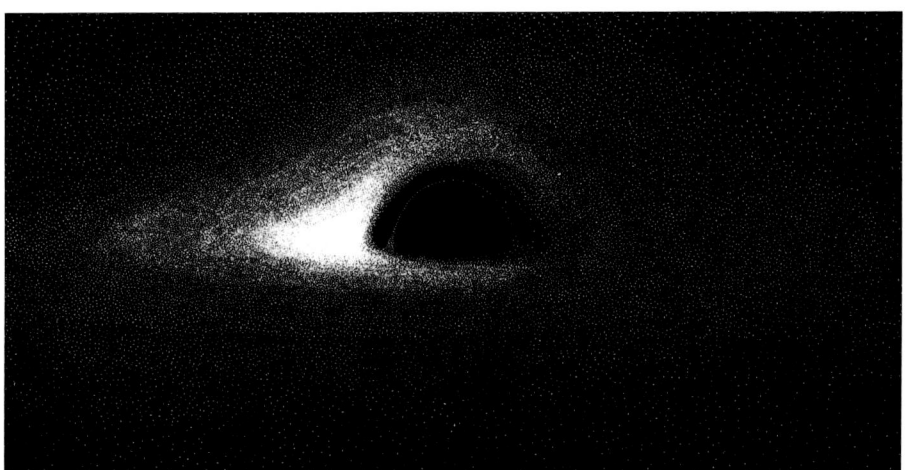

Figure 11. Simulated photograph of a spherical black hole with thin accretion disk, from Jean-Pierre Luminet, "Image of a Spherical Black Hole with Thin Accretion Disk," *Astronomy and Astrophysics* 75 (1979): 235.

Milky Way galaxy, Jean-Pierre Luminet (b. 1951) visualized the appearance of a black hole in the journal *Astronomy and Astrophysics*.[13] Luminet used numerical data from an early transistor computer to inform a drawing of the phenomenon, in which a dark, rounded shape emerges from a luminous halo (Fig. 11).[14] Also in 1979, Disney released the science fiction movie *The Black Hole*, which takes place on a mysterious space station at the edge of a black hole. The advertising poster for the film incorporated a spiraling image of a black hole as the design's focal point. Although Luminet's image and Disney's visualization of the phenomenon are very different, both explore the emergence or disintegration of a shape or an object within an amorphous vortex. Given how images of astronomical phenomena and new discoveries regarding the creation and scope of our universe proliferated across various media channels at the time, it is highly probable that these ideas informed Anthonisen's conception of *Creation*'s composition (Anthonisen admits that he may have been unconsciously inspired by space imagery when sculpting the reverse of *Creation*).[15] One can view *Creation*, therefore, as engaged with a series of creations, from the very intimate—the birth of a child—to the macroscopic—the birth of a universe.

Simultaneously abstract and figural, *Creation* explores ideas of modern art, artistic evolution, material transformation, and cosmic birth. Through this engagement with multiple ideas and definitions of "creation," Anthonisen effectively linked the artist's creative production to the generation of new life and new universes, in order to uphold the significance of the figure and artistic invention within sculptural practice in the 1980s.

NOTES

1. This exhibition marked the first time the museum dedicated its entire 53rd Street headquarters to the works of a single artist, featuring nearly one thousand paintings, sculptures, drawings, collages, prints, ceramics, and costume and theater designs from 152 public and private collections. "*Pablo Picasso: A Retrospective*, May 16–Sep 30, 1980, MoMA," Museum of Modern Art, accessed June 23, 2023, https://www.moma.org/calendar/exhibitions/1818.

2. Picasso and his misogyny have been the subject of recent critical exhibitions and scholarship. See Jason Farago, "With Hannah Gadsby's 'It's Pablo-matic,' the Joke's on the Brooklyn Museum," *New York Times*, June 1, 2023.

3. George Anthonisen, interview by the author, June 14, 2023.

4. Antoinette Le Normand-Romain, ed., *Rodin in the United States: Confronting the Modern* (Williamstown, MA: Sterling and Francine Clark Art Institute, 2022), 194–95.

5. Auguste Rodin, *Rodin: The Man and His Art, with Leaves from His Notebook*, comp. Judith Cladel (New York: The Century Co., 1917), 222.

6. Anthonisen, interview by the author.

7. Roland Barthes, *Image, Music, Text*, trans. Stephen Heath (New York: Hill and Wang, 1977), 146. See Angela L. Miller et al., *American Encounters: Art, History, and Cultural Identity* (Upper Saddle River, NJ: Pearson/Prentice Hall, 2008), 678–79.

8. "Jeff Koons, *New Shelton Wet/Dry Doubledecker*, 1981," Museum of Modern Art, accessed June 25, 2023, https://www.moma.org/collection/works/81090.

9. John Zarobell, "George Anthonisen, Humanist Sculptor," in *The Sculpture of George R. Anthonisen: An Exhibition at Jonathan Edwards College* (New Haven, CT: Jonathan Edwards College, Yale University, 2006), 7.

10. Helge Kragh, "Big Bang: The Etymology of a Name," *Astronomy and Geophysics* 54, no. 2 (April 2013): 2.28–2.30, https://doi.org/10.1093/astrogeo/att035.

11. Walter Sullivan, "Signals Imply a 'Big Bang' Universe," *New York Times*, May 21, 1965.

12. Jim Detjen, "Something New under the Sun: The Theory of a Larger Universe," *Philadelphia Inquirer*, November 7, 1982.

13. Jean-Pierre Luminet, "Image of a Spherical Black Hole with Thin Accretion Disk," *Astronomy and Astrophysics* 75 (1979): 228–35.

14. Steve Dent, "Remembering the First 'Photo' of a Black Hole," *Engadget*, April 19, 2017, https://www.engadget.com/2017-04-19-black-hole-image-jean-pierre-luminet.html.

15. Anthonisen, interview by the author.

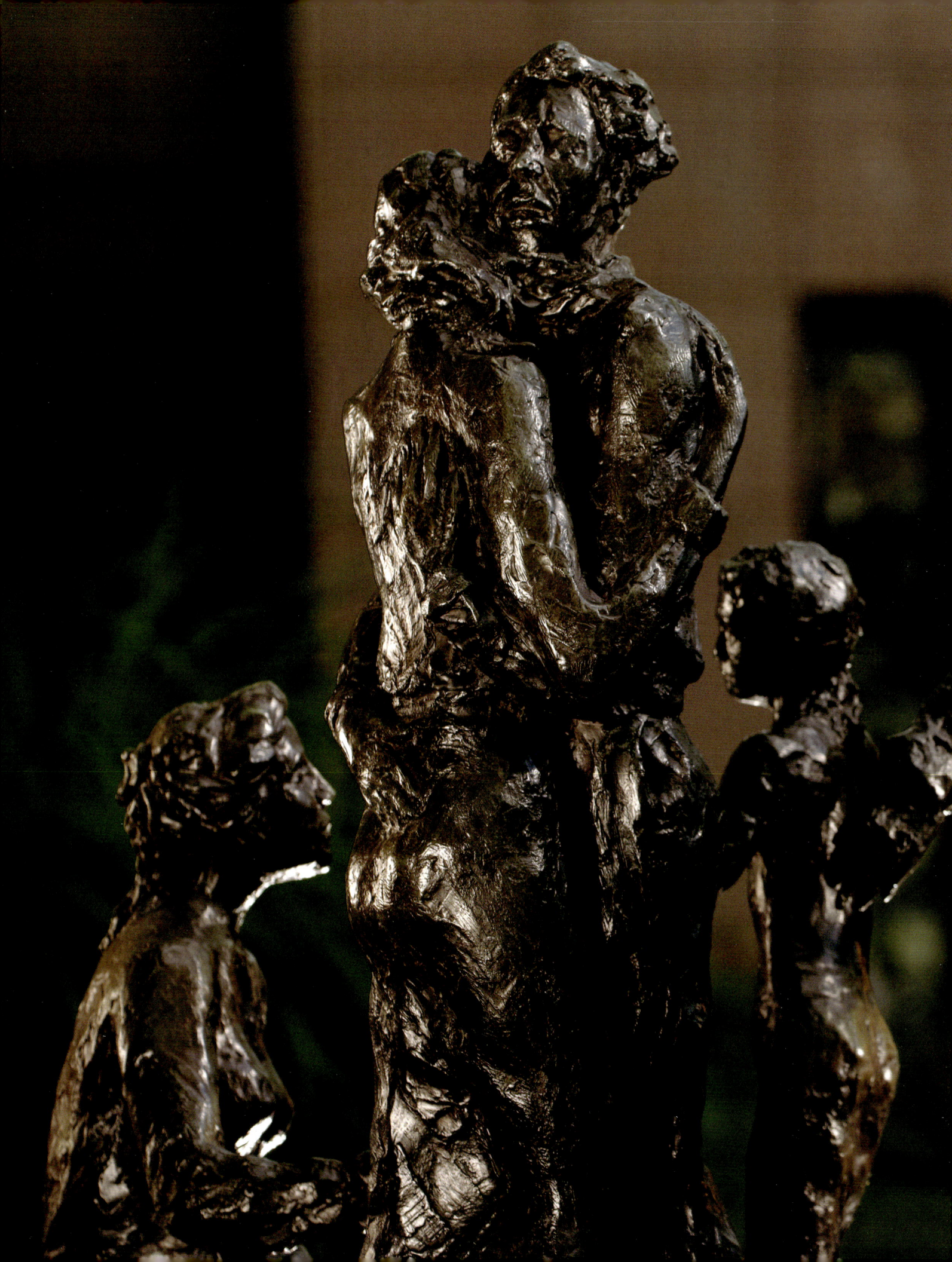

In Conversation with George R. Anthonisen

CLARISSE FAVA-PIZ

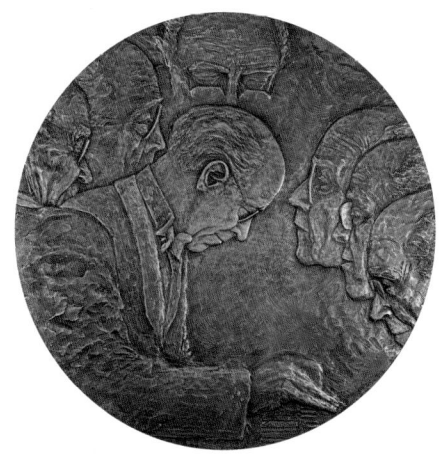

Figure 1. George R. Anthonisen (b. 1936), *Rudolf Serkin*, 1983–84. Aluminum, 23 inches diam. Edition 1/9. Collection of the artist.

Detail of Plate 15.

WHEN I WAS APPROACHED BY THE CURATORIAL TEAM OF THE James A. Michener Art Museum to write an essay on the work of George R. Anthonisen (b. 1936), I immediately thought that an interview with the artist would be the best way to capture his voice and in-depth knowledge of his oeuvre. As a specialist in nineteenth- and early twentieth-century sculpture in Europe and the Americas, I came to this project with a deep interest in analyzing the connections between Anthonisen's work and the tradition of Western sculpture.

The transcript of my conversation with George Anthonisen and his wife, Ellen Anthonisen (b. 1934), highlights the rich repertoire of artistic references—both visual and musical—from which the artist has drawn throughout his career. His lifetime dedication to figurative sculpture is intimately linked to his interest in storytelling and his ability to give form to his thoughts in the sculptural medium. As a young artist in New York City, Anthonisen often visited the Metropolitan Museum of Art, where he was inspired by a vast range of artworks, from Italian Madonnas to eighteenth- and nineteenth-century sculptures by Jean-Antoine Houdon (1741–1828), Auguste Rodin (1840–1917), Augustus Saint-Gaudens (1848–1907), and Daniel Chester French (1850–1931), among others. His artist residency at the Saint-Gaudens National Historical Park shaped his understanding of the bas-relief format and informed his future sculptural experimentations, like the medallion depicting Rudolf Serkin (1903–1991) (Fig. 1). Anthonisen admired his predecessors, and in particular Saint-Gaudens, for their use of soft and heavier contours of the bas-relief as a vehicle for narration.

Anthonisen does not consider figurative sculpture to be an art of the past. He belongs to a lineage of artists who revisit myths to bring a universal dimension to their work. His sculptures comment on societal and political concerns of his time, as seen in *Antigone* (Pls. 33–34), *Death and Starvation* (Pl. 8), and *I Set Before You This Day* (Pls. 13–15). Themes of trauma and suffering function as a leitmotif throughout his oeuvre—placing him in the lineage of modern sculptors like Käthe Kollwitz (1867–1945), Wilhelm Lehmbruck (1881–1919), and Alberto Giacometti (1901–1966).

41

My conversation with George and Ellen Anthonisen took place on May 24, 2023.

What are the artworks that best characterize your oeuvre?

GEORGE R. ANTHONISEN: *I Set Before You This Day, Give Us Grace* [Pls. 42–43], and *Caryatid* [Pls. 47–48] are important declarations. These three sculptures stand alone, but shown together, each complements the other. As a whole, they make a statement about the human family. Within these three sculptures are themes that appear throughout my body of work. Each sculpture leads viewers to reflect on the human condition.

In past interviews, you insist on your inspiration from the tradition of nineteenth- and early twentieth-century sculpture. Artists usually like to detach themselves from the past—perhaps out of fear of having their works perceived as derivative. How do you negotiate this?

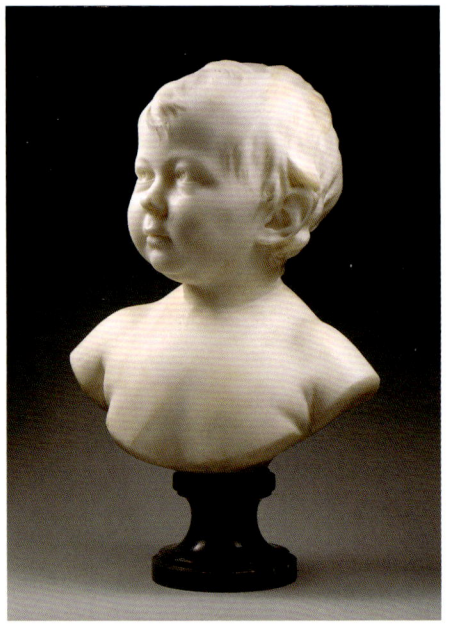

Figure 2. Jean-Antoine Houdon (1741–1828), *Sabine Houdon*, 1788. White marble, 10¾ × 8⅞ × 5⅞ inches. The Metropolitan Museum of Art, Bequest of Mary Stillman Harkness, 1950, 50.145.66.

GRA: I love the idea that I am derivative.

Jean-Antoine Houdon was a big influence and still is. In doing bas-relief, his awareness of details and the finesse of some of the modeling is remarkable [Fig. 2]. I have always equated making sculpture overall with music and the fine high notes. Houdon had an exquisite ability to render very fine notes and he did not neglect the heavy, deep notes either.

My favorite artist is Beethoven [1770–1827]. I think his range of emotions is wonderful; I think every note he uses conveys sentiment. What I look for in my art and the art of others is communication of emotion using the vocabulary of the figure.

Have you made a portrait of Ludwig van Beethoven?

GRA: It is always in the back of my mind. There is a grandeur about him but also a simplistic aspect. Whether in a symphony or concerto, broad ideas are communicated, but Beethoven does not lose sight of nuance, the smallest part of the puzzle, the light, fine texture on top of a larger, more obvious form. He understands humanity. To manage to bring these things together in an image is a wonderful challenge.

Could you describe the sculptural group I Set Before You This Day *and the circumstances of its creation?*

ELLEN ANTHONISEN: George was asked by a Holocaust survivor, who had seen two other works by George—*Death and Starvation* and *Murder: Cain and Abel* [Pl. 5]—if he could do a sculpture that asked the question that he had been haunted by ever since he managed to live through the Holocaust. "What would I do if I were in a situation where helping your fellow man meant that you and your family were threatened with certain death? Would you choose to help, or would you choose to ignore those persons in need?"

GRA: There is a range of choices made for helping and not helping, in terms of Jews in jeopardy and who would help and who would not. The couple standing and intertwined, they are people who understand the severity of the situation, but they have chosen to turn their backs. On the other side, there is a father and a daughter. They both have their garments torn on their right shoulder and look to be in deep distress. And the kneeling woman is taking the daughter into her arms. She is committed to helping the Jews.

The focus of this group is the dead or dying Holocaust figure. His arm is wrapped around the leg of another man, who is the leader and certainly of the oldest generation of the people who are refusing to help. In between, there is a mother with a little child, and the child—a young boy—is innocently reaching out to help. But the mother is doing two things at once; she is keeping him from joining the group, but allowing him to bear witness. It is a duality that is so difficult for the person: she knows that she could be helping, but she is not going to jeopardize her child in the process.

On the other side, the father in the middle is doing two things at once: he is handing off his daughter to the safety of the woman who is kneeling, and he is a reflection of the man standing next to him. That man is asking, with open arms, "Can you not help us?" And the Jewish father is facing us and asking the same question: "Can you help us?"

What I have set up is a lot of different choices for the viewer. And of course, no one, including myself, knows how one would react in this situation.

EA: George's dream is to do this piece seven feet high.

GRA: Like Auguste Rodin's *The Burghers* [Fig. 3]!

> *Related to the history of multifigure sculpture, did you have Rodin's* The Burghers of Calais *in mind? Or was it the idea of monumentality that you were exploring in your piece?*

GRA: Both factors are true. In *The Burghers*, there are multiple figures, and they are not sequential. The story is of different aspects of humanity willing to sacrifice—some under pressure and others voluntarily. Rodin is a remarkable sculptor. I love crediting him. The connections are obvious and I am certainly not going to deny it. I use this influence to tell my story.

> *I am interested in what you were saying about scale. Would you like to have this piece of much larger scale, and why?*

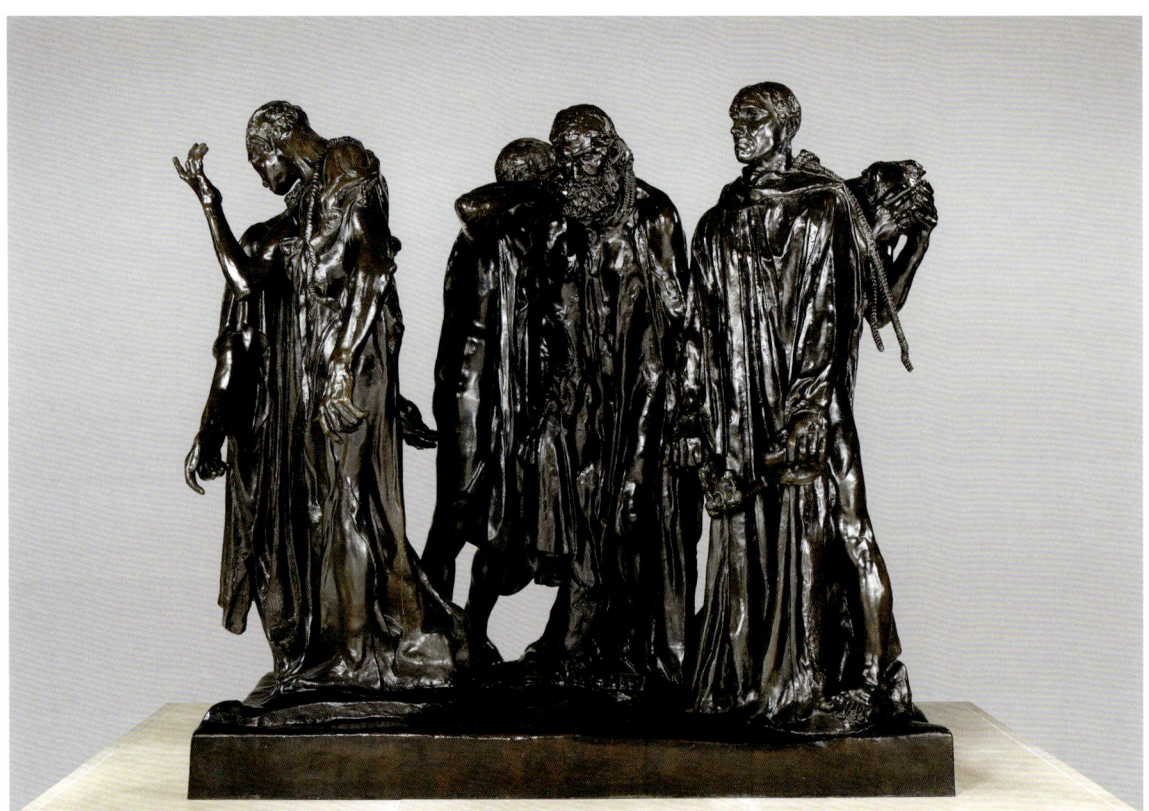

GRA: Yes, I would like to enlarge this sculpture group. I want people to experience it as the burghers were mounted. You can almost fit into that sculpture, you become part of it. In the many years since I executed this work, I have evolved the thesis, and I have been commissioned to do a reduction of *I Set Before You This Day*.

In the original grouping, the daughter is rendered helpless and totally diminished. If she is to regain a sense of humanity, it is through the help of people who are making that gesture. In the newest interpretation, titled *The Choice* [Pl. 69], the figures are much smaller, and they are more ambivalent. They understand the consequences of their actions much more thoroughly than in the original sculpture.

The father is anchored in the present, the here and now. And the little girl, in my new rendering of her, is aware that she somehow is the future. There is a meditative quality in her that the original little girl does not have.

I am working with the idea of duality in the person.

The kneeling figure is in contrast to everybody else. She became much more significant in terms of reflection, prayer, and support. The gesture of kneeling, humbling herself, is very significant, and that carries through the original work and in *The Choice*.

Figure 3. Auguste Rodin (1840–1917), *The Burghers of Calais*, modeled 1884–95, cast 1985. Bronze, 82½ × 94 × 95 inches. The Metropolitan Museum of Art, Gift of Iris and B. Gerald Cantor, 1989, 1989.407.

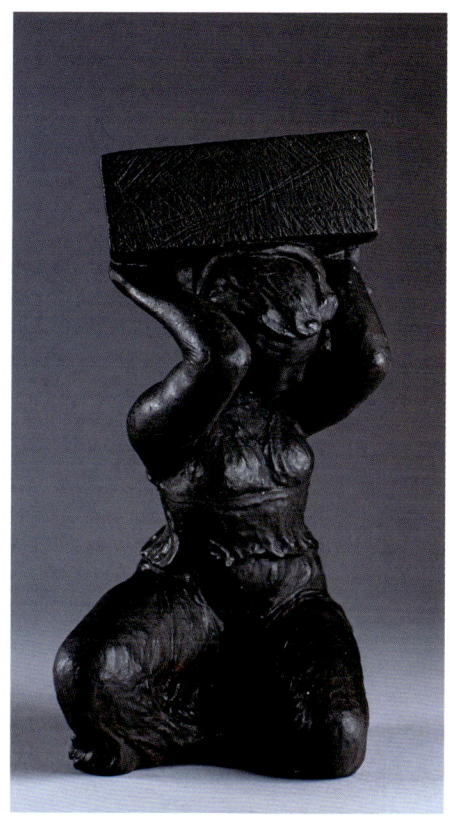

Figure 4. George R. Anthonisen (b. 1936), *Johnson Caryatid (Bucks County Volunteer of the Year Award)*, 1984. Bronze, 9 × 4½ × 4½ inches. Edition 10/10. Collection of the artist.

I Set Before You This Day is sited today in the Michener Art Museum courtyard. In front of the museum is Caryatid. *What is the origin of this figure?*

GRA: In 1984, I was winner of a competition to create an award for the Volunteer of the Year in Bucks County, Pennsylvania, the region where we live. The competition was sponsored by the Johnson Companies in cooperation with Ad World, *Advance of Bucks County, Bucks County Courier Times, Daily Intelligencer, Quakertown Free Press*, and the WBCB and WBUX radio stations. The figure [Fig. 4] was nine inches tall and was derived from the John Donne quote "For whom the bell tolls." The caryatid was inspired by Greek sculpture. The sculpture was cast in bronze and awarded to an individual for ten years before the program dissolved.

Subsequently, I created a midsize caryatid where she became Black and removed the quote inscribed on the piece, because I understood the quote by John Donne should be linked to Ernest Hemingway's *For Whom the Bell Tolls* and [a line from] Martin Luther King's ["I Have a Dream"] speech, "Let freedom ring." Caryatid carries a bell. The bell is also a symbol of churches, and we think of churches as bastions of good. The bell is always in the church belfry. It is ultimately the Liberty Bell. The concept of a bell is so expansive in terms of its connotations. The Black woman is transposed as a heroine representing all humanity in democracies where liberty is cherished.

Did you work with a Black model to make that piece?

GRA: I do not work with live models. I work with my imagination, memory, intuition, and what I observe in real life, movies, and anatomy books. I worked and studied live models for four years and dissected a cadaver at Dartmouth Medical School.

Occasionally, I reference Ellen. The female figures I have developed are tastefully sensual, childbearing, intelligent, dynamic, and physically strong.

It seems to me that your references are in the broader realm of artistic references, not only within the history of sculpture.

GRA: I think what you are saying is artists tell a story. I interpret the story as directly as I possibly can, not making an elaborate overcomplexity when there is a simpler, direct rendering at hand.

Can you talk about the time when you were a sculptor in residence at the Saint-Gaudens National Historical Park?

GRA: That was very important because I was at a crossroads. I had been living in New York, and galleries and collectors were favoring "avant-garde" works, and by that time, I had recognized that I had a real facility for modeling. And in fact, an image that I was only formulating in my head would jump into a reality in clay, which just astounded me. I was wondering, How the hell do I fit into this art scene? Can I?

So, when I came to the Saint-Gaudens National Historic Site, most of [Saint-Gaudens's] works that are now cast in bronze were at that time only in plaster. And I saw the deterioration of a seated Lincoln that was the full monumental size he had done for Chicago. It was just fading away, sitting there, and did in fact become extinct, but you sure could see where Daniel Chester French got his idea for the Lincoln Memorial.

The big thing for me was seeing how remarkably alive the work of Augustus Saint-Gaudens was. And it was right up my alley.

Bas-relief was a new concept to me. Because I had been so enthralled about being able to do three-dimensional work, I had not even considered bas-relief. And to see [Saint-Gaudens's] portraits in this format gave new dimension to the story. I think of [the depiction of] Sargent's sister [Fig. 5]. It is a big bas-relief, and has been cast in bronze as well as cut in stone. She is sitting and playing the guitar. The other work, *The Children of Jacob H. Schiff* [Fig. 6], consists of two children and Saint-Gaudens's dog. Each relief is colossal with the information it contains. Earlier in our conversation, I told you about Houdon and the musical scale of his work, and the same thing applies to these reliefs. Large, heavy forms are present in contrast with light, high, beautiful detail of delicate forms. It is wonderful to see images that are not small but in a size that I believe is accessible to storytelling.

EA: In studying Saint-Gaudens's reliefs, George loved the soft quality of the plaster of paris. Plaster is similar to stone; both are soft and nonreflective to light hitting the surface. The surface of bronze is naturally light reflective.

Although some reliefs by Saint-Gaudens have now been cast into bronze, George has continued to use plaster of paris as the primary medium for his current relief work. They are beautiful, showing off the delicacy of the modeling because it is so direct; no foundry is involved. I do not know anyone who creates relief quite like George.

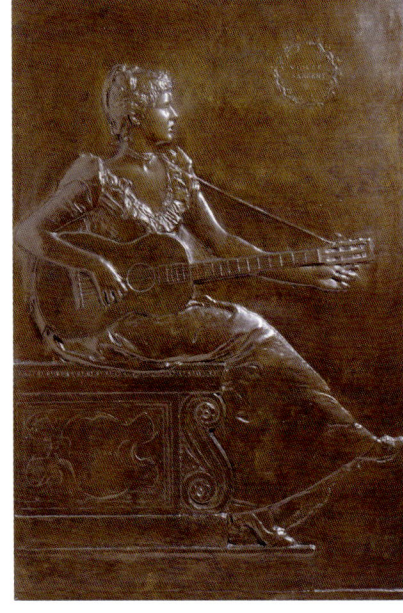

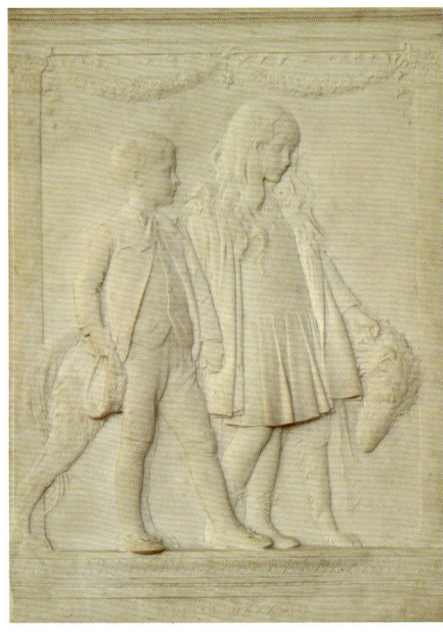

Figure 5. Augustus Saint-Gaudens (1848–1907), *Violet Sargent*, 1890. Bronze, 50 × 34 inches. Smithsonian American Art Museum, Gift of Rose Pitman Hughes, 1970.39.

Figure 6. Augustus Saint-Gaudens (1848–1907), *The Children of Jacob H. Schiff*, 1884–85, carved 1906–07. Marble, 68⅞ × 51 inches. The Metropolitan Museum of Art, Gift of Jacob H. Schiff, 1905, 05.15.3.

GRA: When I studied Saint-Gaudens, I learned that he used to cut cameos to support his family, and from that he developed the bas-relief. But the bas-relief itself has a very unique surface because it has an undulation, a fluidity, to it.

Could you tell me the story behind your bas-relief portrait of Rudolf Serkin?

GRA: We were in Marlboro, Vermont . . . , where Rudolf Serkin was affiliated with the Marlboro Music School, and where professionals and elite students played music together. We would go to concerts on a regular basis. There was an informality to this environment.

EA: When we saw Serkin at concerts, he was tall and very gangly. He would sit down at the keyboard, and everything came into sync. Then we saw him at a family restaurant. Serkin was playing with his grandchild who was under the table, and he was totally casual, had his shoes off, having fun with his family. He was very human. After that incident, George said, "I know what I am going to do."

GRA: There was a staff photographer at Marlboro and I requested photographs he took of Serkin in action.

EA: [*Describing the work*] All the faces around the medallion are Serkin. On the left-hand side, you see two figures joined with a single arm playing the piano, but all aspects of Serkin's personality are depicted in the relief.

Do you see any links between this piece and the Saint-Gaudens bas-reliefs we talked about earlier?

GRA: Every bas-relief I have done relates to him. It's not that I was under pressure with any deadlines with this residency. I was young, ambitious, and had energy. The Serkin piece is the result of that and is a high note. It's like when I told you that I'd like to sculpt Beethoven; I think one of the things that scares me is if I would do Beethoven justice in whatever rendering I manage. I won't try to duplicate the Serkin format. I will be very simple and direct.

Are you thinking of portraying Beethoven in a bas-relief?

GRA: Yes, a relief of Beethoven, not three-dimensional. There are a number of photographs [taken] throughout his life, and they are all so very different, it is just amazing. It's up to me to select from those images and determine what to elaborate on my own. I see an amalgamation of the qualities that allowed him to be as humble and as self-confident as he was with his music. Delicate and fine on the one hand, and strong and powerful on the other.

Could you describe your studio? Do you work with studio assistants on your compositions?

GRA: I do not have an atelier like Chester French or Saint-Gaudens. I do my own work, except I do not do the bronze casting. Once I model the clay and cast it in plaster, I refine the material. Ellen and I then take it to the foundry, and we monitor the process. After the foundry makes a mold, we do casting editions of either six or nine. After they construct the mold, they do a wax impression, and they refine it, and we come up again and do a quality check. At this stage, Ellen is better than I am in assessing the work, because I am so happy to be getting to the bronze stage, I lose my critical eye. Ellen maintains her focus on the piece. In the wax, I would sign and number and copyright, and then they'd take it back and pour the bronze from that. The resulting sculpture would just be cold bronze, no patina.

EA: George is very hands-on at the foundry. The artisans, with George, would work with the patina, and we were most fortunate that the patinists were artists themselves.

GRA: They had been trained as artists; they were people who had art degrees and were also technical people. We were at one foundry for a very long time, and as we grew, they grew, and they outgrew us, and we had to change foundries. They had artisans I completely relied on, both in patina and in wax, and among the things I did, and I am very glad, is to have them sign on the piece.

What is the story of your Antigone?

EA: That's my favorite piece, because in every work that George has done, it is the sensuality and strength of the woman, the issue of trauma, that is encapsulated here.

 The sculpture is based on Sophocles's play; Jean Anouilh (1910–1987) updated the story in the 1940s where the soldiers were Germans. *Antigone* is a universal narrative that has been examined throughout history.

GRA: Kent State University in Ohio was a site of confrontation between soldiers and protesters during the Vietnam War. I first created a small maquette of *Antigone* [Fig. 7], where the figures are nude, and Antigone's right hand is raised, and her fist is clenched.

Why the change of her arm's position?

GRA: When her hand is down and clenched, she has in her fist the dirt that will commit her to the burial of her brother, and this made it more dramatic in terms of her making a commitment.

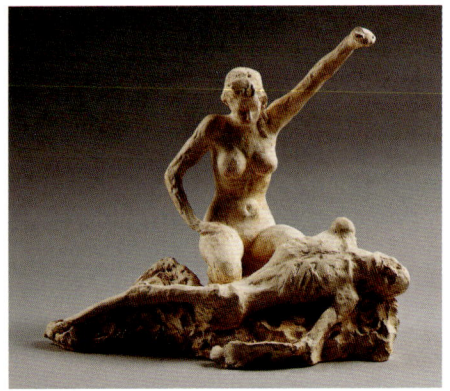

Figure 7. George R. Anthonisen (b. 1936), *Antigone* (maquette), 1987. Plaster, 14 × 15¼ × 9 inches. The Philip and Muriel Berman Museum of Art at Ursinus College.

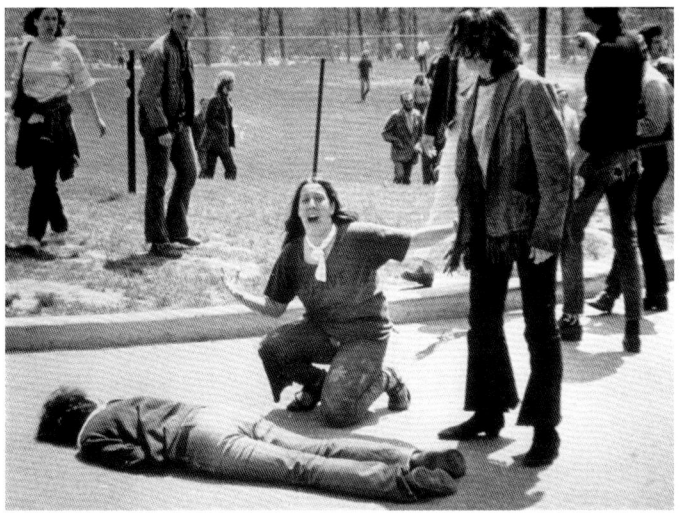

Figure 8. John Paul Filo (b. 1948), *Mary Ann Vecchio Kneeling over the Body of Jeffrey Miller on May 4, 1970, on the Campus of Kent State University, Kent, Ohio*, 1970.

Was Antigone *made in the context of the Kent State University confrontation?*

GRA: Yes, this girl was kneeling over a boy who had been killed by a soldier. There is a very famous photograph [Fig. 8]. It was so awful that this kind of confrontation was happening in our country, let alone on a college campus.

What do you think about the capacity of the medium of sculpture to function as social commentary?

GRA: Ellen is a big reader of the news, and I am not, because I have an understanding of how horrific human beings can be in any context as well as how wonderful they can be in any context, and I carry that with me as a shield, a shield of understanding. But when I hear over and over again something that hits my sensibility, I have to do something about it, and what I do is create an art object.

What about the story and background of Death and Starvation?

GRA: I am very proud of this sculpture and its tenets. I knew its execution had to do with a rage I had about famine and inequities of peoples, but I had no idea if the image I was contemplating would be palatable for public exposure.

EA: With *Death and Starvation*, George felt very strongly about the famine and death in Biafra in 1976. It was not a commission piece. Interest developed in 1985, during the Ethiopian famine, and a client visited the studio and requested information about this work. The client knew that a world conference on the alleviation of poverty and starvation was scheduled to take place at the World Health Organization [WHO] in Geneva, Switzerland. Subsequently, he presented a photograph of the image and information on George to Nobel Prize winner Norman Borlaug [1914–2009]. Borlaug contacted a Japanese philanthropist, Mr. Ryoichi Sasakawa, who liked the sculpture. Subsequently, a meeting was scheduled in New York for us to meet a representative for Mr. Sasakawa. The work was used as the figurehead for the WHO conference, where it still resides. That is my favorite story, really.

Can you tell me more about the relationship between this piece and the motif of the pietà?

GRA: Not so much the pietà, but a Madonna, for sure. In the Metropolitan Museum of Art, I was struck by the back of a Madonna [Figs. 9–10]; it is almost a shadowy image. Madonnas for me, and particularly in Florence, are symbolic

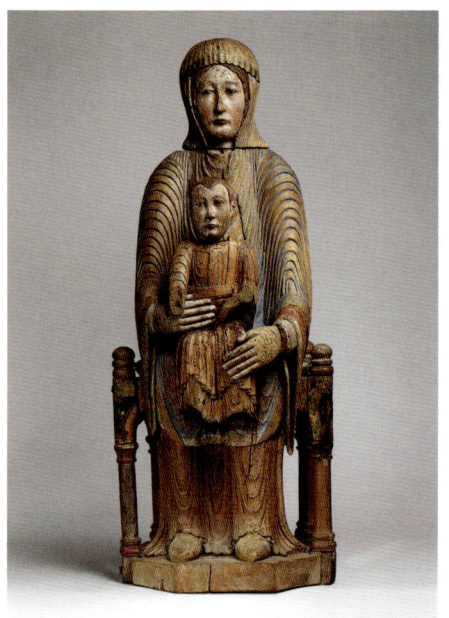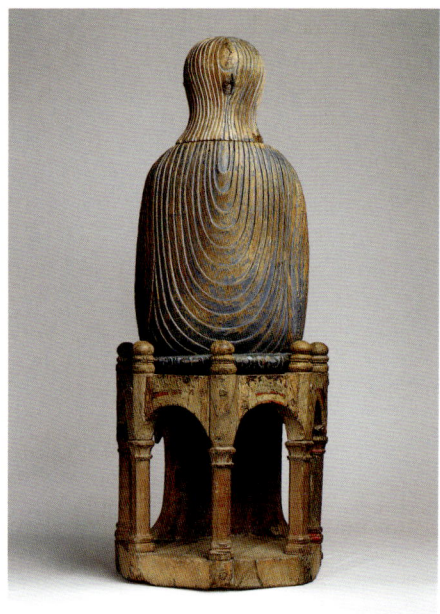

Figures 9–10. Artist unknown, *Virgin and Child in Majesty* (front and back), ca. 1175–1200. Walnut with paint, tin relief on a lead white ground, and linen, 31⁵/₁₆ × 12½ × 11½ inches. The Metropolitan Museum of Art, Gift of J. Pierpont Morgan, 1916, 16.32.194a, b.

of an institutionalized comment on the responsibility of humanity to protect the weak, as in the protection of the mother for the baby. *Death and Starvation* is a perversion of that concept; it becomes an image of death in the guise of caretaker for this neglected, starving child.

Did you also look at artists such as Käthe Kollwitz?

GRA: Absolutely. Käthe Kollwitz [Fig. 11] and also Wilhelm Lehmbruck [Fig. 12]. He made sense with his depictions of despair; he uses elongated arms that become so heavy that I can imagine his own sense of immobility, the difficulty to lift one's arm. Alberto Giacometti also utilizes lengthened torsos and arms with a surface that is modeled as if crushed by the environment around them. There is a loneliness to these figures.

Any final reflections?

GRA: I understand how wonderful life can be because I have had a wonderful life. When I joined the National Sculpture Society, I saw all these monuments to the glory of war, to the glory of leaders, to the glory of heroes, but nothing that reflected the negative nature in humanity. I hope I have not overdone it, but in expressing both the beautiful things and the awful side of humanity, I try to bring balance. Generations have dealt with conflict, genocide, enslavement, and we have to come to terms with it. My sculptural efforts seek to capture moments that should remind us of these cruel things but also reflect hope for the best of humanity.

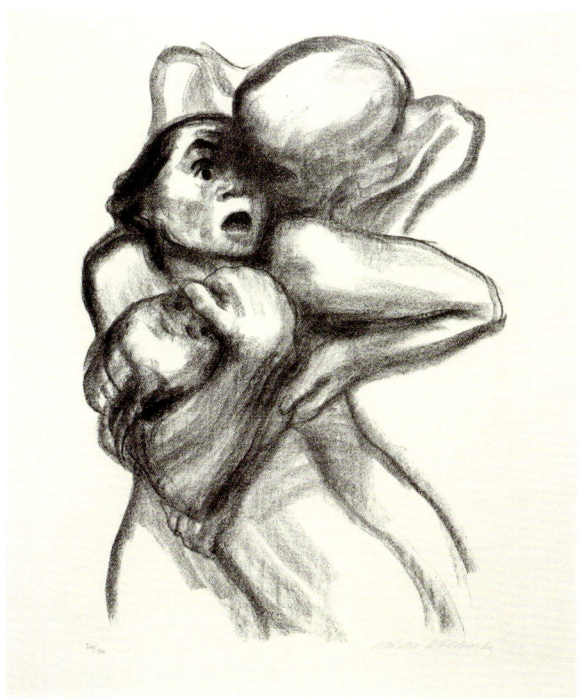

Figure 11. Käthe Kollwitz (1867–1945), *Death Seizes a Woman*, 1934. Crayon lithograph on paper, 24¾ × 19¾ inches. RISD Museum, 2005.142.7.

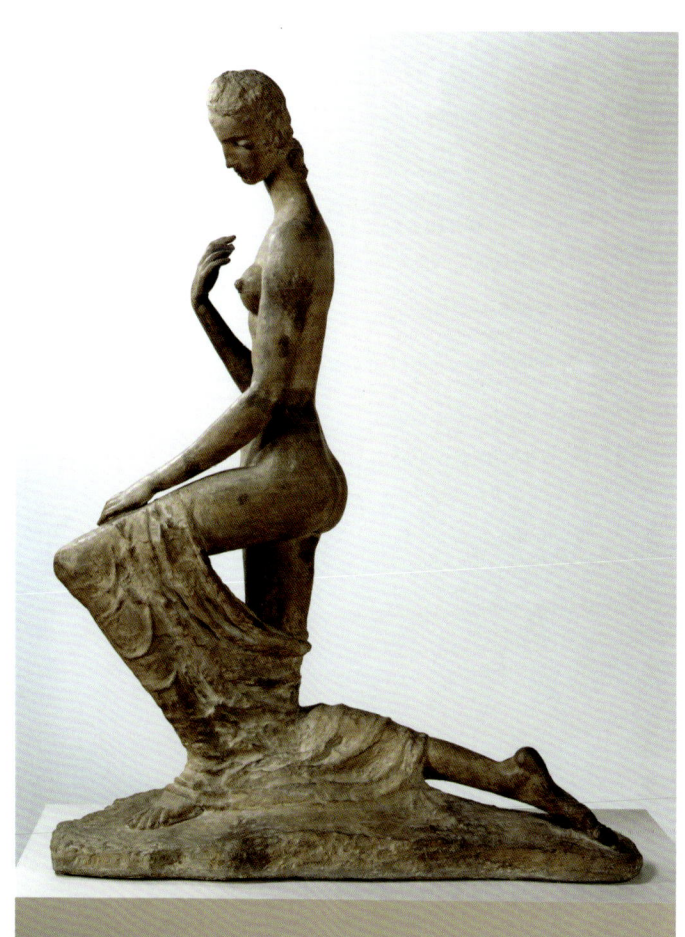

Figure 12. Wilhelm Lehmbruck (1881–1919), *Kneeling Woman*, 1911. Cast stone, 69½ × 56 × 27 inches. Museum of Modern Art, Abby Aldrich Rockefeller Fund, 268.1939.

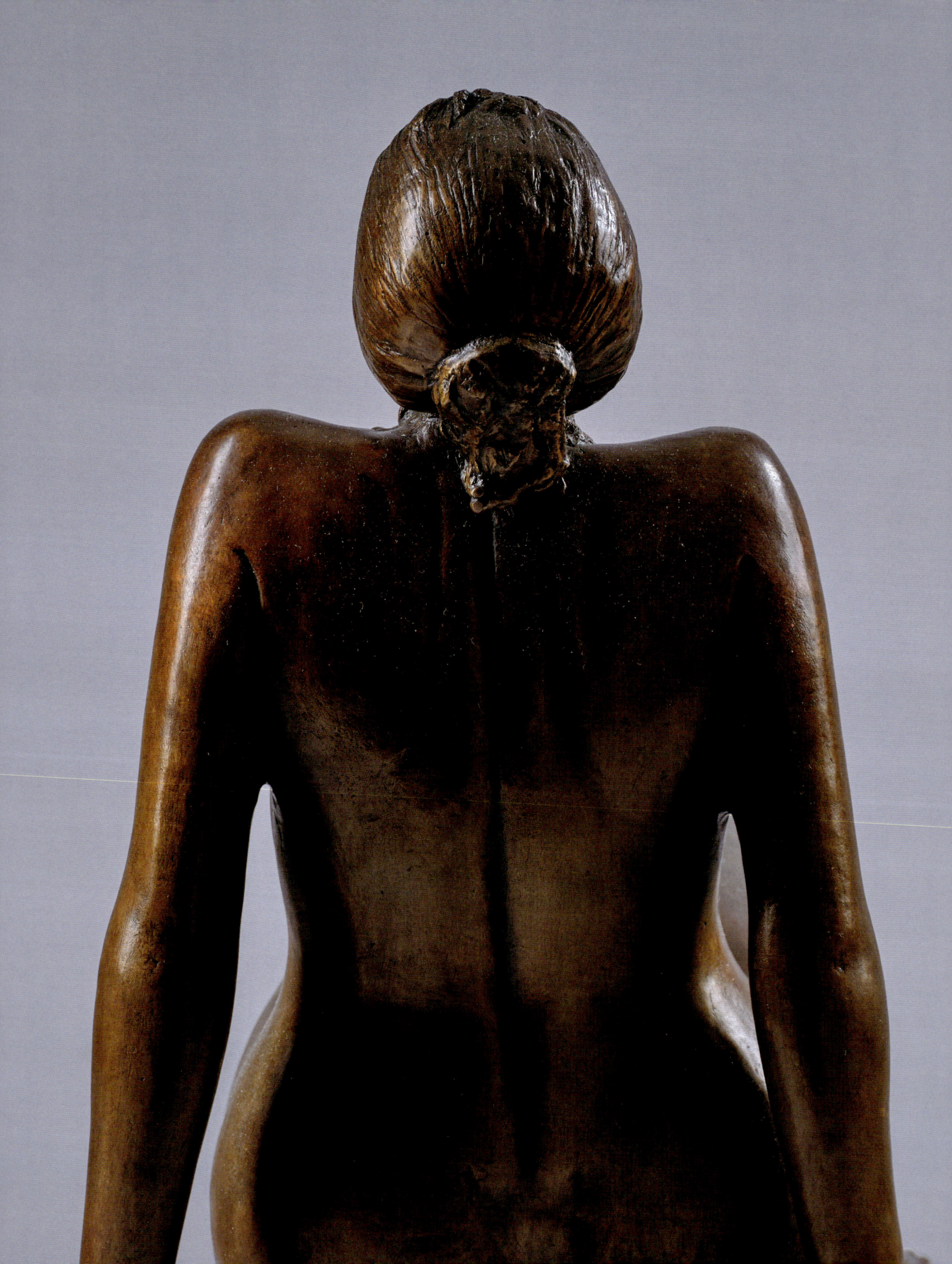

Exhibition Checklist

George R. Anthonisen (b. 1936), *Solomon*, 1972–74. Plaster, 26 × 21 × 12 inches. The Philip and Muriel Berman Museum of Art at Ursinus College.

George R. Anthonisen (b. 1936), *George Gershwin*, 1969–72. Bronze, life-size. Edition 4/15. Collection of Lucille and James Amadie.

George R. Anthonisen (b. 1936), *Dynamic Torso*, 1975–76. Bronze, 34 × 25 × 16 inches. Edition 2/3. Collection of Robert L. and Joyce Byers.

George R. Anthonisen (b. 1936), *Senator Ernest Gruening*, 1976. Plaster, 26¾ × 17¼ × 15½ inches. The Philip and Muriel Berman Museum of Art at Ursinus College.

George R. Anthonisen (b. 1936), *Murder: Cain and Abel*, 1975–76. Bronze, 38 × 13½ × 12½ inches. Edition 2/6. James A. Michener Art Museum, Anonymous gift, 2000.26.

George R. Anthonisen (b. 1936), *Death and Starvation*, 1976. Bronze, 22 × 17 × 20 inches. Edition 3/6. The Philip and Muriel Berman Museum of Art at Ursinus College.

George R. Anthonisen (b. 1936), *Nightmare*, 1977. Bronze, 13 × 10½ × 15 inches. Edition 1/6. Collection of the artist.

George R. Anthonisen (b. 1936), *Nude Undressing*, 1979–80. Bronze, 16 × 12½ × 11 inches. Edition 4/6. Collection of the artist.

George R. Anthonisen (b. 1936), *I Set Before You This Day (Study I: Kneeling Woman Rescuer)*, 1979–80. Plaster, 14 × 7 × 7½ inches. The Philip and Muriel Berman Museum of Art at Ursinus College.

George R. Anthonisen (b. 1936), *I Set Before You This Day (Study I: Mother with Son)*, 1979–80. Plaster, 17½ × 6½ × 8½ inches. The Philip and Muriel Berman Museum of Art at Ursinus College.

George R. Anthonisen (b. 1936), *I Set Before You This Day (Study I: Hostile Leader)*, 1979–80. Plaster, 17½ × 13 × 11 inches. The Philip and Muriel Berman Museum of Art at Ursinus College.

George R. Anthonisen (b. 1936), *I Set Before You This Day (Study I: Rescuer with Refugee Father and Daughter)*, 1979–80. Plaster, 19½ × 17 × 7 inches. The Philip and Muriel Berman Museum of Art at Ursinus College.

George R. Anthonisen (b. 1936), *Creation*, 1981–82. Bronze, 24 × 24 × 14 inches. Edition 3/9. Collection of Carol and Louis Della Penna.

George R. Anthonisen (b. 1936), *Picasso*, 1982–84. Bronze, 16 × 14 × 11 inches. Edition 1/1. Collection of Carol C. Turbow.

George R. Anthonisen (b. 1936), *Rudolf Serkin*, 1983–84. Aluminum, 23 inches diam. Edition 1/9. Collection of the artist.

George R. Anthonisen (b. 1936), *I Set Before You This Day*, 1979–87. Bronze, 37 × 29 × 28 inches. Edition 1/9. Collection of Helene and Mark Hankin.

George R. Anthonisen (b. 1936), *Antigone* (maquette), 1987. Plaster, 14 × 15¼ × 9 inches. The Philip and Muriel Berman Museum of Art at Ursinus College.

George R. Anthonisen (b. 1936), *Antigone*, 1988–91. Bronze, 27½ × 32 × 24 inches. Edition 1/9. Collection of the artist.

George R. Anthonisen (b. 1936), *Sunnyside Up*, 1988–91. Bronze, 11 × 47 × 16 inches. Edition 1/9. Collection of Kathy and Ted Fernberger.

George R. Anthonisen (b. 1936), *Give Us Grace (Study 3: Grandfather and Granddaughter Dancing)*, 1991. Plaster, 16 × 8⅛ × 5¼ inches. The Philip and Muriel Berman Museum of Art at Ursinus College.

George R. Anthonisen (b. 1936), *Give Us Grace (Study 6: African American Couple Dancing)*, 1991. Plaster, 16½ × 4½ × 4½ inches. The Philip and Muriel Berman Museum of Art at Ursinus College.

George R. Anthonisen (b. 1936), *Give Us Grace (Study 7: Male Couple Dancing)*, 1991. Plaster, 16¼ × 10¼ × 5⅛ inches. The Philip and Muriel Berman Museum of Art at Ursinus College.

George R. Anthonisen (b. 1936), *Dawn*, 1994. Bronze, 22 × 11½ × 9 inches. Edition 4/9. James A. Michener Art Museum, Gift of Henry W. Pfeiffer, 2014.1.

George R. Anthonisen (b. 1936), *Caryatid* (maquette), 1992–94. Plaster, 17⅞ × 8 × 9½ inches. Collection of Rachel Anthonisen Gates.

George R. Anthonisen (b. 1936), *Meditation* (maquette), 1994. Bronze, 36½ × 13 × 8 inches. Edition 2/9. Collection of Cherry and Eddie Robinson.

George R. Anthonisen (b. 1936), *Give Us Grace*, 1994–96. Bronze, 78 × 60 × 14 inches. Edition 1/5. James A. Michener Art Museum, Gift of George and Ellen Anthonisen, 2016.13.1.

George R. Anthonisen (b. 1936), *Game Over*, 1995–96. Bronze, 19 × 28 × 9 inches. Edition 1/9. The Philip and Muriel Berman Museum of Art at Ursinus College.

George R. Anthonisen (b. 1936), *Tea Party* (maquette), 1996–97. Bronze, 20 × 32 × 19 inches. Edition 1/9. Collection of the artist.

George R. Anthonisen (b. 1936), *Transcendence (Caryatid Head)*, 1996–2022. Plaster, 24 × 14 × 14 inches. Collection of the artist.

George R. Anthonisen (b. 1936), *Raoul Wallenberg II*, 1998–2000. Plaster, 27 × 15 × 15 inches. Collection of the artist.

George R. Anthonisen (b. 1936), *Caryatid*, 1994–2000. Bronze, 74 × 43 × 39 inches. Edition 1/5. James A. Michener Art Museum, Gift of George and Ellen Anthonisen, 2016.13.2.

George R. Anthonisen (b. 1936), *Torso III Drape*, 2001. Bronze, 15 × 5 × 4 inches. Edition 2/9. Collection of the artist.

George R. Anthonisen (b. 1936), *Dialogue*, 2003–04. Bronze, 29 × 20 × 20 inches. Edition 1/9. Collection of Carol and Louis Della Penna.

George R. Anthonisen (b. 1936), *Three Nudes (Graces)*, 2006–07. Bronze, 31⅜ × 36½ inches. Edition 2/9. James A. Michener Art Museum, Donated in memory of William J. Smart, 2023.26.2.

George R. Anthonisen (b. 1936), *Aspiration*, 2007–08. Bronze, 35 × 30 × 29 inches. Edition 2/9. James A. Michener Art Museum, Donated in memory of William J. Smart, 2023.26.1.

George R. Anthonisen (b. 1936), *Five Women*, 2010–12. Bronze, 15 × 14½ × 6 inches. Edition 2/9. Collection of Brenda and John Bray.

George R. Anthonisen (b. 1936), *The Choice*, 2022–24. Bronze, 16 × 12½ × 12 inches. Edition 1/9. Collection of Anne K. MacDowell and Martin R. Quigley.

FRESCOES

George R. Anthonisen (b. 1936), *Evolving Images*, 1987. Mineral colors, limewater, and casein on plaster, 28 × 30 inches. James A. Michener Art Museum, Gift of Tom Spain, 2014.8.

George R. Anthonisen (b. 1936), *Origins*, 1987. Mineral colors, limewater, and casein on plaster, 49¼ × 37¼ inches. Collection of the artist.

George R. Anthonisen (b. 1936), *Arrangement IV*, 1993. Mineral colors, limewater, and casein on plaster, 23 × 25¼ inches. Private collection.

George R. Anthonisen (b. 1936), *Armitage Road, Solebury*, 2000. Mineral colors, limewater, and casein on plaster, 24 × 32 inches. Collection of Ann and Daniel Bernstein.

PAINTINGS

Paul Matthews (1933–2019), *Portrait of George Anthonisen*, 1985. Oil on canvas, 31 × 26 inches. From the home of Brent and Janet Anthonisen.

Daniel Anthonisen (b. 1970), *Union*, 2015. Casein on gesso panel, 8 × 10 inches. Collection of George and Ellen Anthonisen.

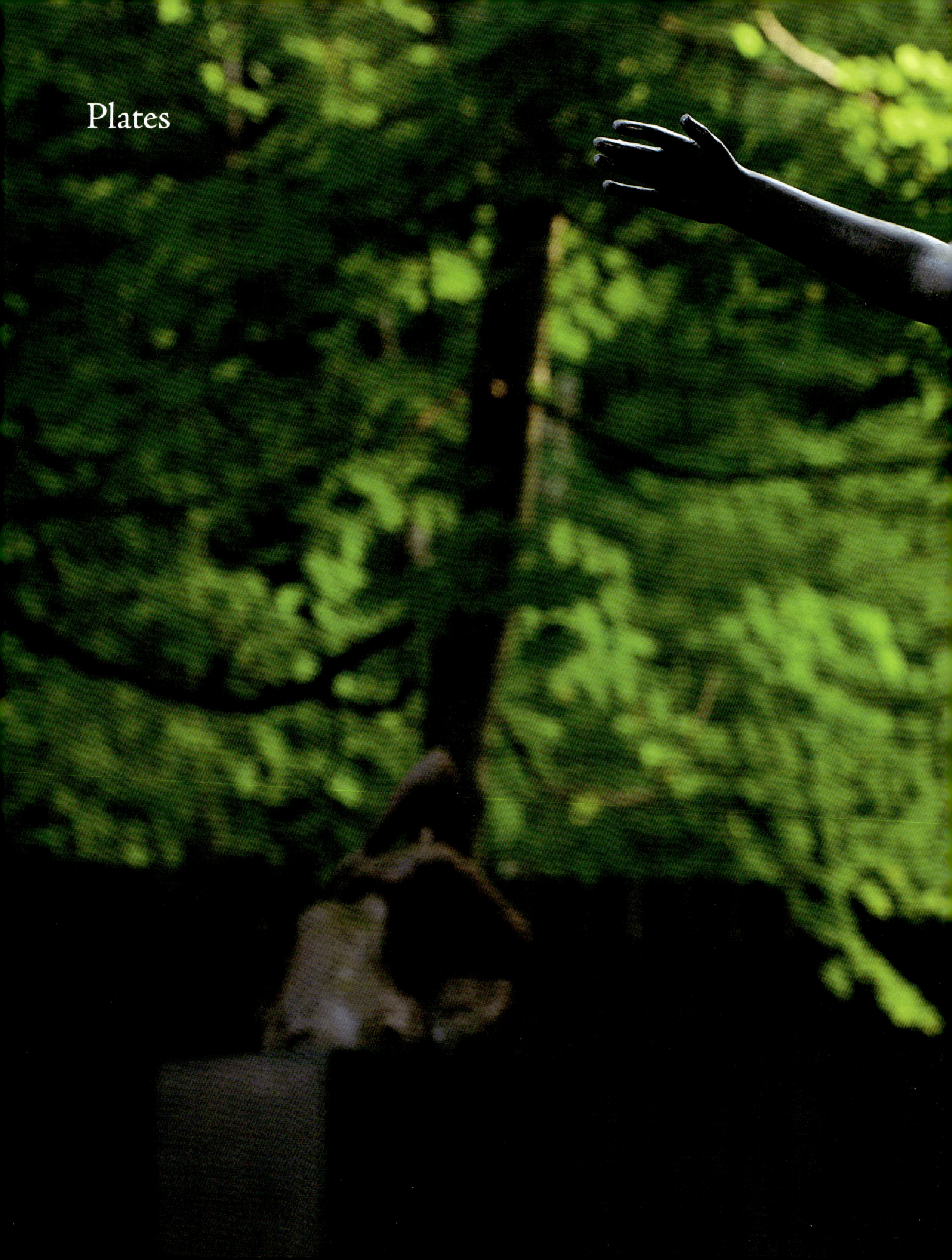

Plates

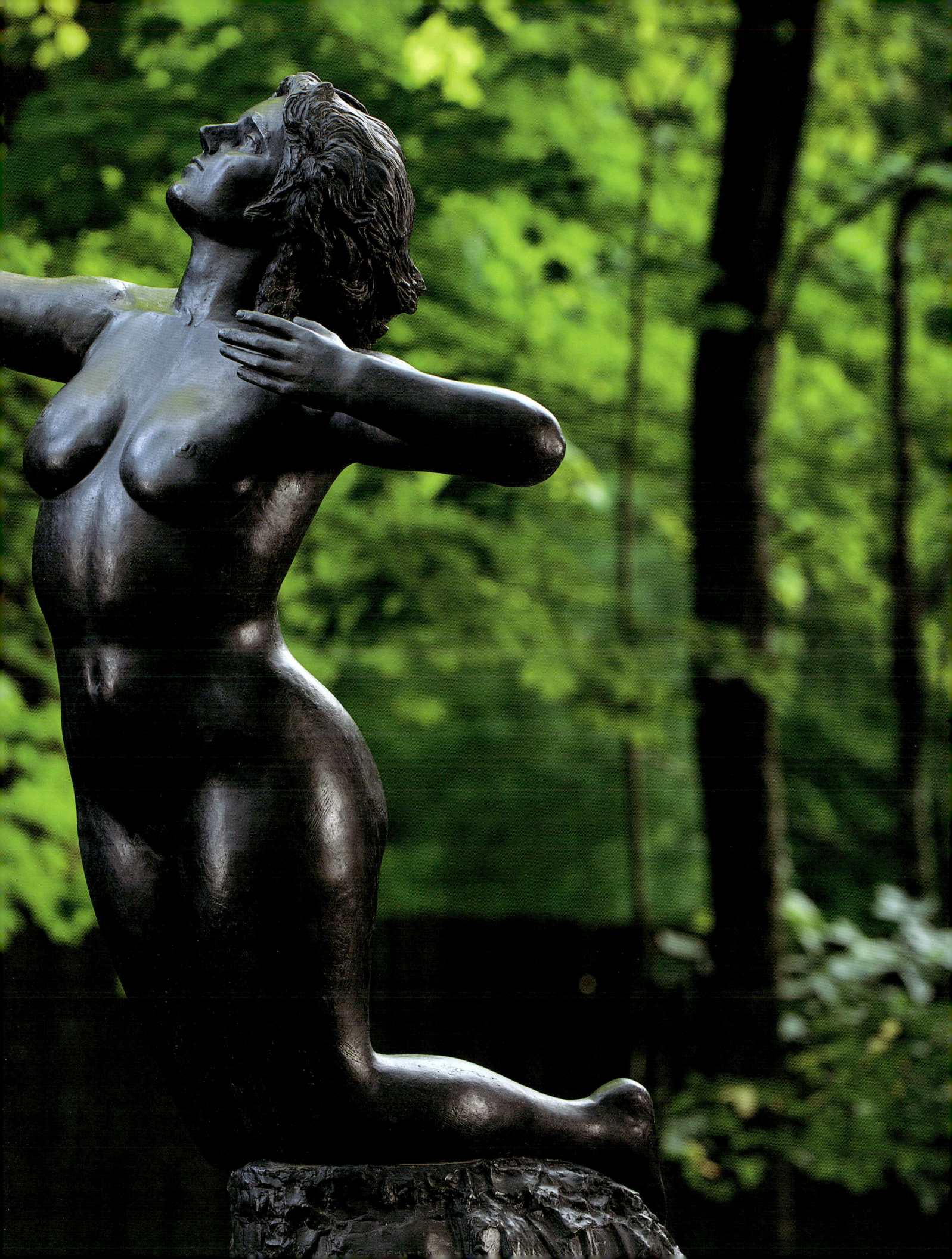

Sculpture

PLATE I

Heroic Torso, 1966–69

Bronze, 49 × 16 × 23 inches. Edition 1/1
The Philip and Muriel Berman Museum of Art at Ursinus College

58   GEORGE R. ANTHONISEN: MEDITATIONS ON THE HUMAN CONDITION

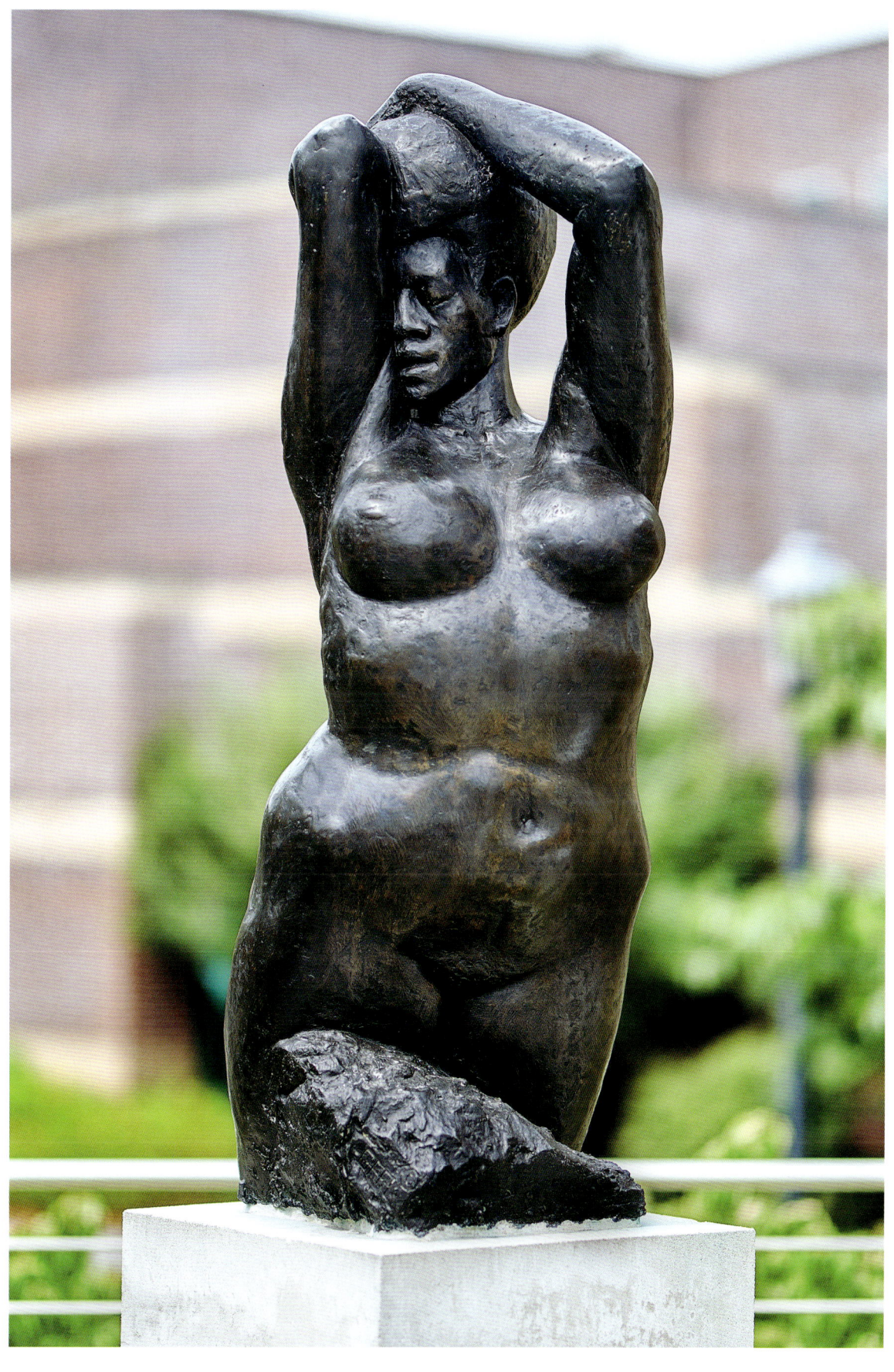

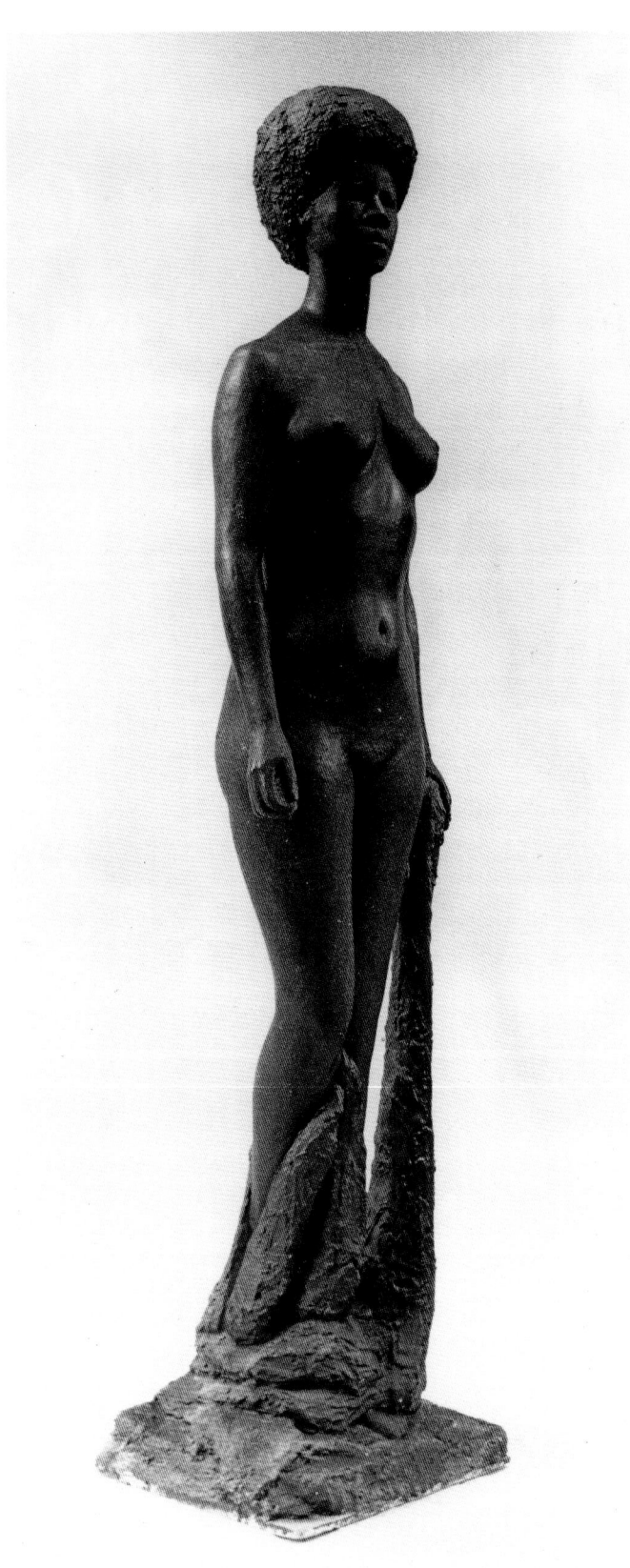

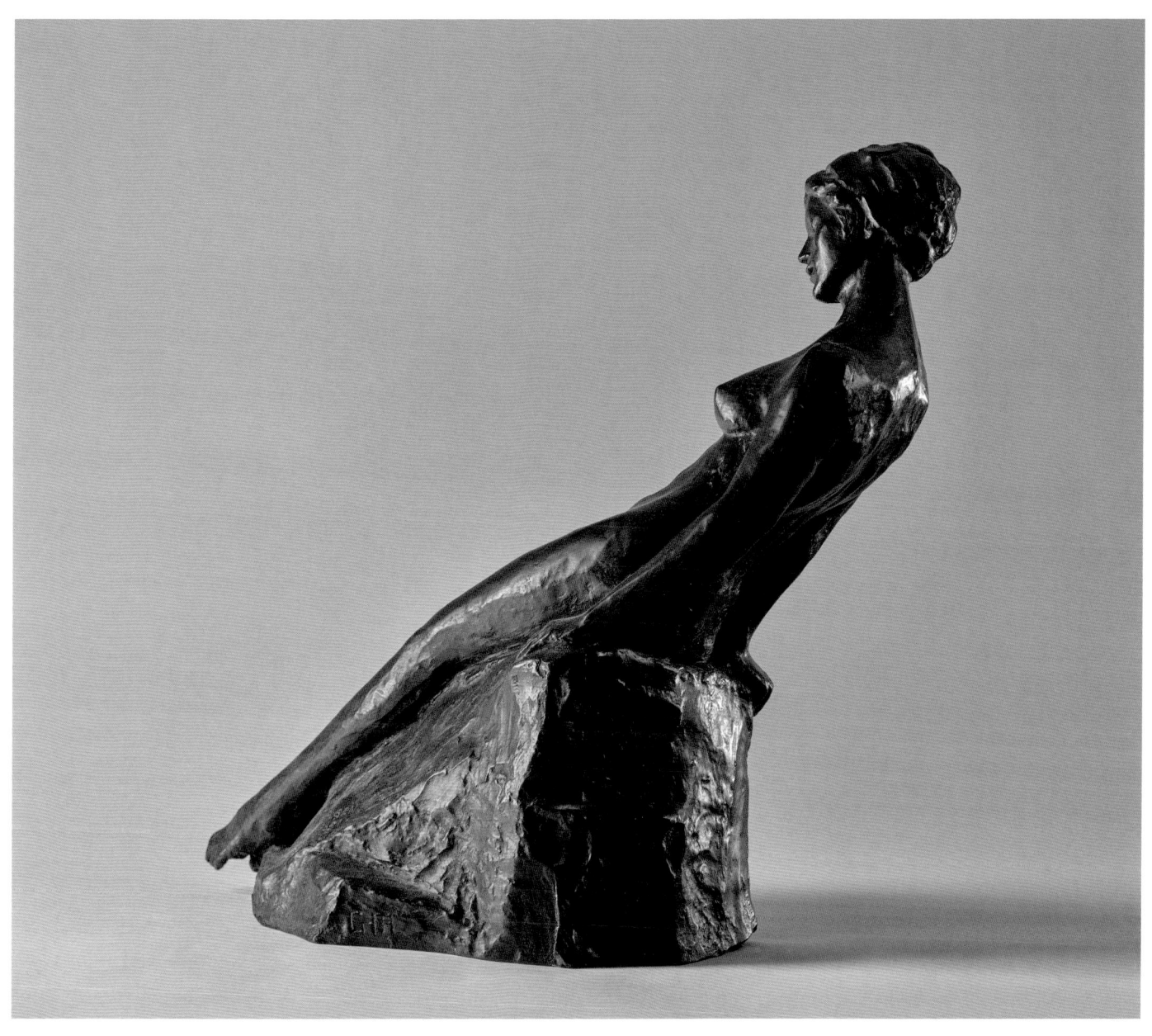

PLATE 3
Semi-Reclining Nude, 1968

Bronze, 18 × 19 × 7 inches. Edition 6/6
Collection of the artist

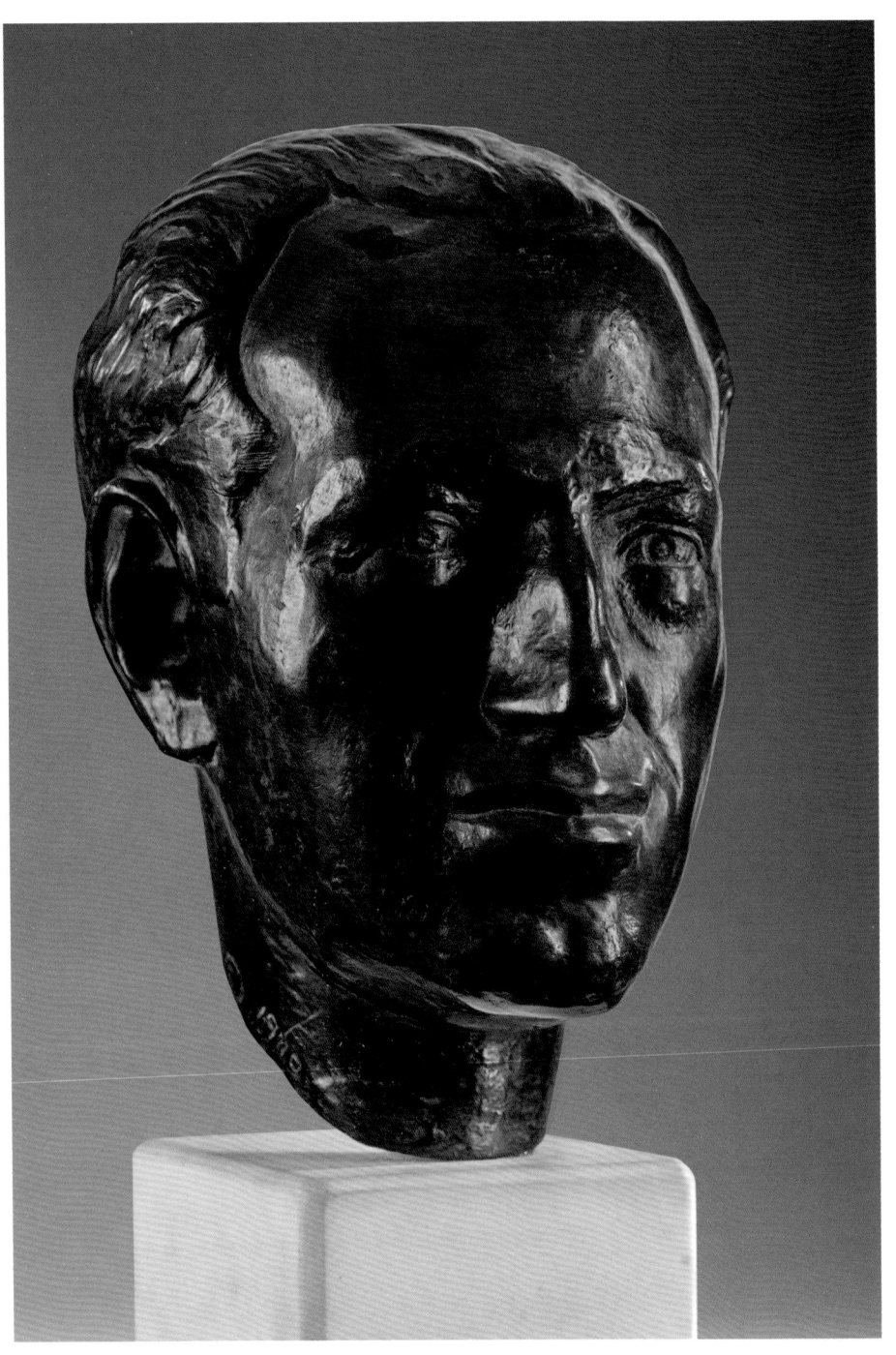

PLATE 4
George Gershwin, 1969–72
Bronze, life-size. Edition 4/15
Collection of Lucille and James Amadie

PLATE 5
Murder: Cain and Abel, 1975–76
Bronze, 38 × 13½ × 12½ inches. Edition 2/6
James A. Michener Art Museum, Anonymous gift,
2000.26

62   GEORGE R. ANTHONISEN: MEDITATIONS ON THE HUMAN CONDITION

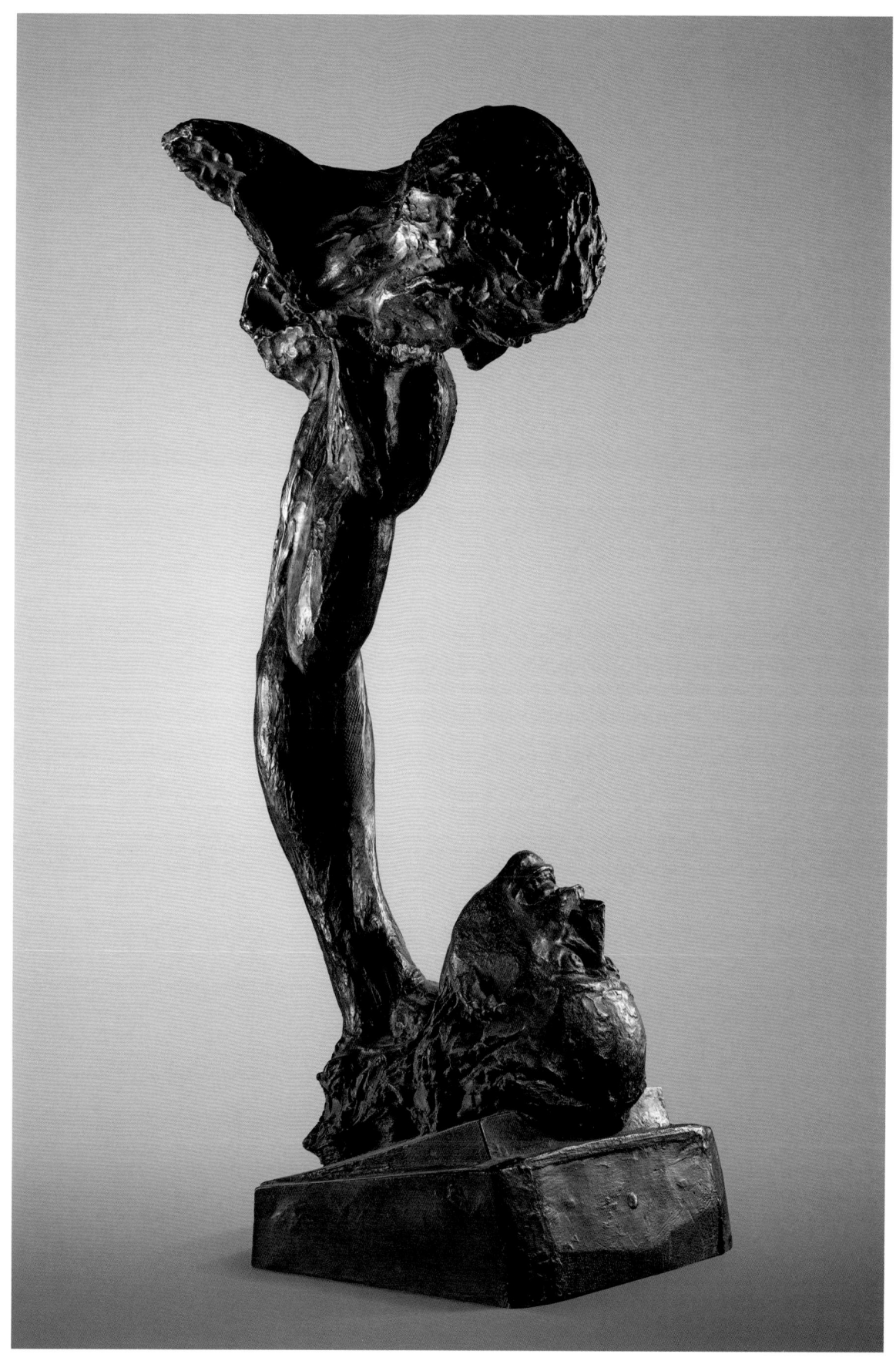

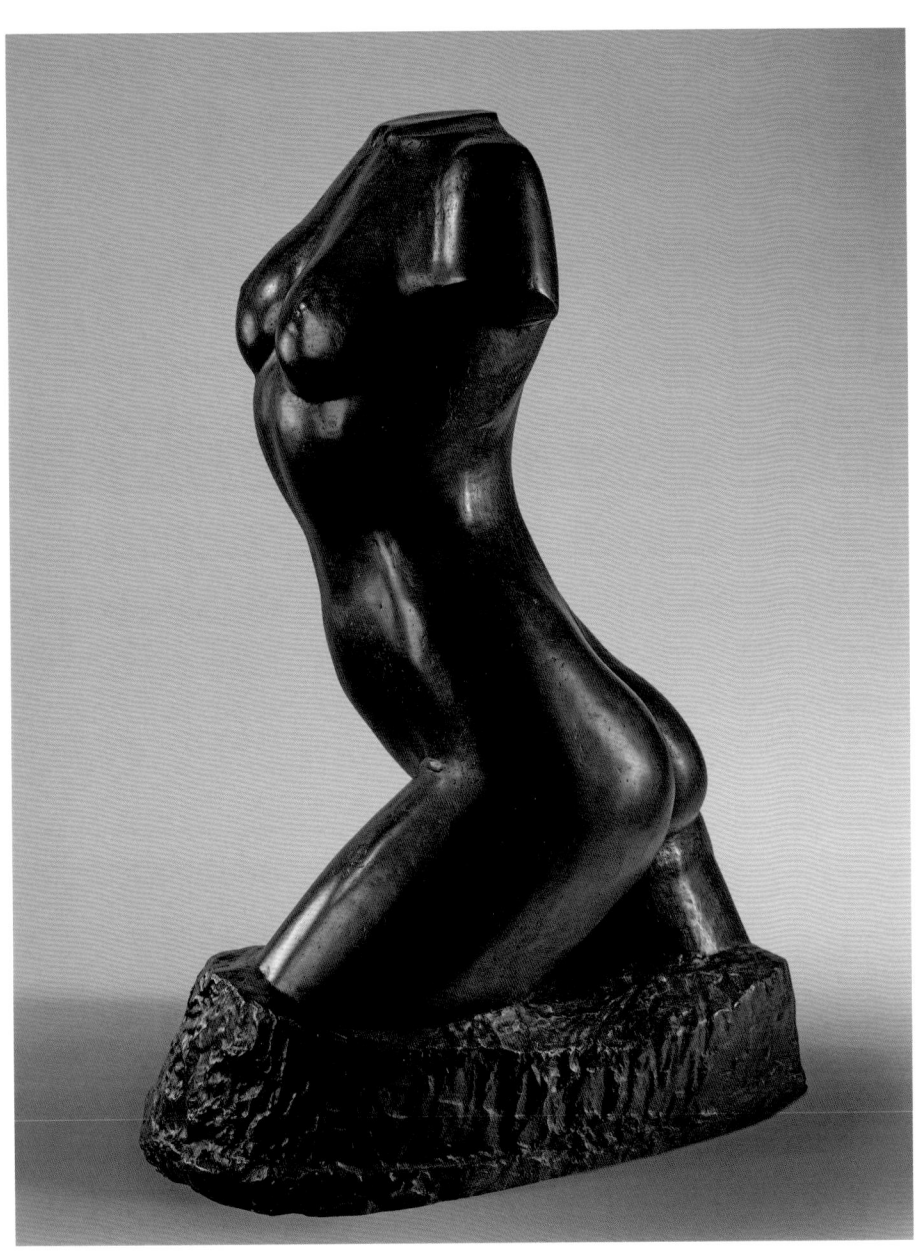

Dynamic Torso, 1975–76

Bronze, 34 × 25 × 16 inches. Edition 2/3
Collection of Robert L. and Joyce Byers

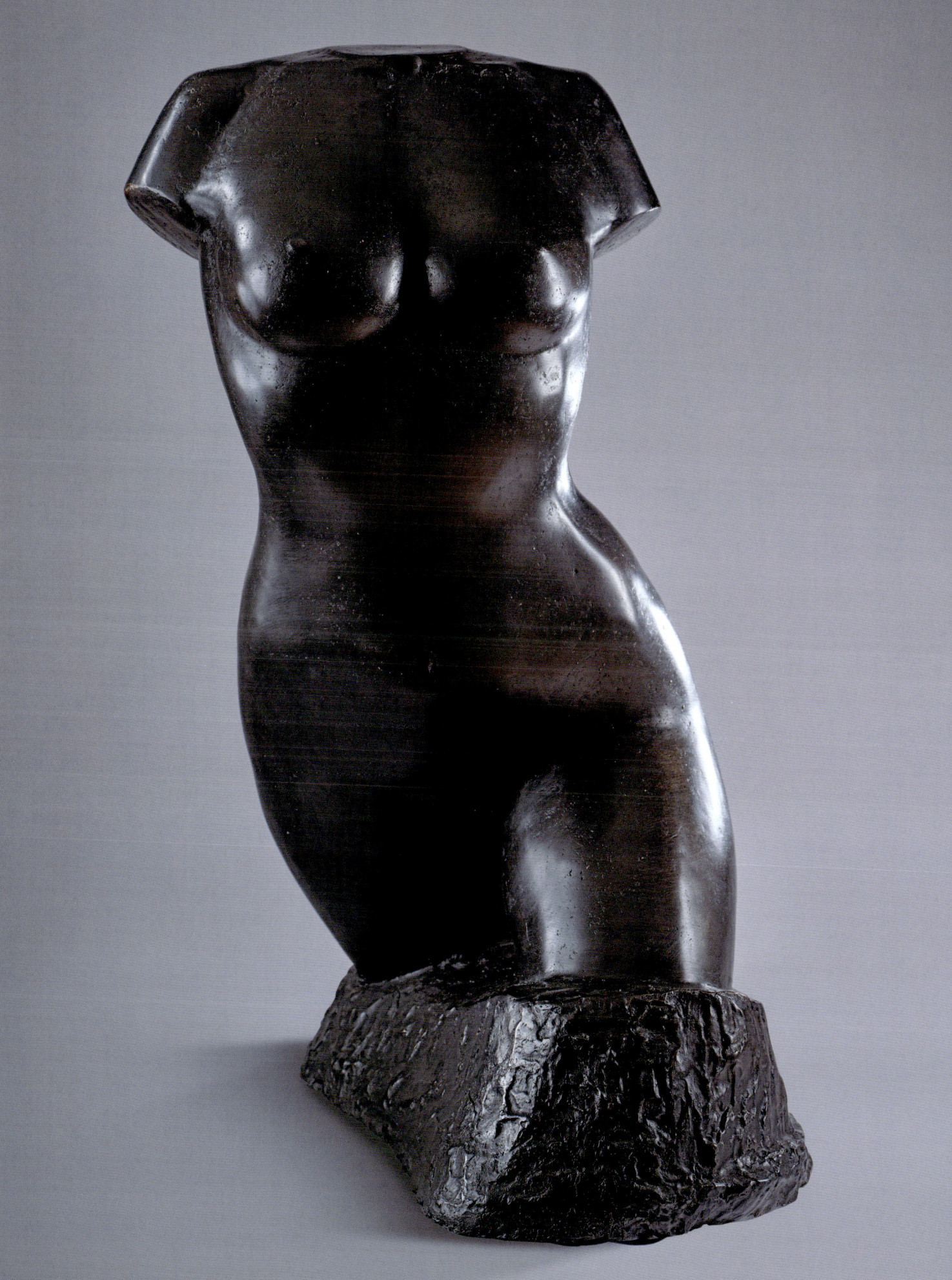

PLATE 8

Death and Starvation, 1976

Bronze, 22 × 17 × 20 inches. Edition 3/6
The Philip and Muriel Berman Museum of Art at Ursinus College

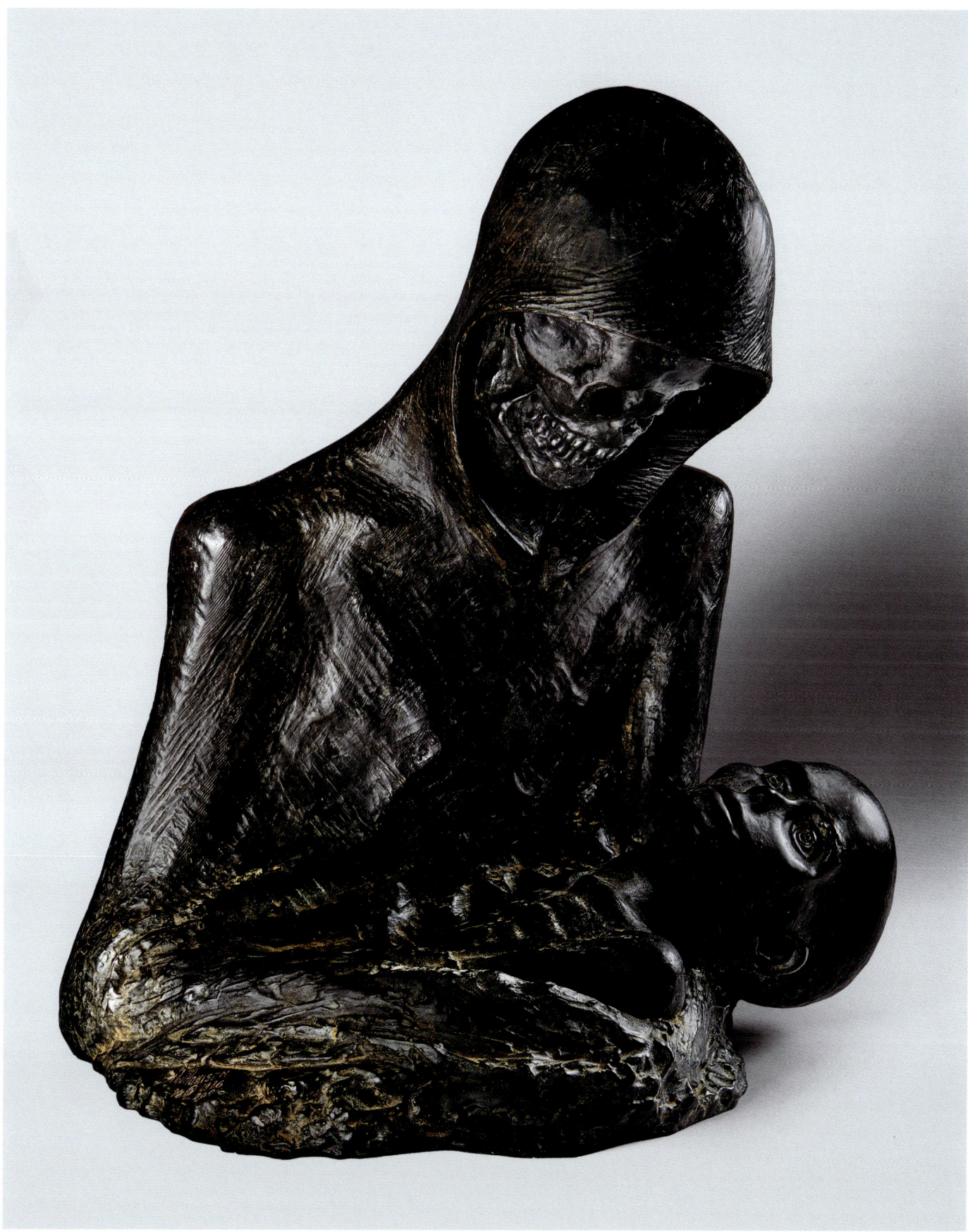

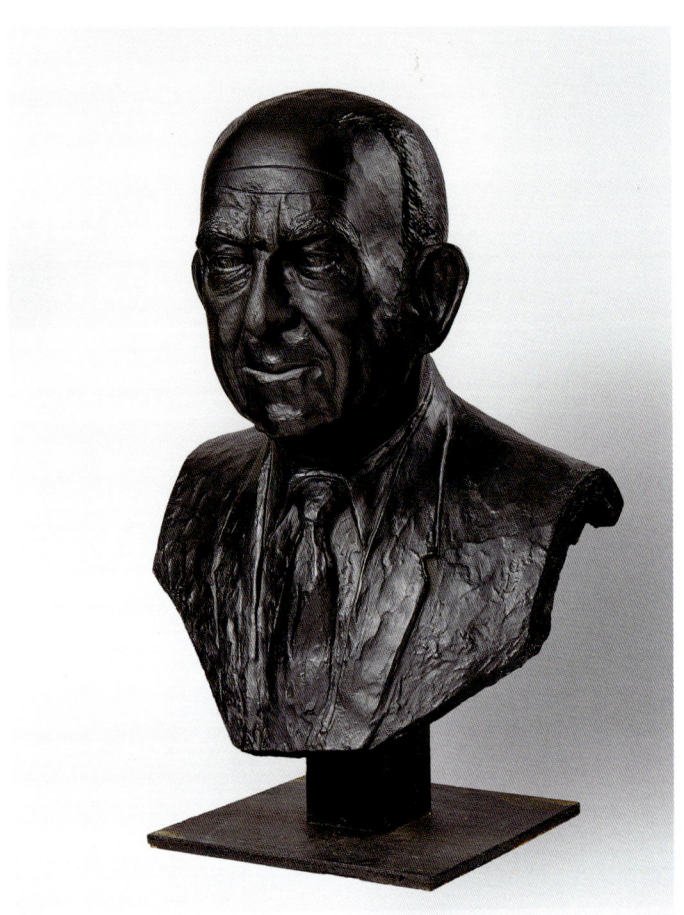

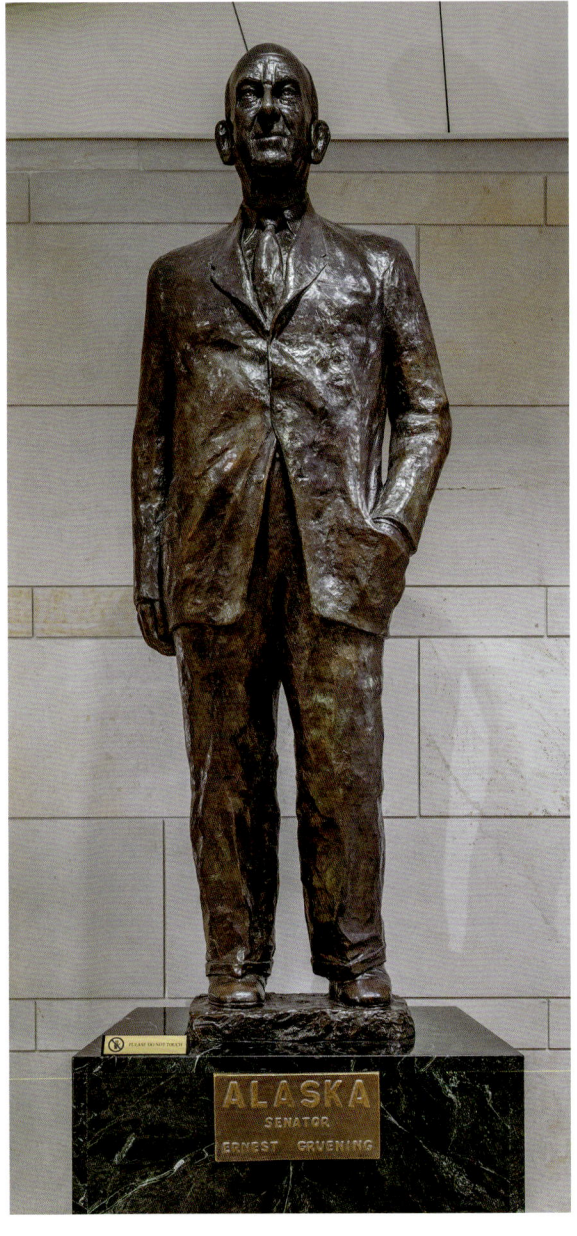

PLATE 9
Senator Ernest Gruening, 1976
Plaster, 26¾ × 17¼ × 15½ inches
The Philip and Muriel Berman Museum of Art
at Ursinus College

PLATE 10
Senator Ernest Gruening, 1976–77
Bronze, 7 feet high. Edition 1/1
Alaska State Council on the Arts for US Capitol Building,
Architect of the Capitol

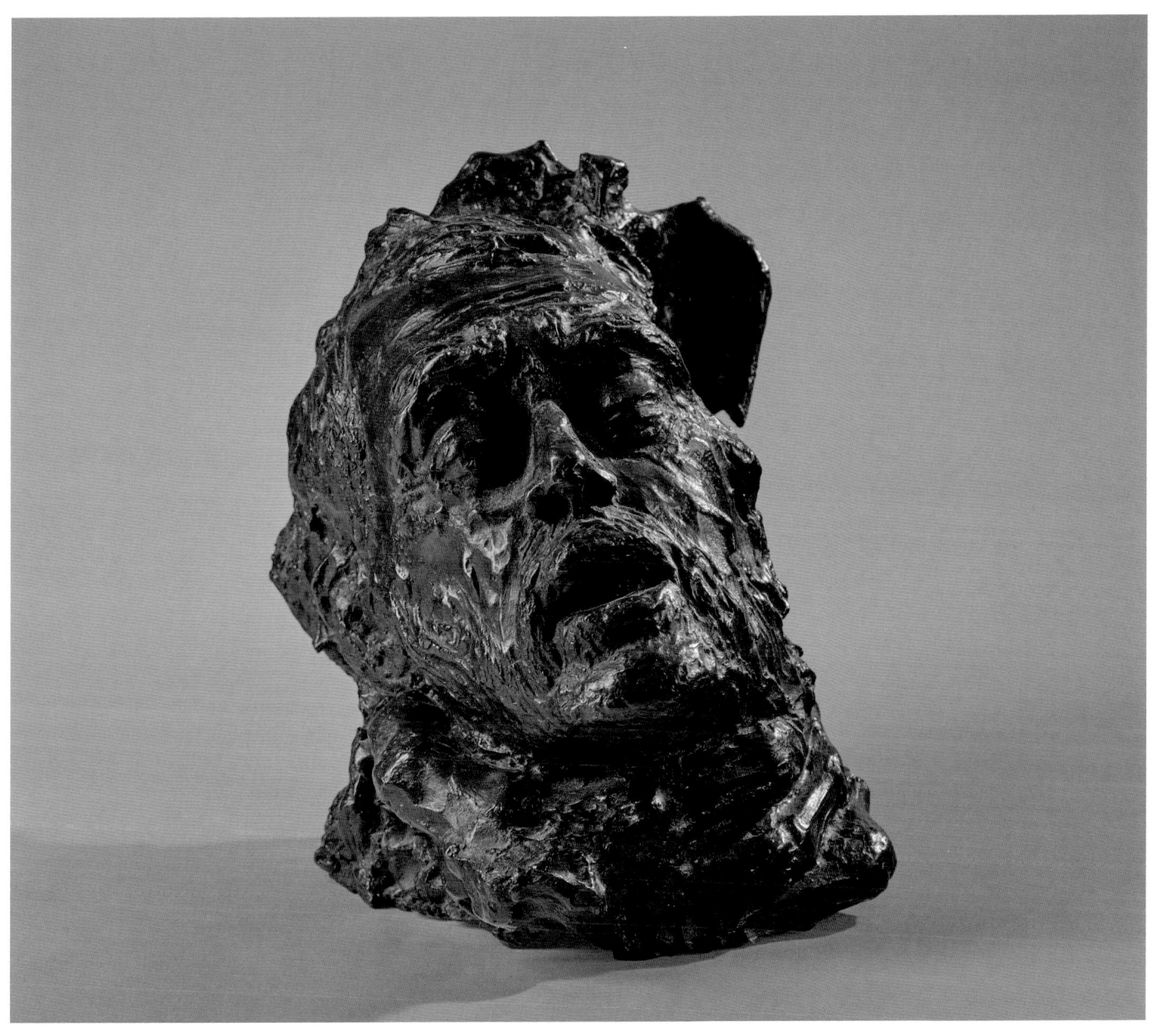

PLATE II

Nightmare, 1977

Bronze, 13 × 10½ × 15 inches. Edition 1/6
Collection of the artist

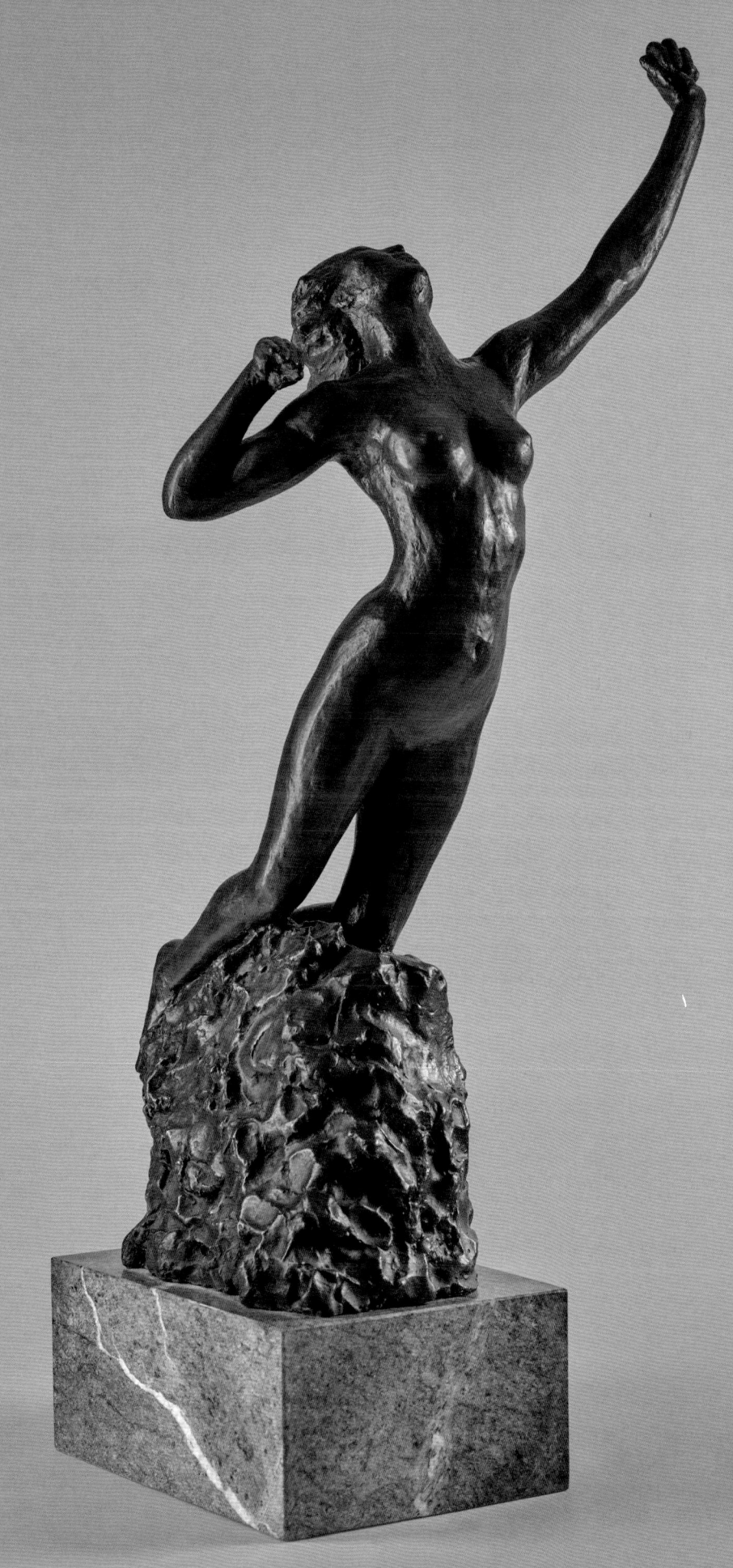

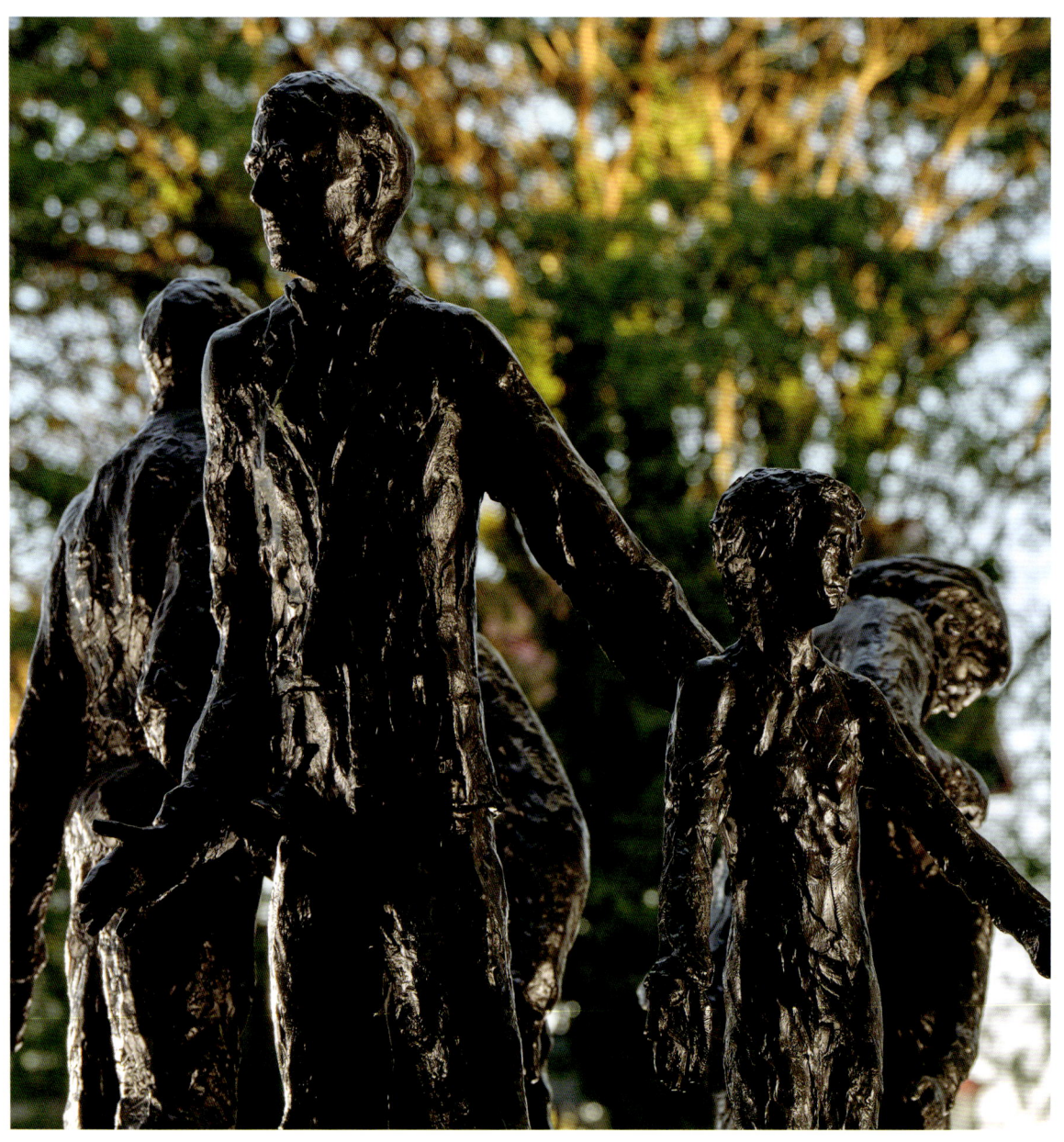

I Set Before You This Day, 1979–87

Bronze, 37 × 29 × 28 inches. Edition 1/9
Collection of Helene and Mark Hankin

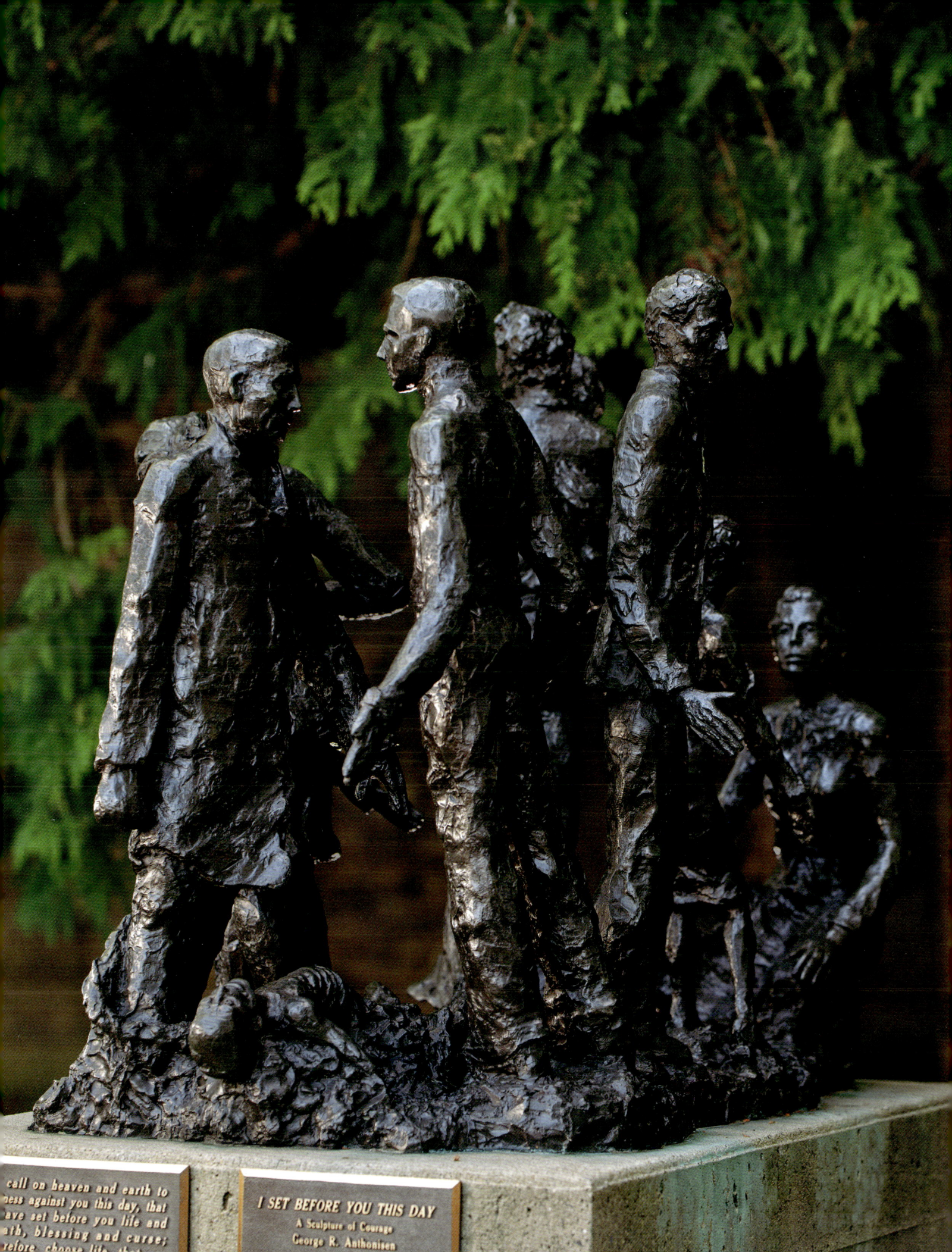

call on heaven and earth to
...ness against you this day, that
...ave set before you life and
...ath, blessing and curse;
...fore choose life, that...

I SET BEFORE YOU THIS DAY
A Sculpture of Courage
George R. Anthonisen

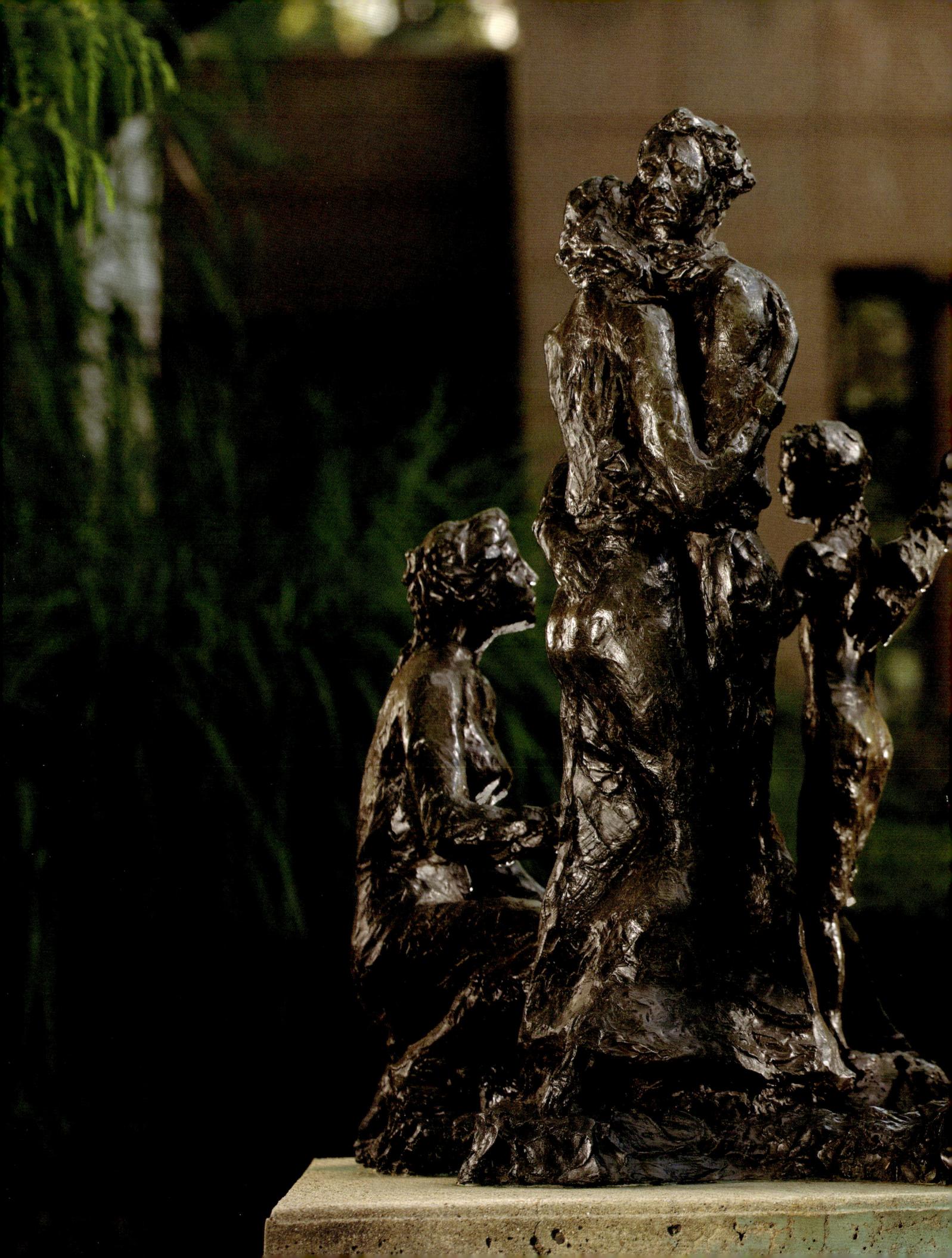

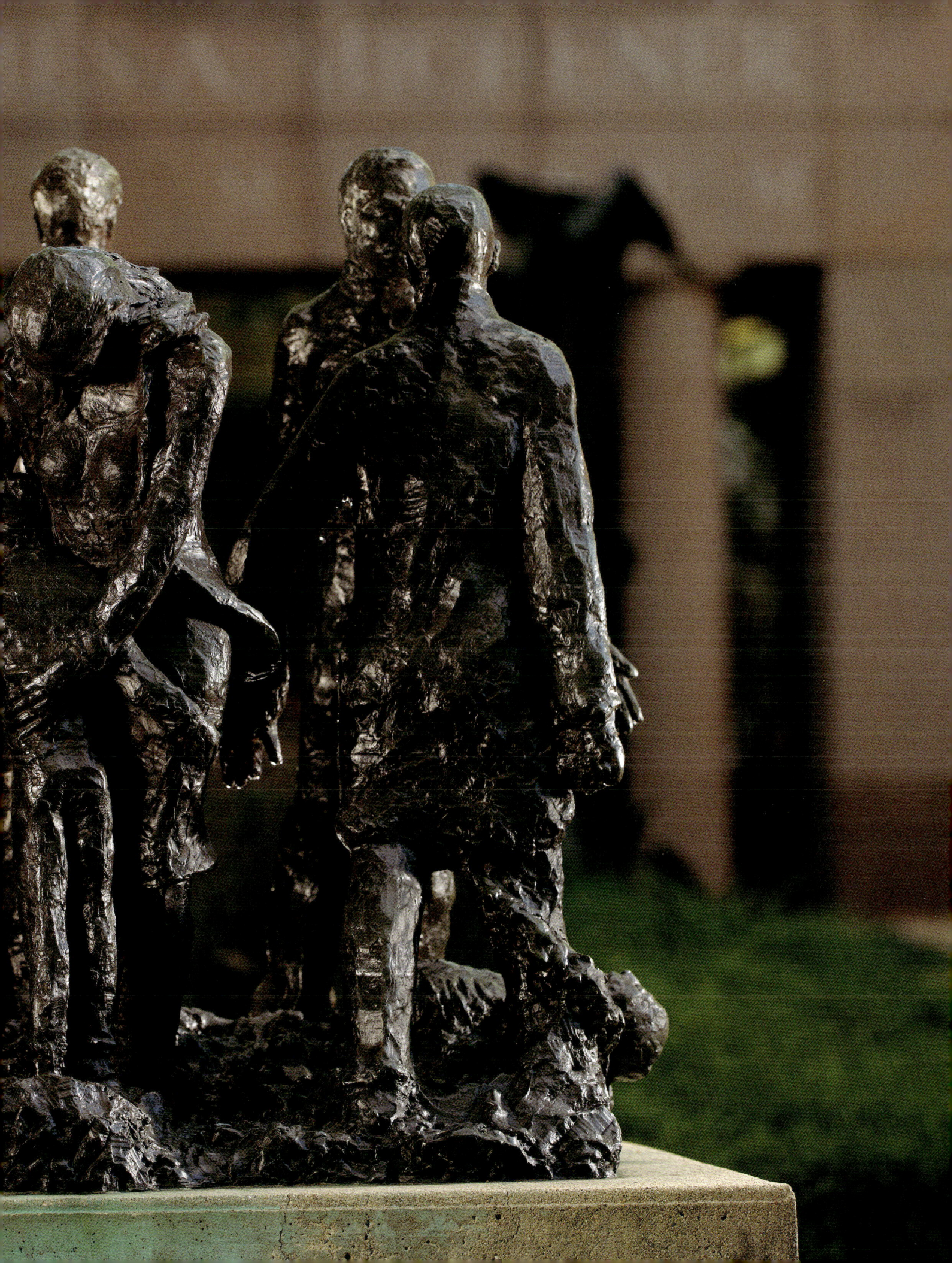

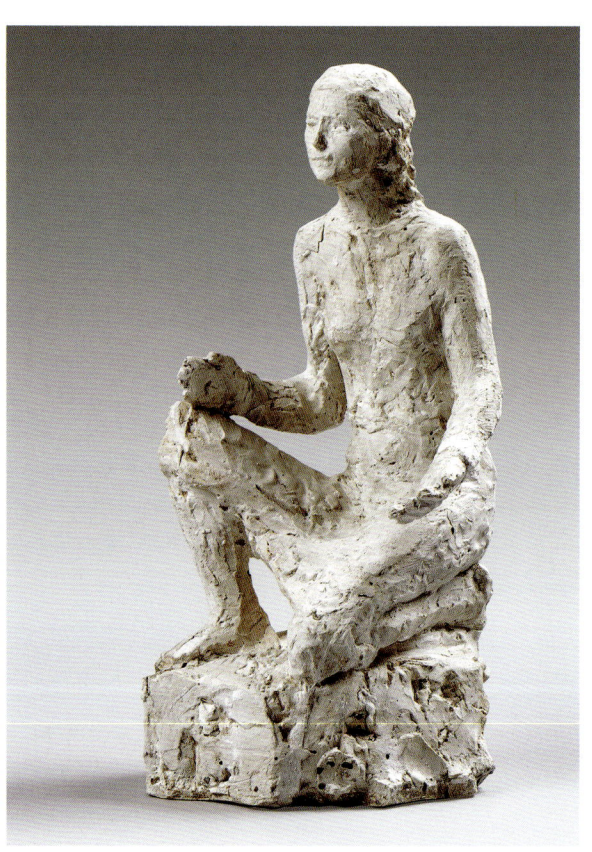

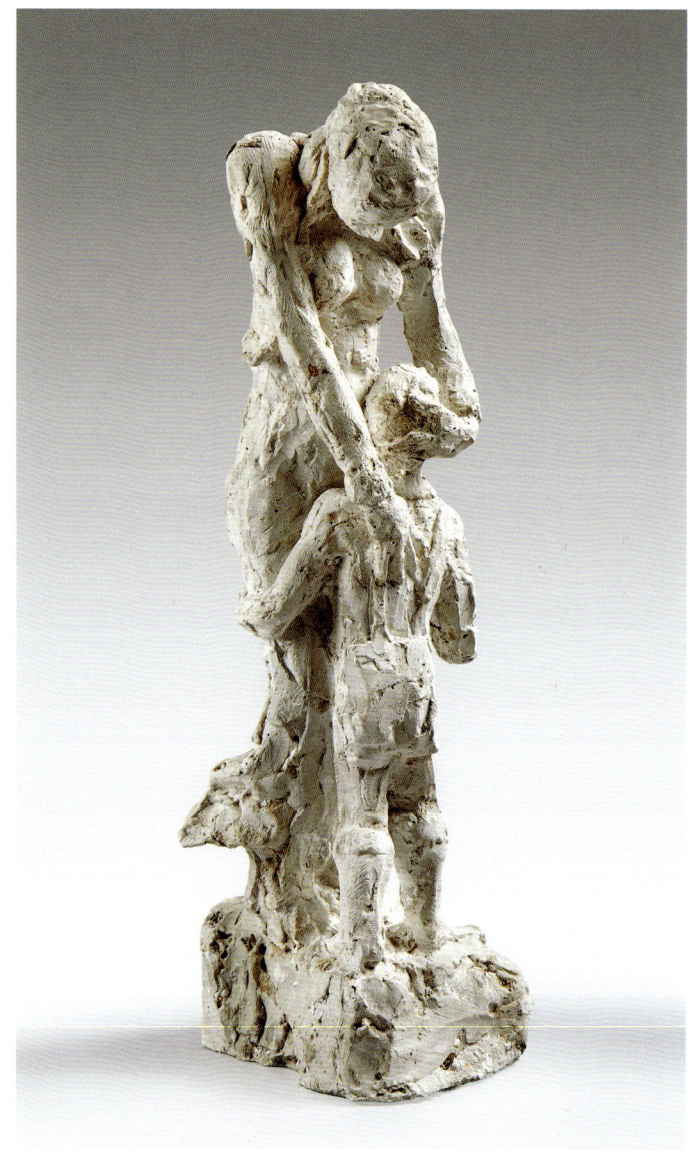

PLATE 16

I Set Before You This Day (Study I: Kneeling Woman Rescuer), 1979–80

Plaster, 14 × 7 × 7½ inches
The Philip and Muriel Berman Museum of Art at Ursinus College

PLATE 17

I Set Before You This Day (Study I: Mother with Son), 1979–80

Plaster, 17½ × 6½ × 8½ inches
The Philip and Muriel Berman Museum of Art at Ursinus College

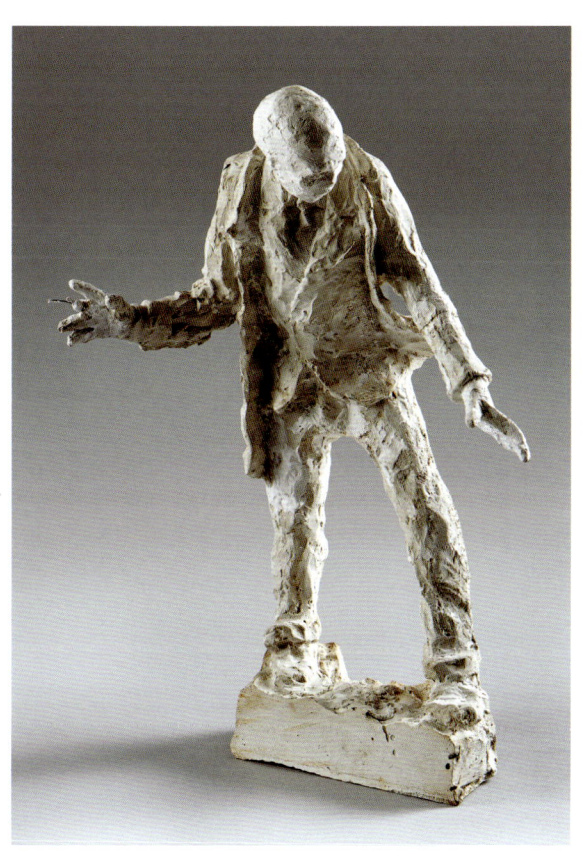

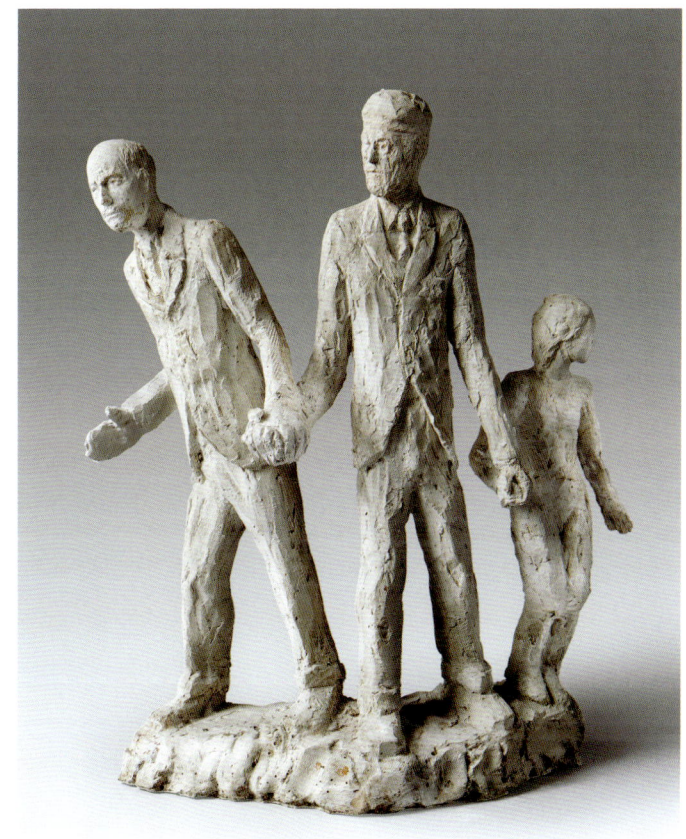

PLATE 18

I Set Before You This Day (Study I: Hostile Leader), 1979–80

Plaster, 17½ × 13 × 11 inches
The Philip and Muriel Berman Museum of Art at Ursinus College

PLATE 19

I Set Before You This Day (Study I: Rescuer with Refugee Father and Daughter), 1979–80

Plaster, 19½ × 17 × 7 inches
The Philip and Muriel Berman Museum of Art at Ursinus College

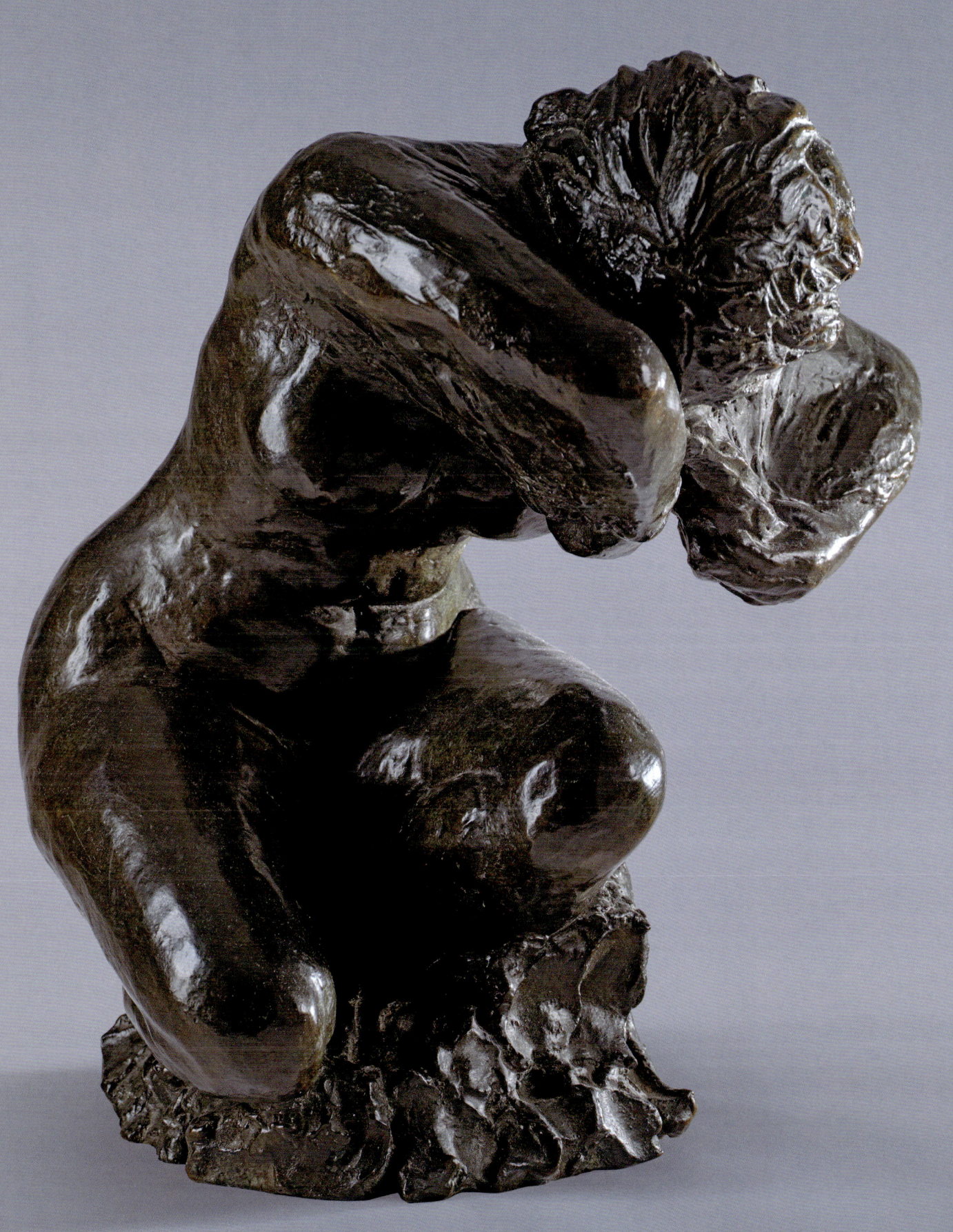

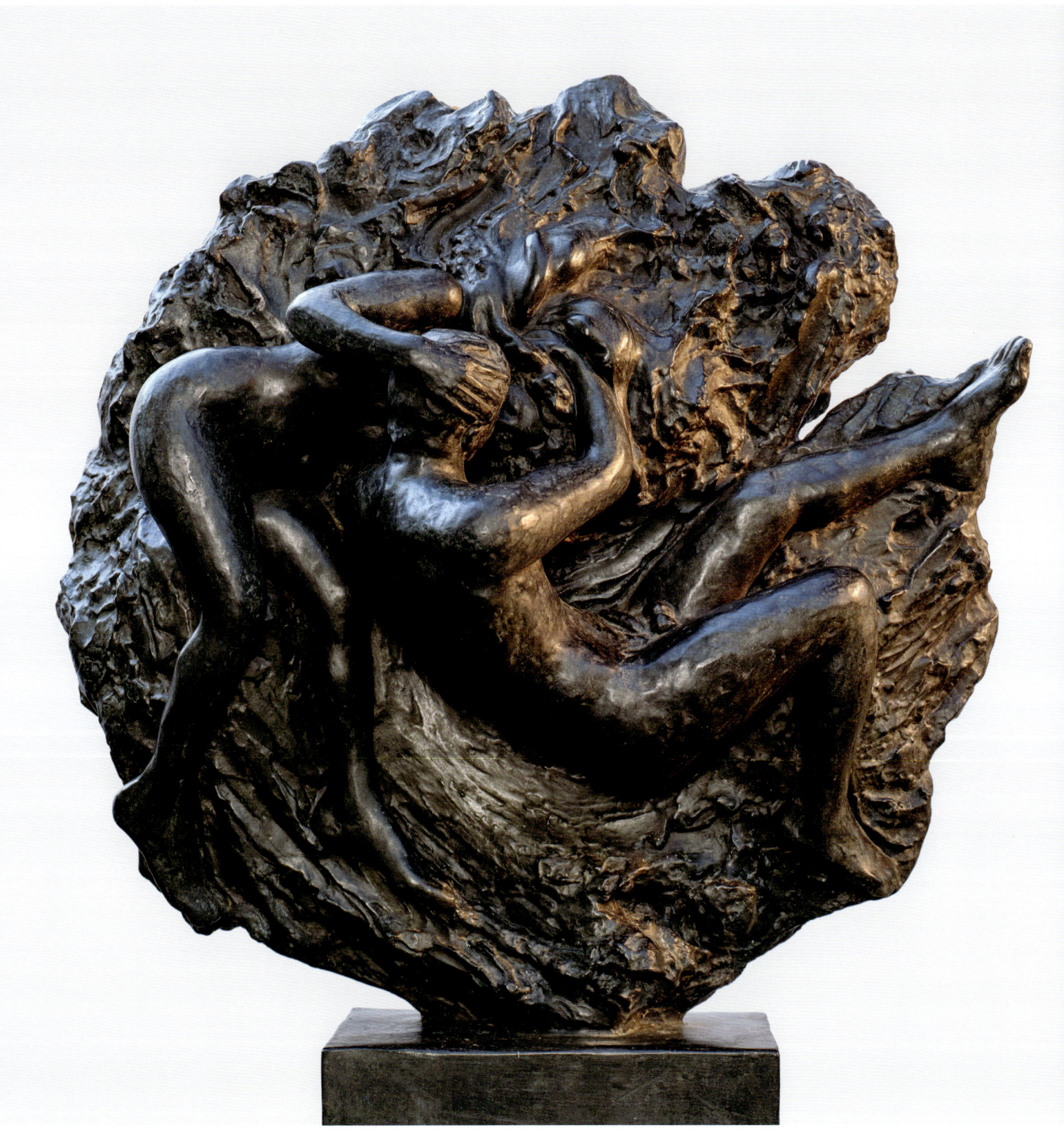

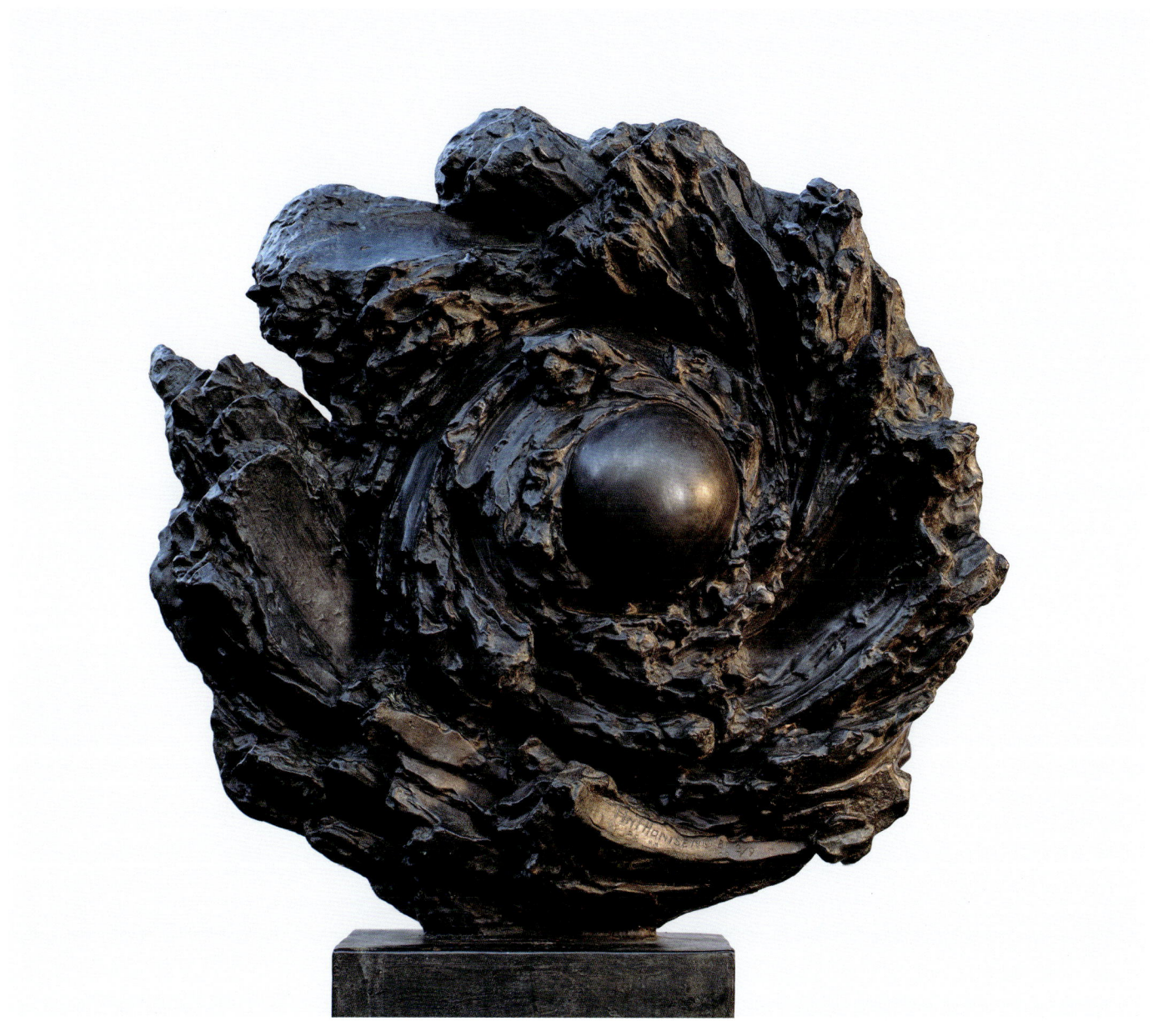

Creation (front and back), 1981–82

Bronze, 24 × 24 × 14 inches. Edition 3/9
Collection of Carol and Louis Della Penna

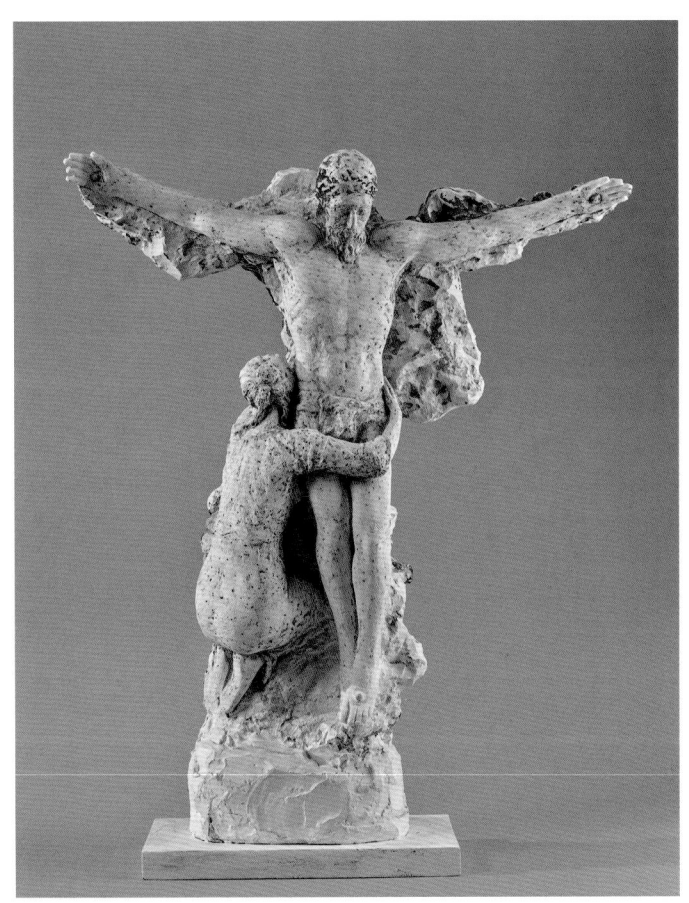 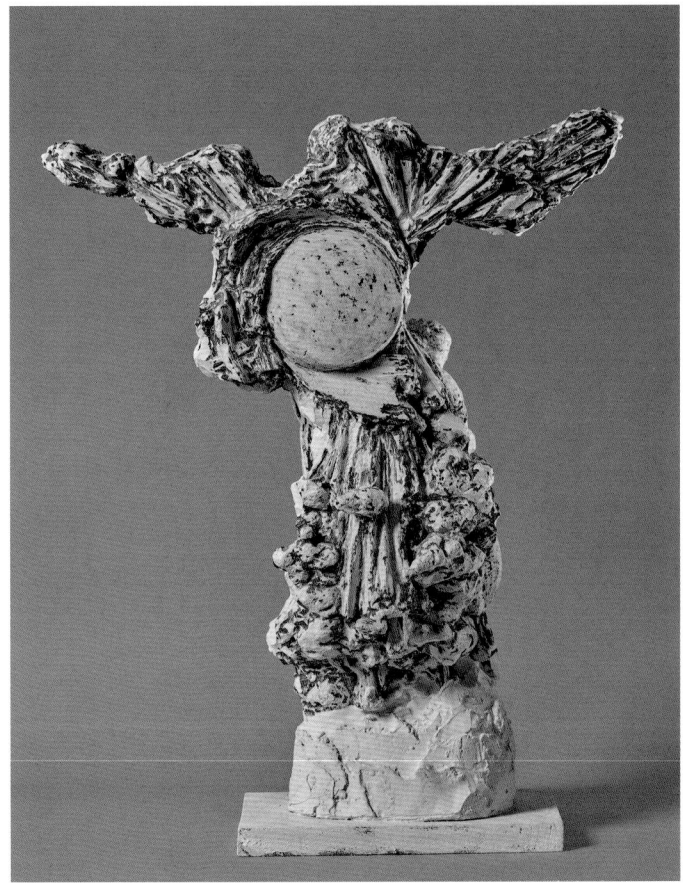

PLATES 23–24

Crucifixion I: Christ and Mary Magdalene
(front and back), 1982

Hydrostone, 25½ × 22 × 7 inches. Edition 2/9
Collection of the artist

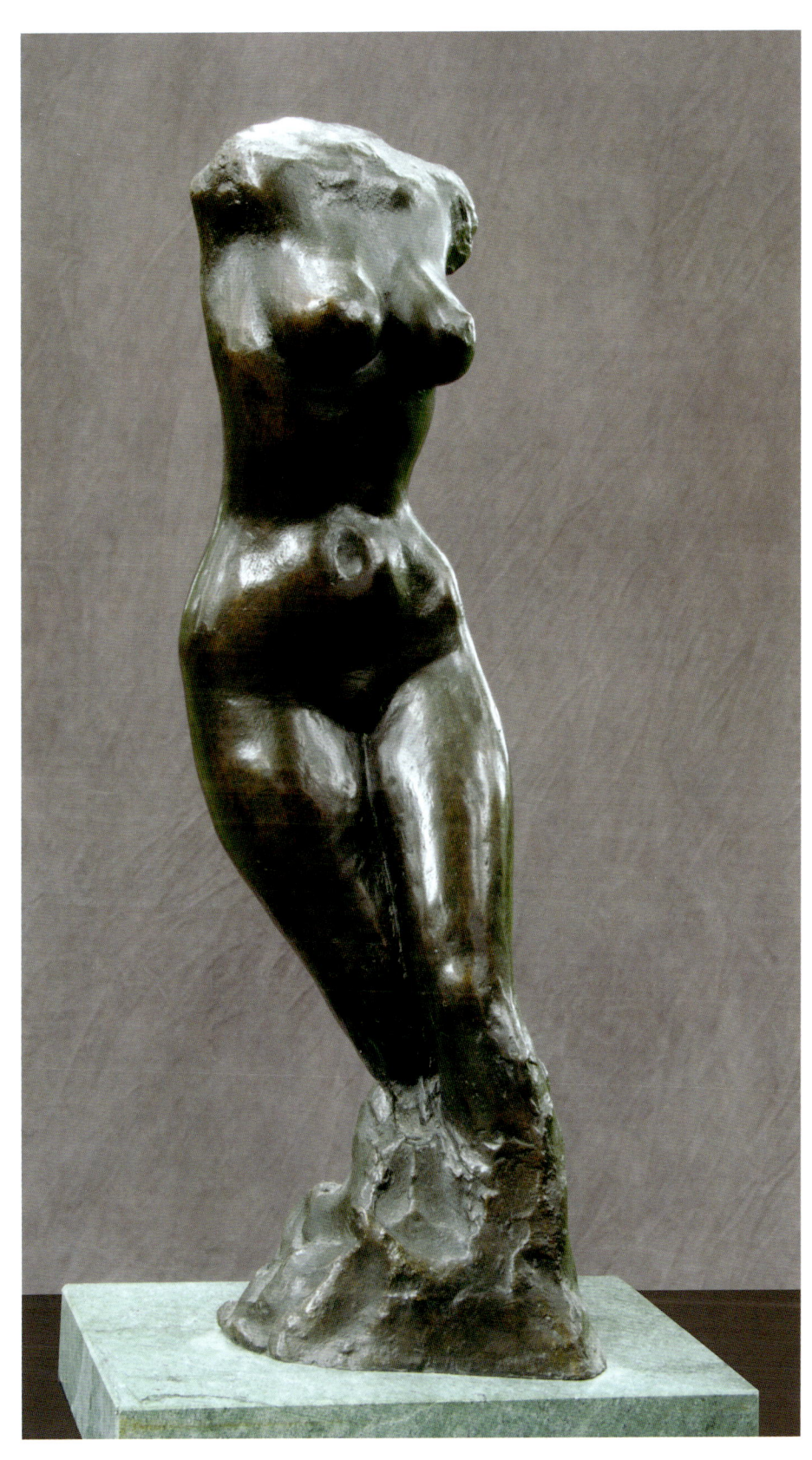

PLATE 25
Torso in Motion, 1982–85
Bronze, 12 × 3 × 3 inches. Edition 6/9
Private collection

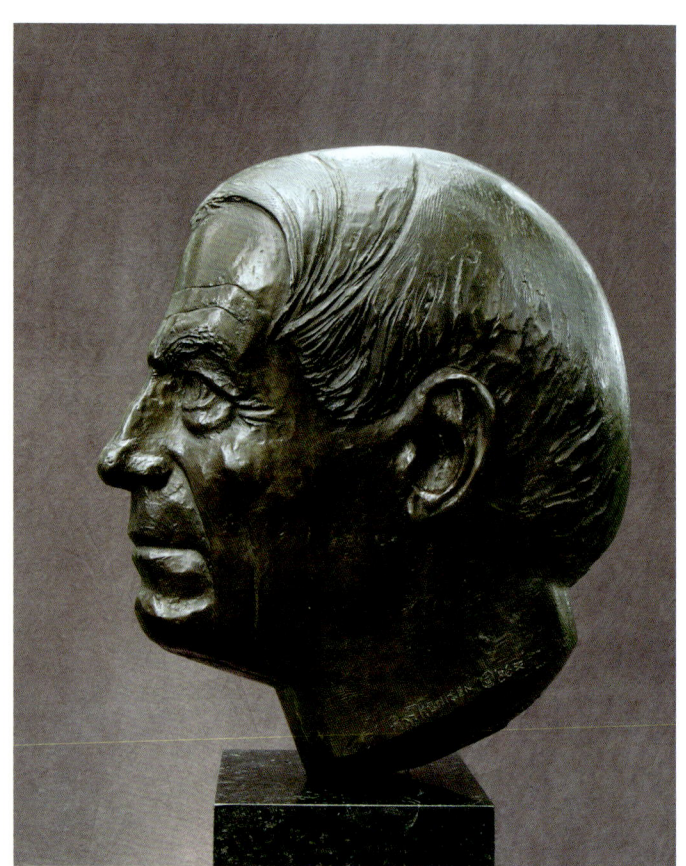
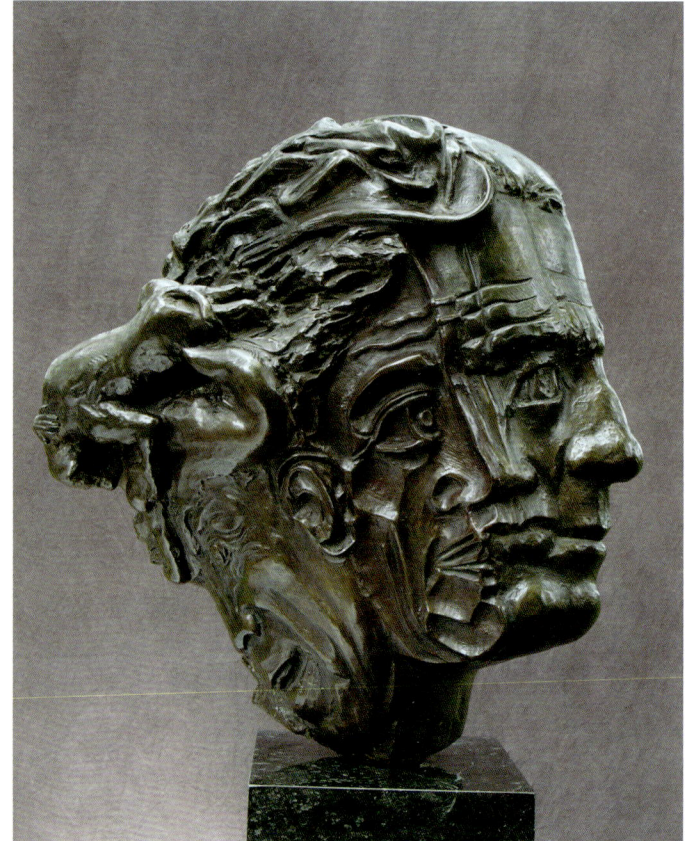

PLATES 26–28

Picasso (side and front), 1982–84

Bronze, 16 × 14 × 11 inches. Edition 1/1
Collection of Carol C. Turbow

84   GEORGE R. ANTHONISEN: MEDITATIONS ON THE HUMAN CONDITION

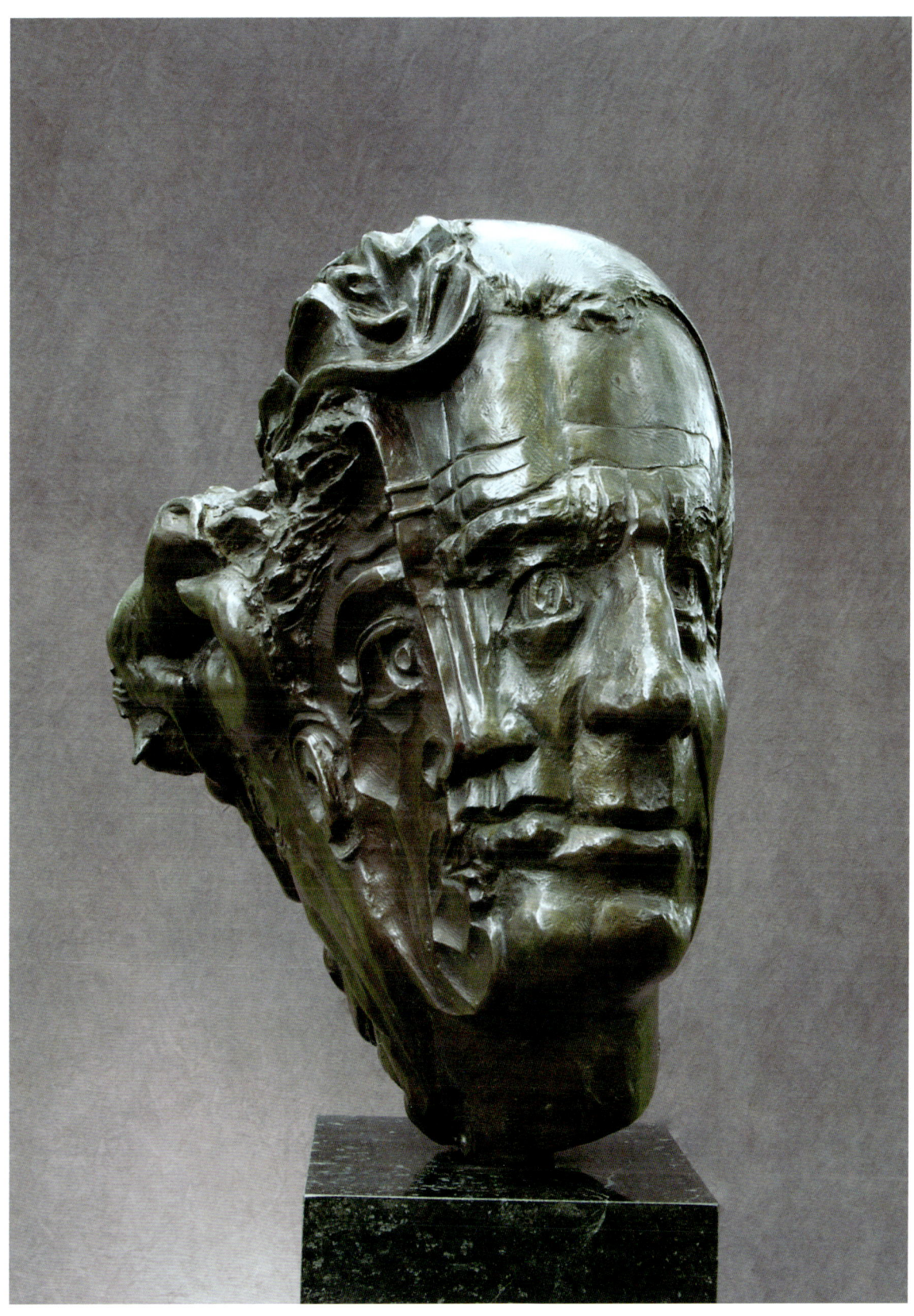

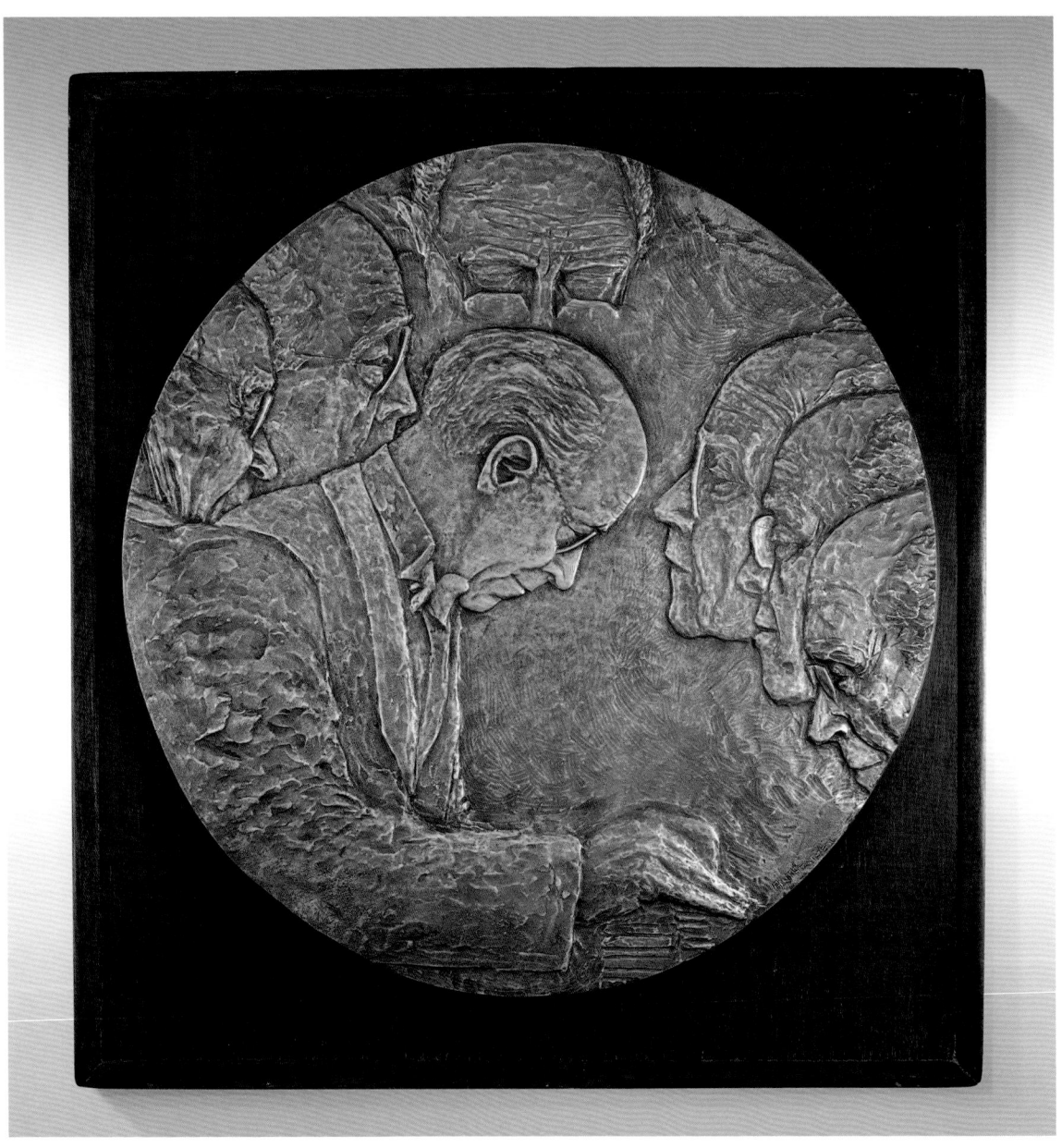

PLATE 29

Rudolf Serkin, 1983–84

Aluminum, 23 inches diam. Edition 1/9
Collection of the artist

PLATE 30

*Johnson Caryatid (Bucks County
Volunteer of the Year Award),* 1984

Bronze, 9 × 4½ × 4½ inches. Edition 10/10
Collection of the artist

86   GEORGE R. ANTHONISEN: MEDITATIONS ON THE HUMAN CONDITION

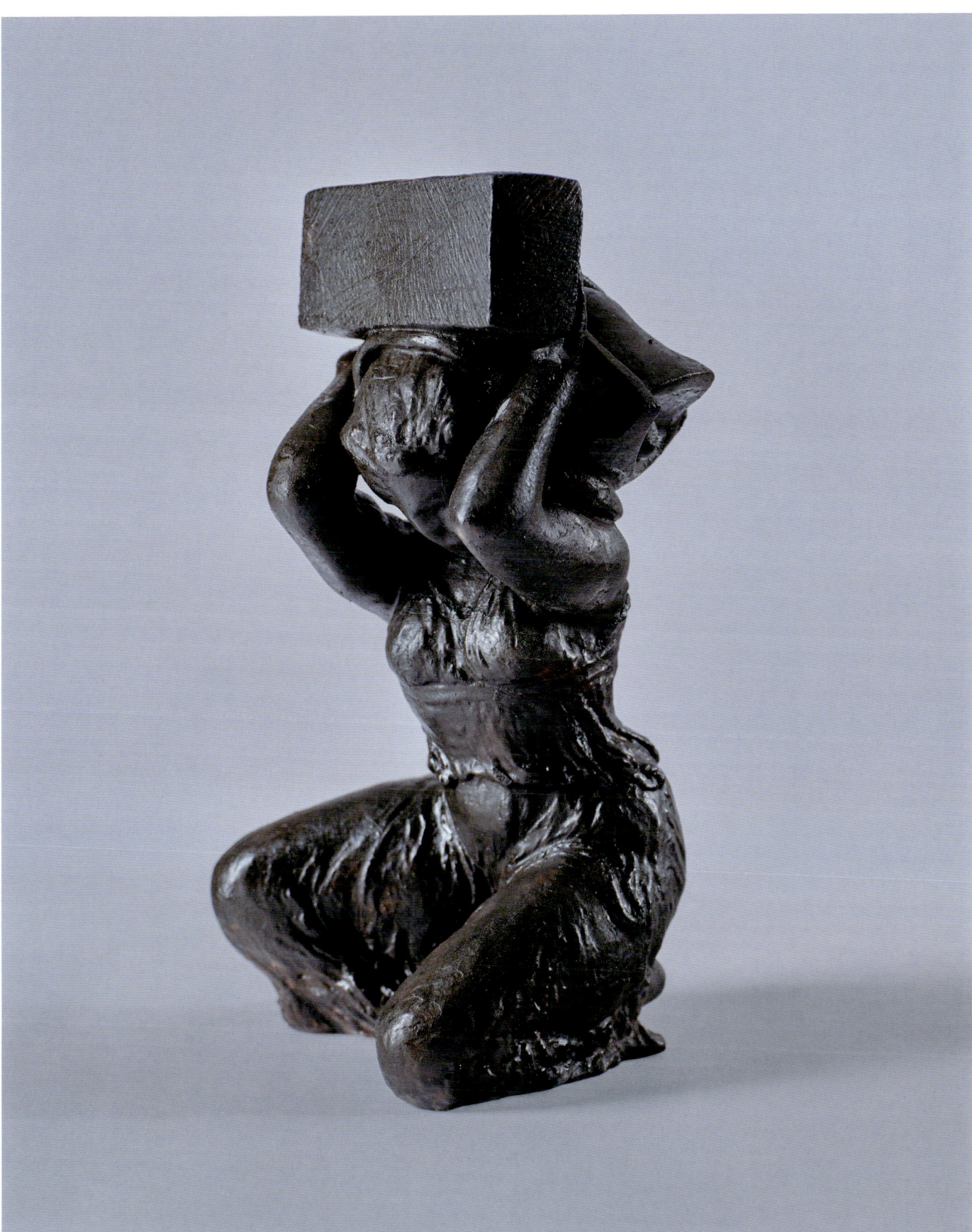

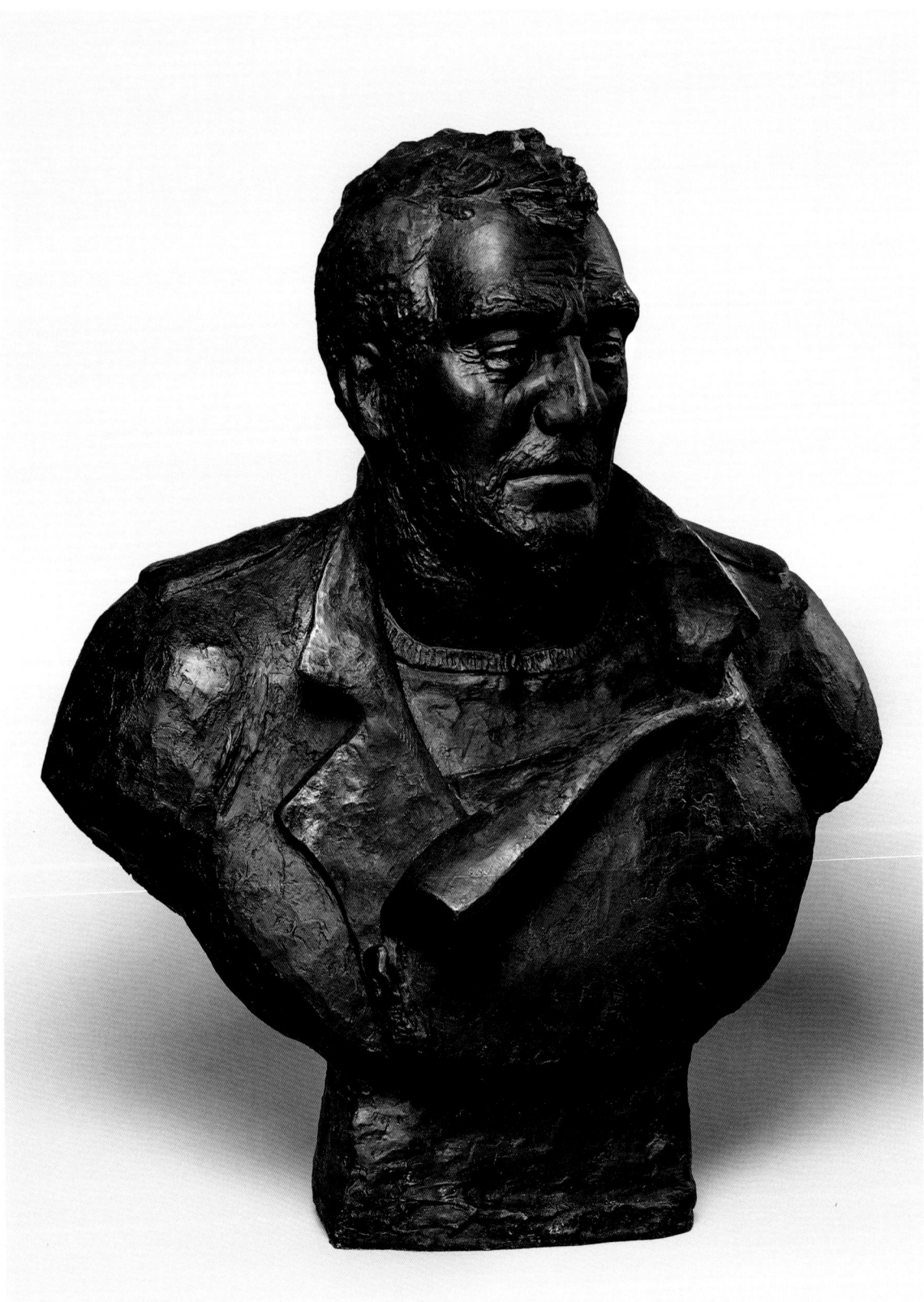

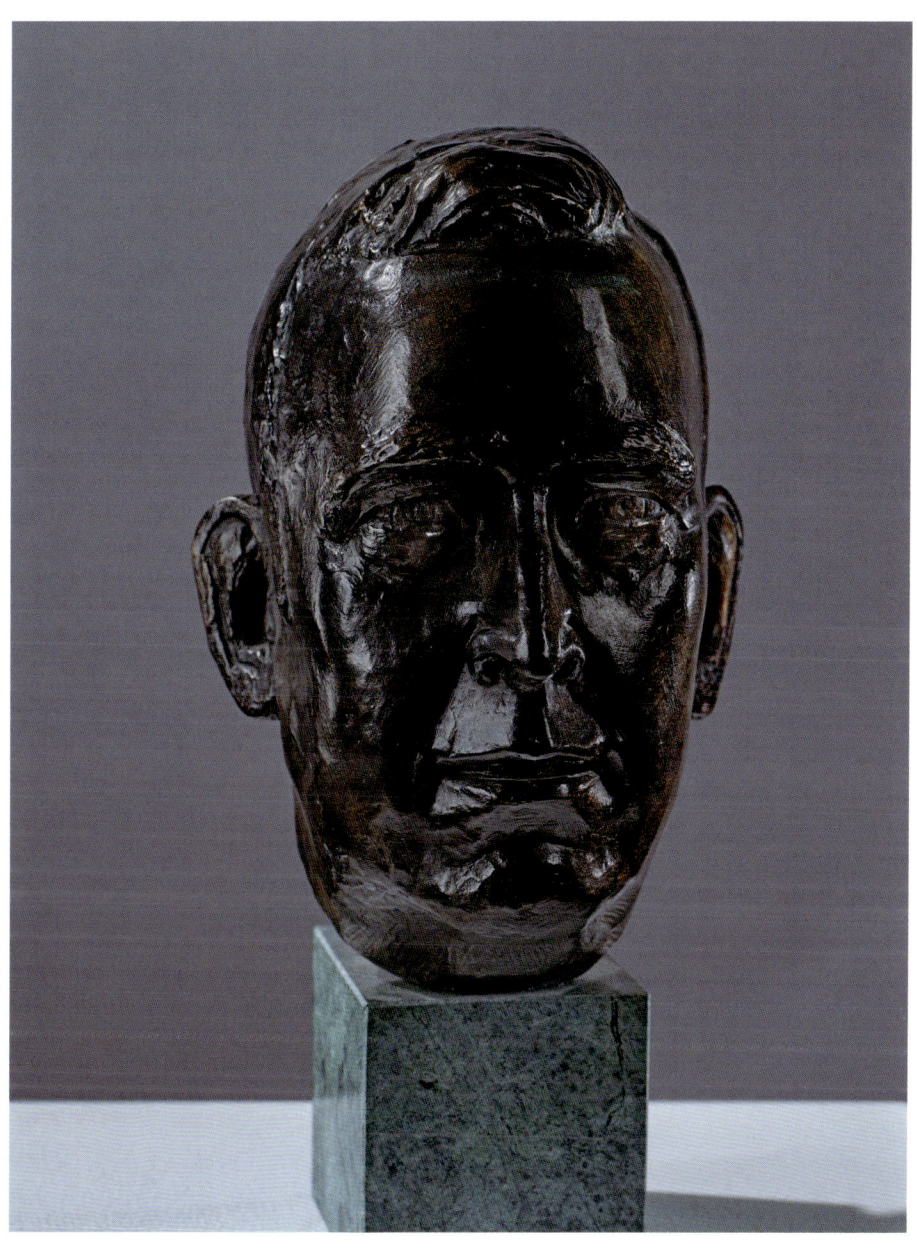

PLATE 31
Warrior, 1985

Plaster, 27 × 22 × 16 inches
The Philip and Muriel Berman
Museum of Art at Ursinus College

PLATE 32
Robert L. Byers, 1990

Bronze, life-size. Edition 1/1
Collection of Robert L. and Joyce Byers

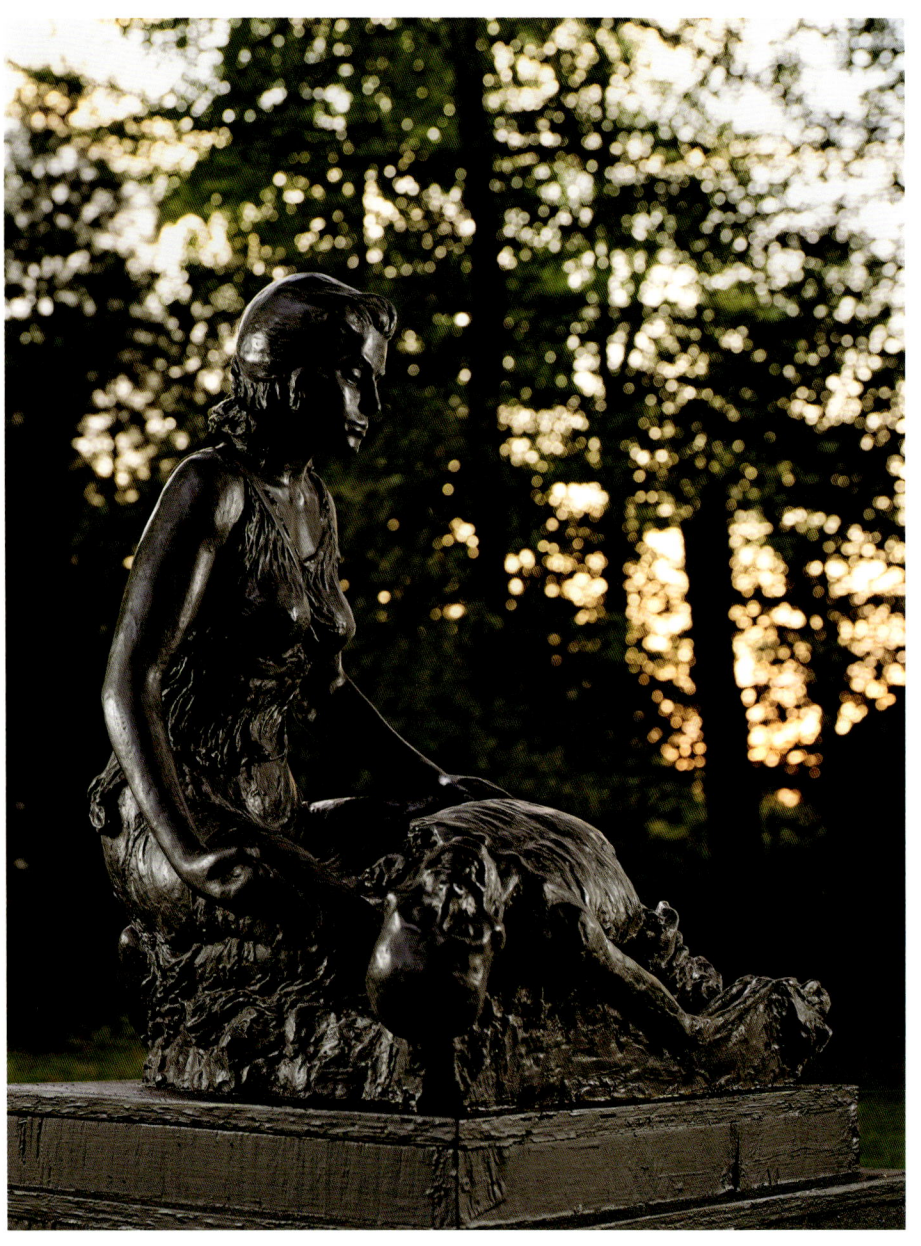

PLATES 33–34

Antigone, 1988–91

Bronze, 27½ × 32 × 24 inches. Edition 2/9
Collection of the artist

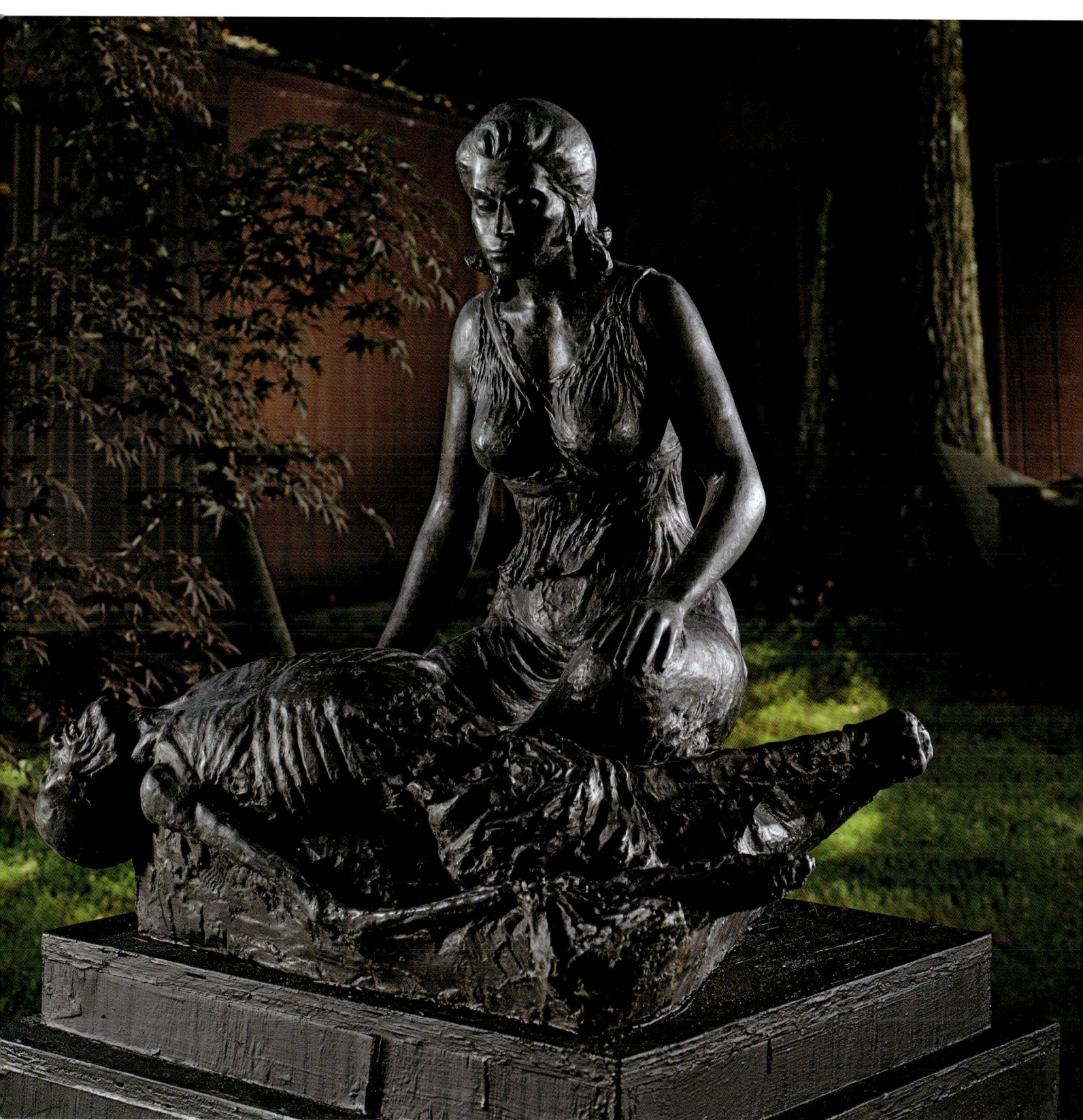

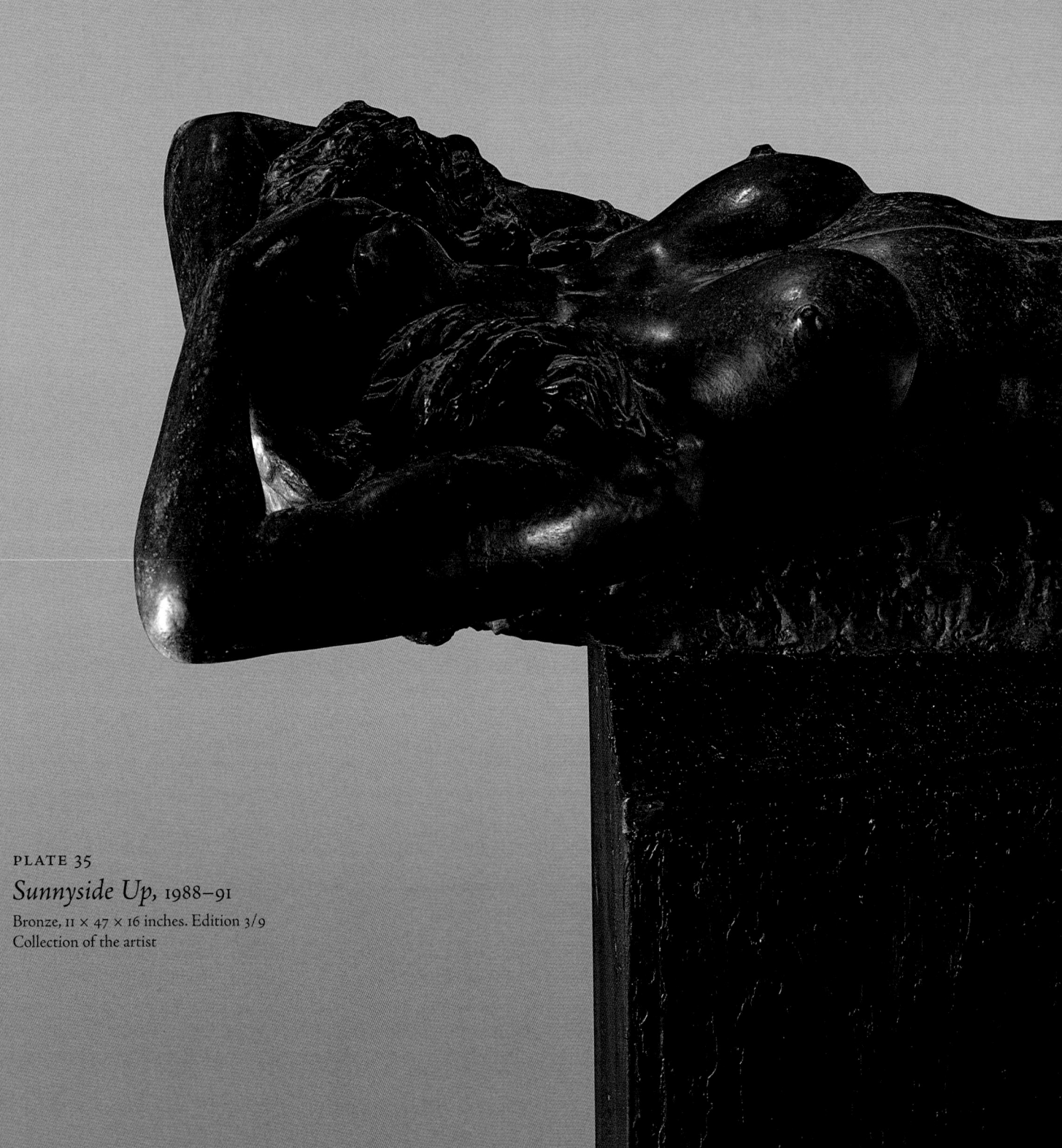

PLATE 35
Sunnyside Up, 1988–91
Bronze, 11 × 47 × 16 inches. Edition 3/9
Collection of the artist

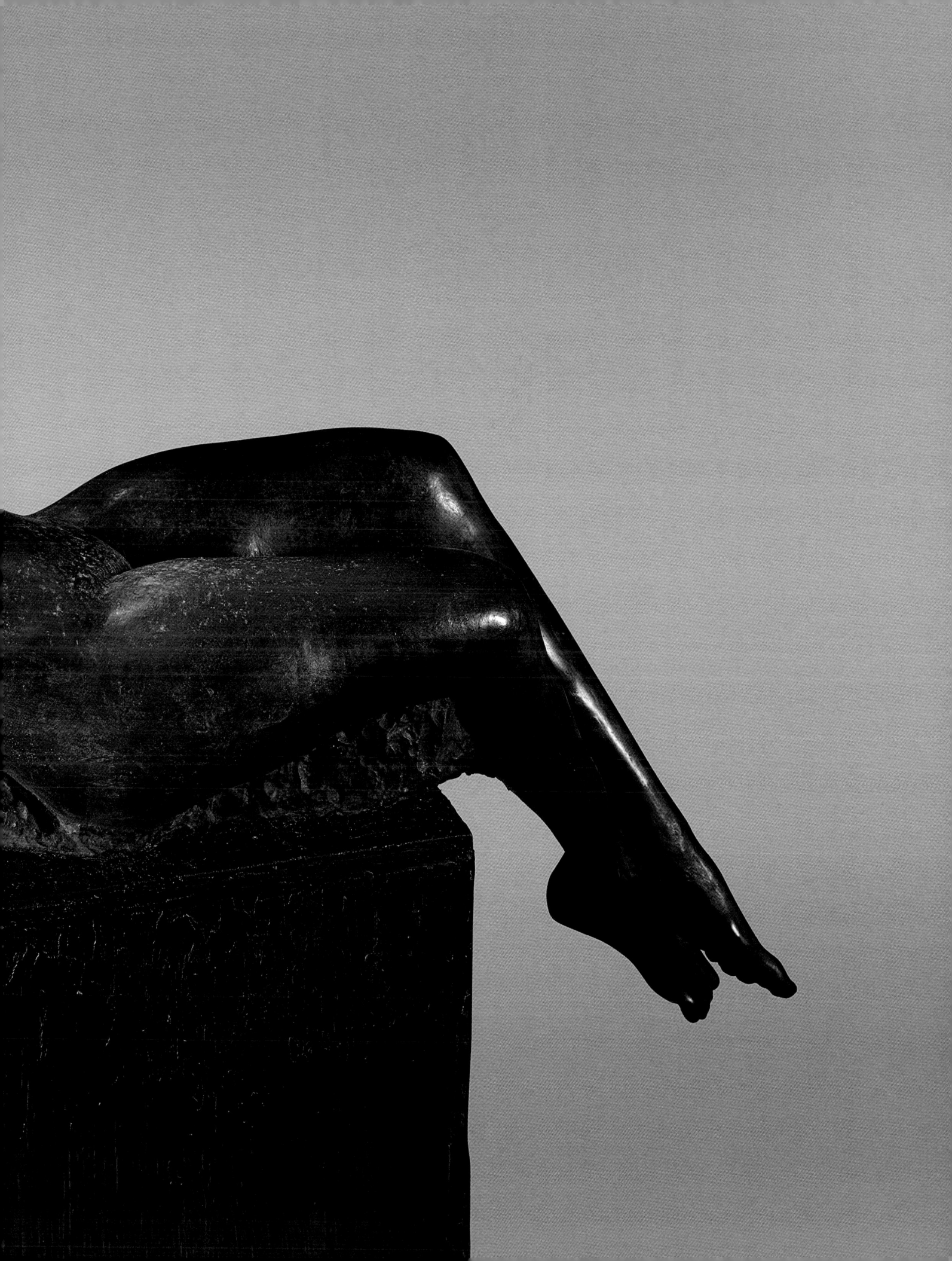

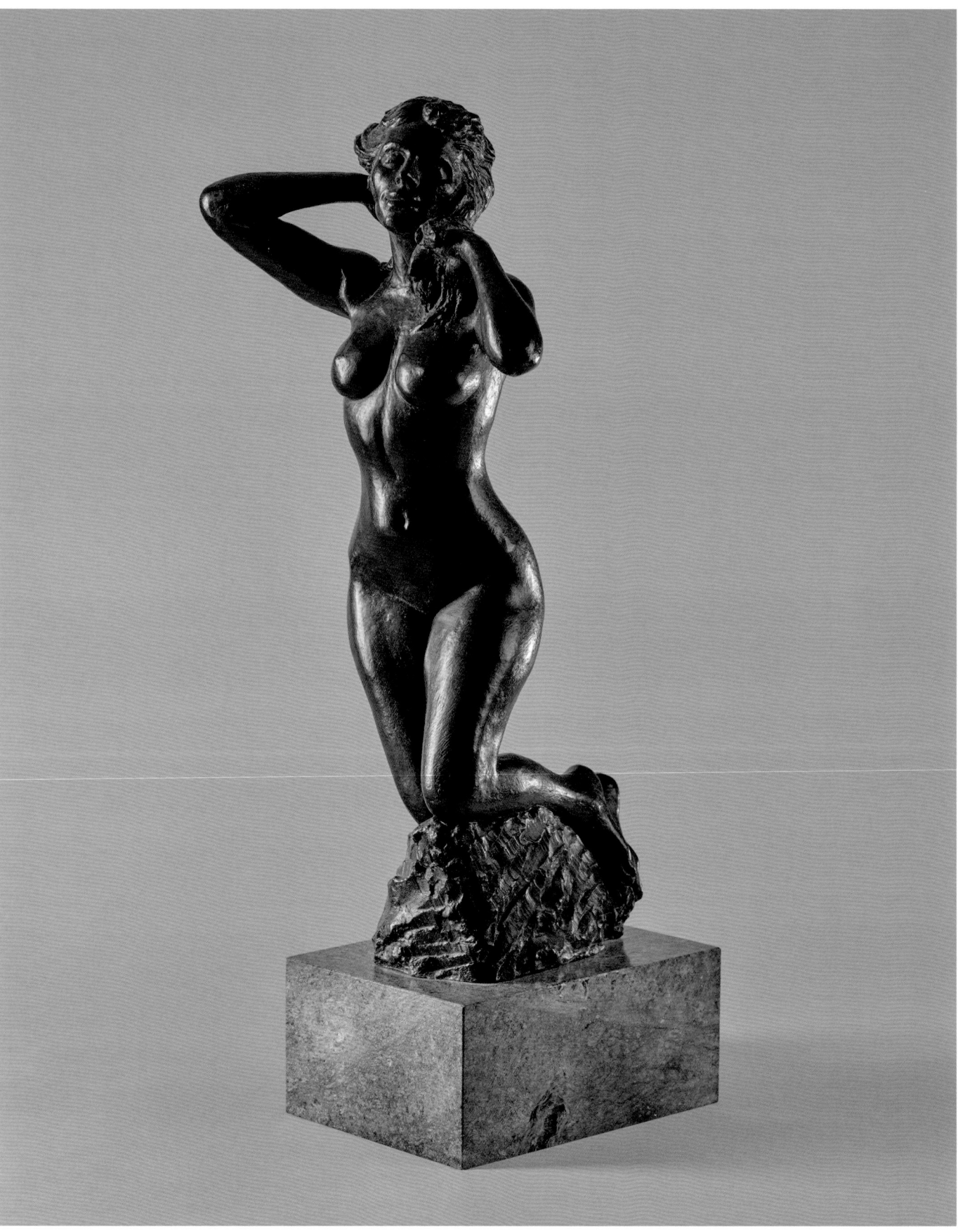

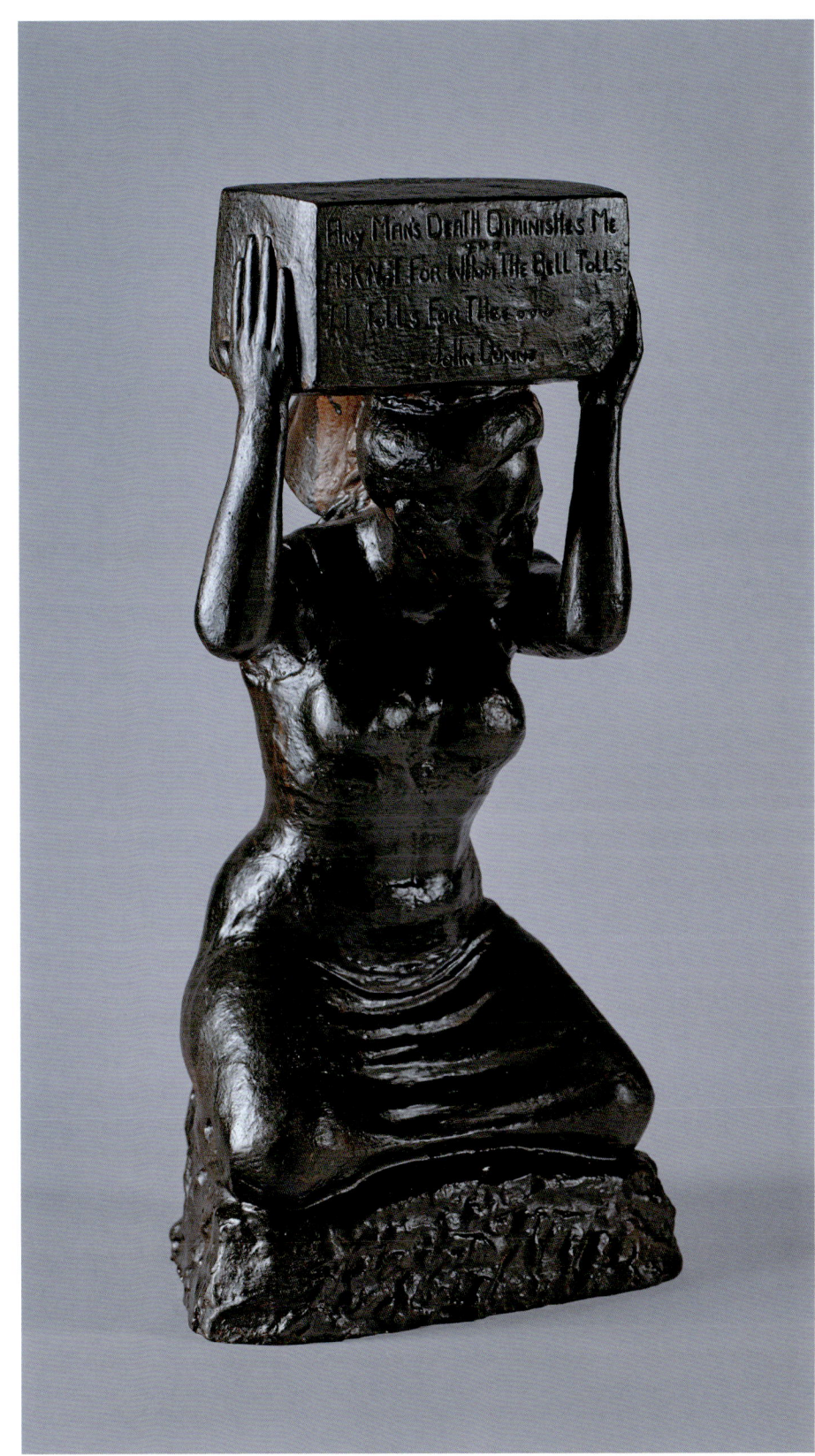

PLATE 36

Quiescence, 1989–90

Bronze, 22 × 11½ × 9 inches. Edition 4/9
Collection of the artist

PLATE 37

Caryatid (maquette), 1992–94

Plaster, 17⅞ × 8 × 9½ inches
Collection of Rachel Anthonisen Gates

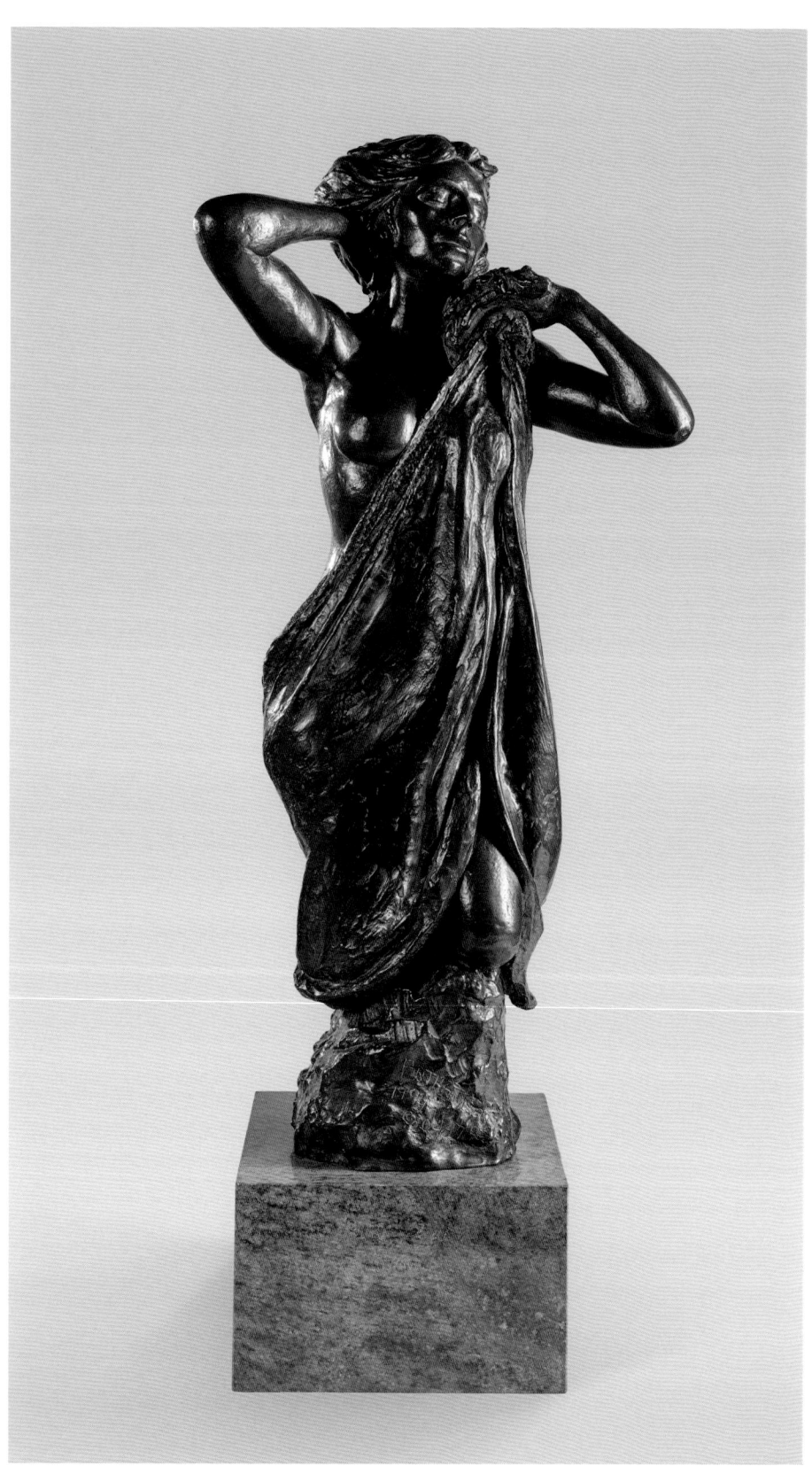

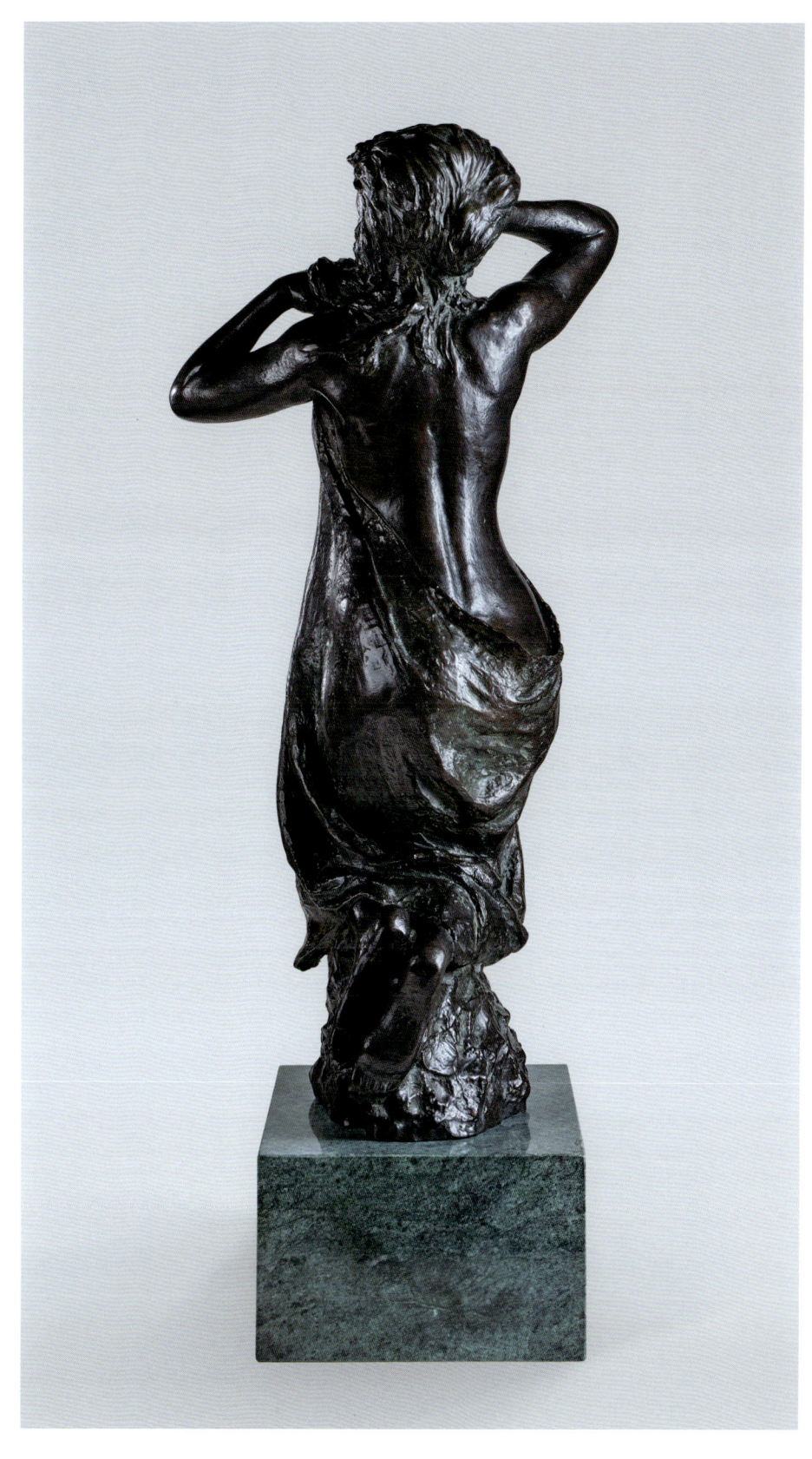

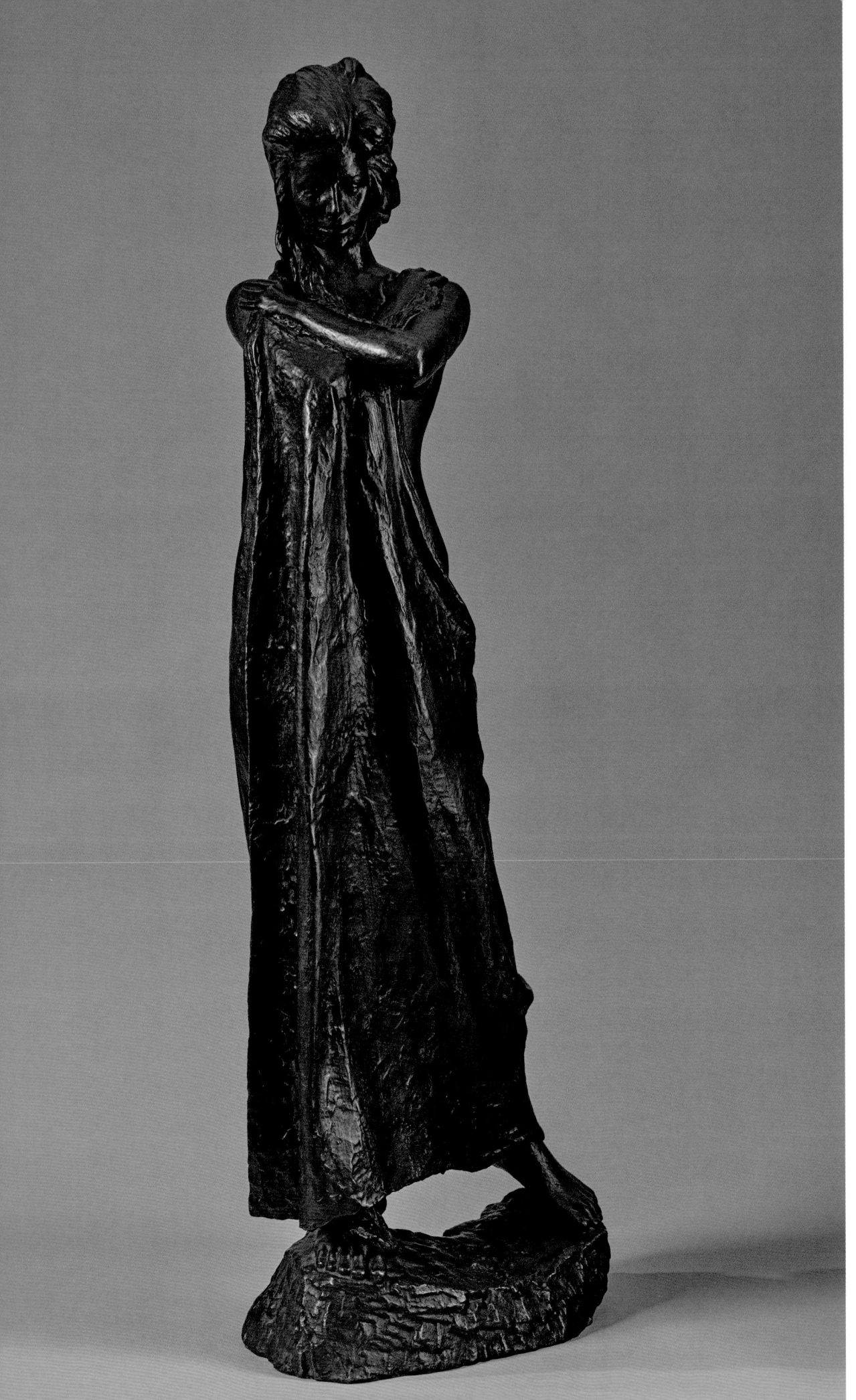

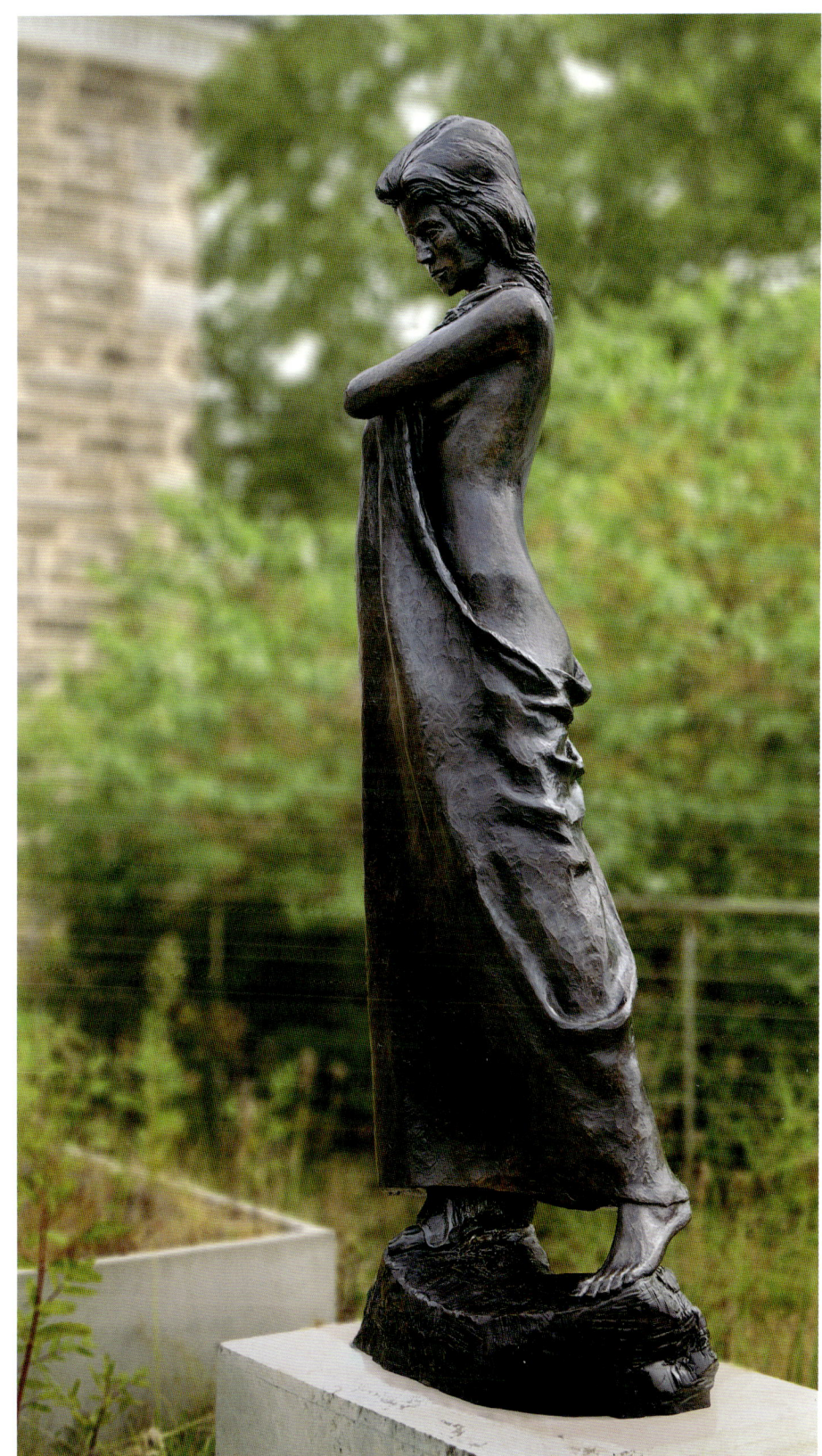

PLATE 40
Meditation (maquette), 1994
Bronze, 36½ × 13 × 8 inches. Edition 4/9
Collection of the artist

PLATE 41
Meditation, 1994–95
Bronze, 79½ × 28 × 18 inches. Edition 2/3
The Philip and Muriel Berman Museum of Art
at Ursinus College

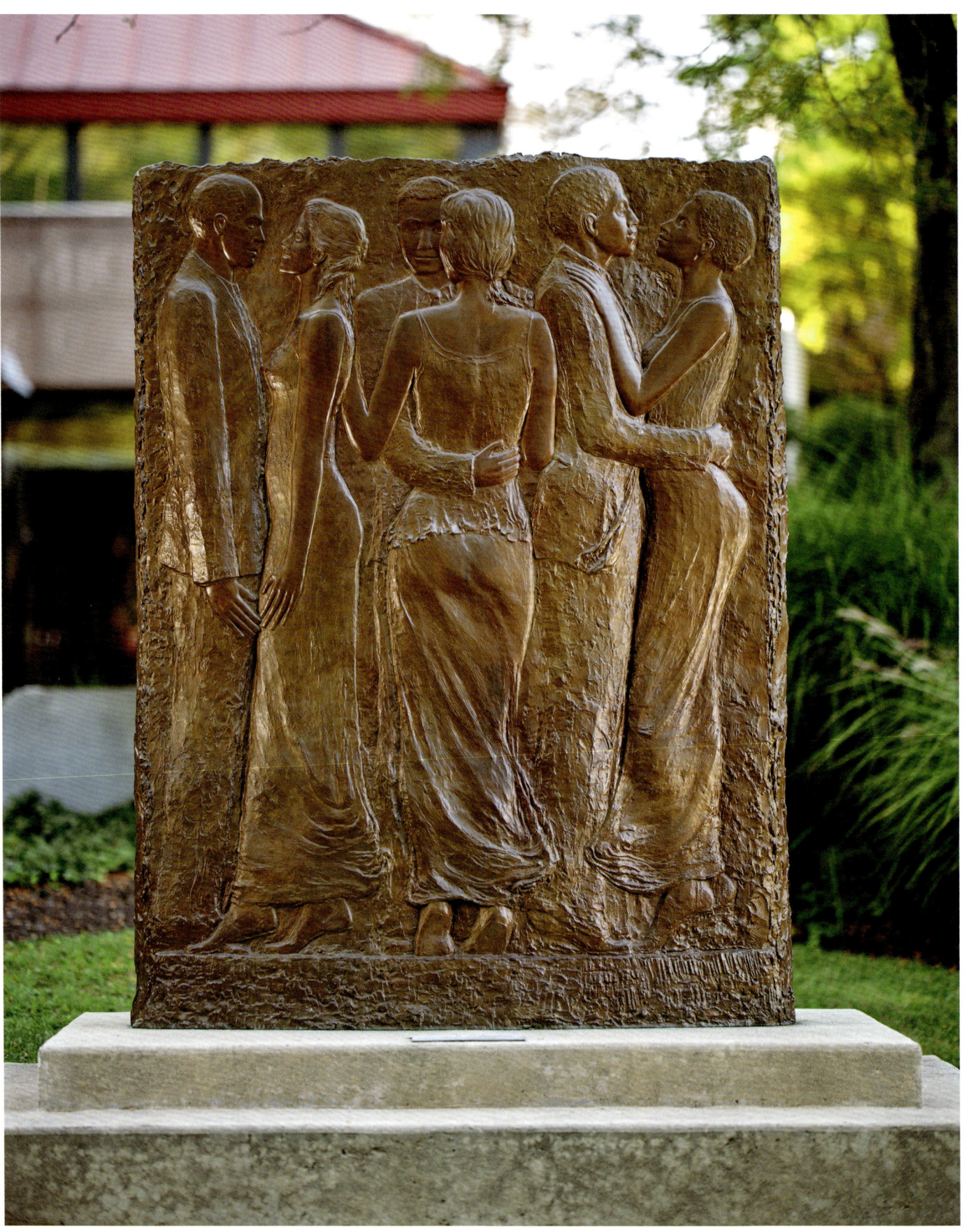

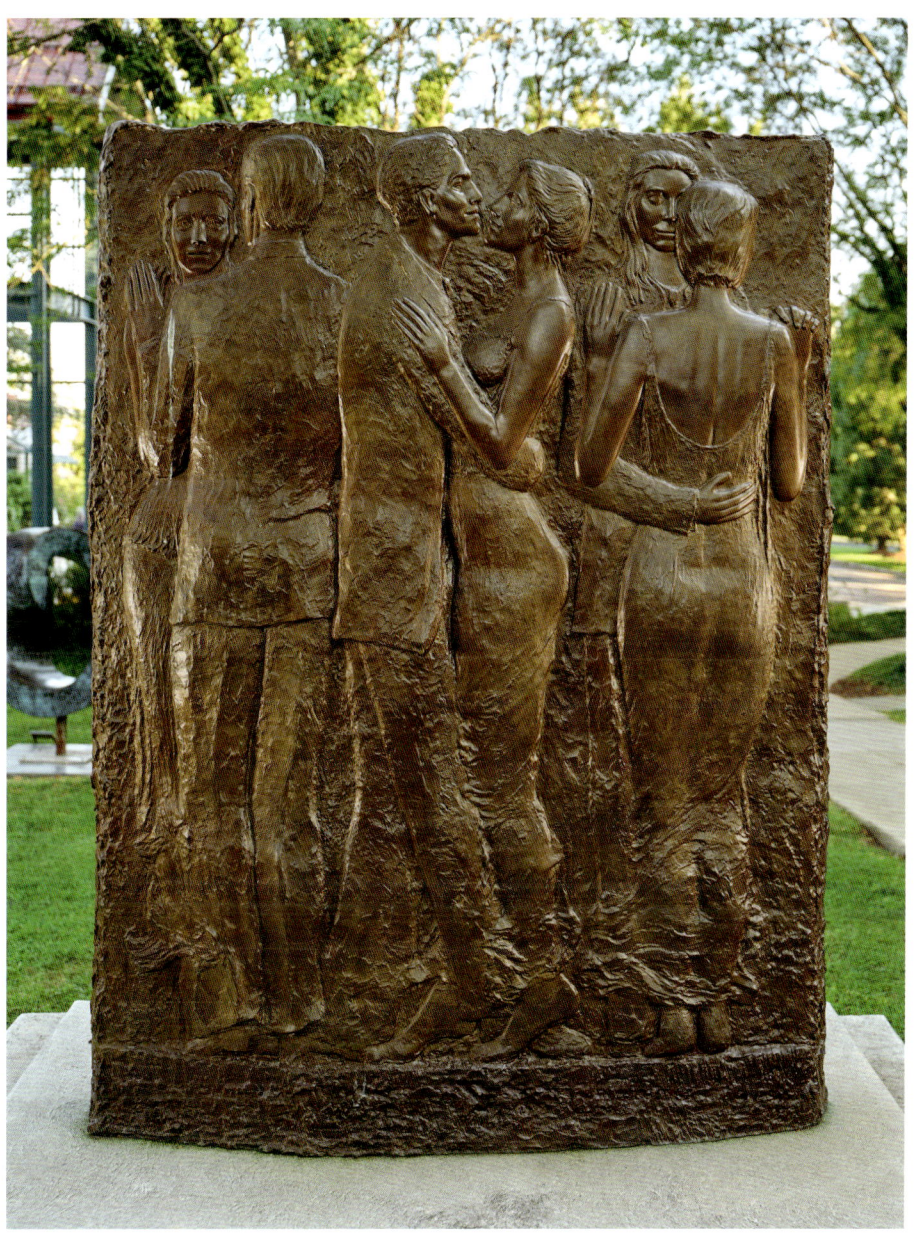

PLATES 42–43

Give Us Grace (front and back), 1994–96

Bronze, 78 × 60 × 14 inches. Edition 1/5
James A. Michener Art Museum, Gift of George and Ellen Anthonisen,
2016.13.1

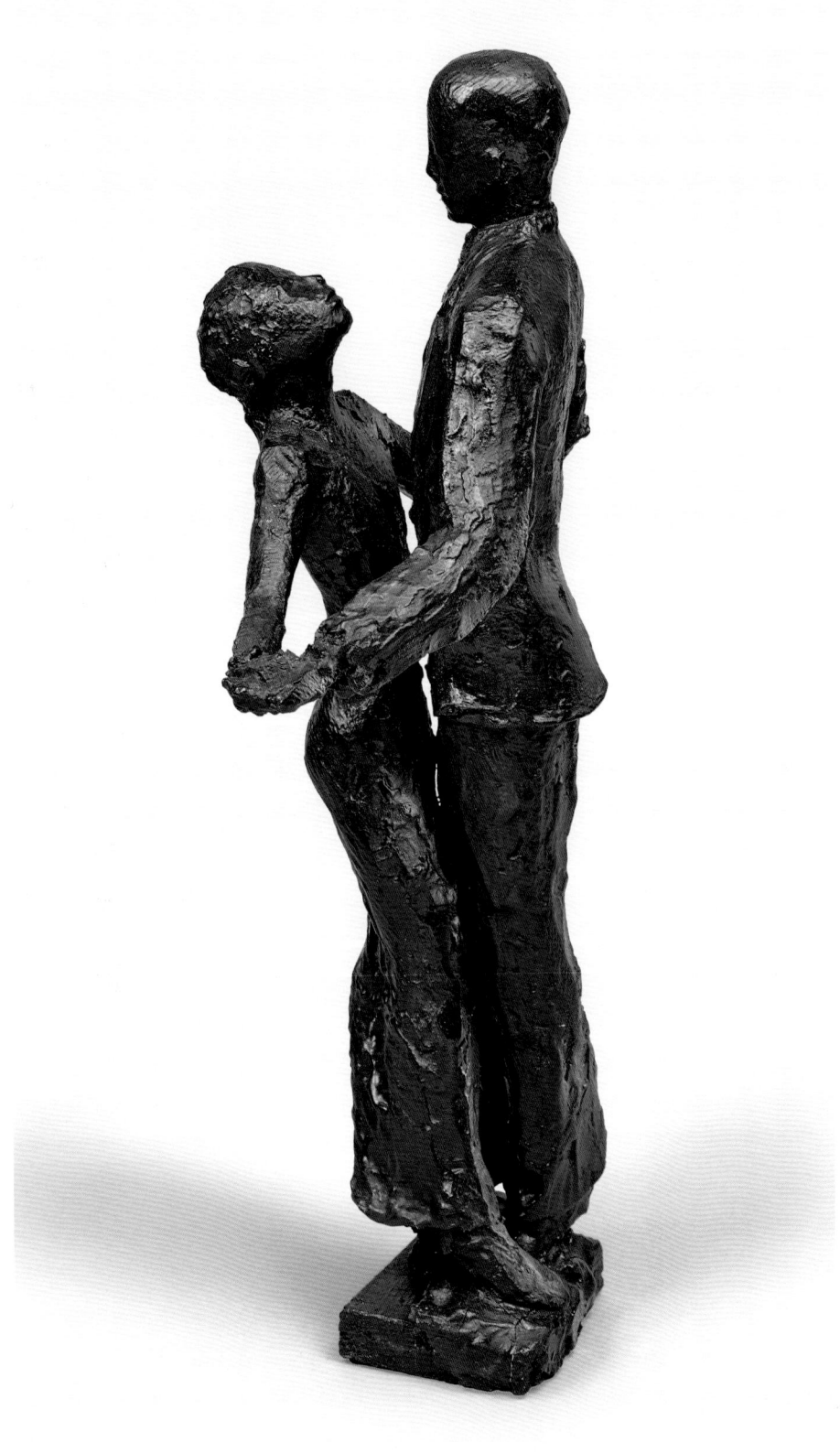

PLATE 44
*Give Us Grace
(Study 3: Grandfather and
Granddaughter Dancing)*, 1991
Plaster, 16 × 8⅛ × 5¼ inches
The Philip and Muriel Berman Museum of Art
at Ursinus College

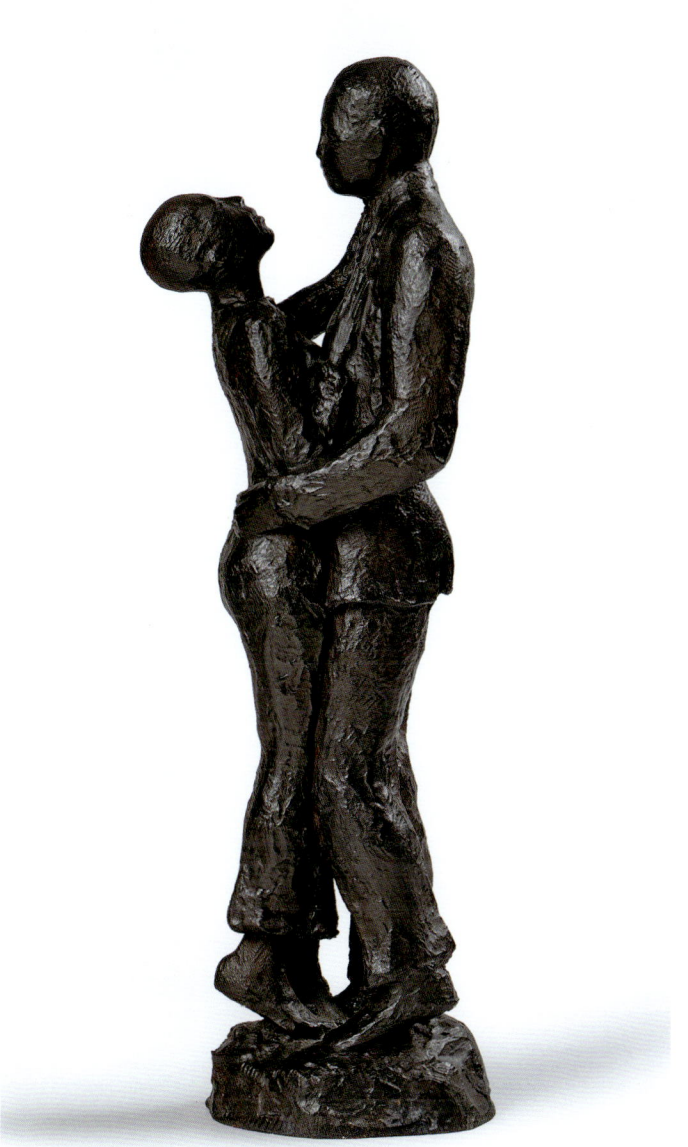

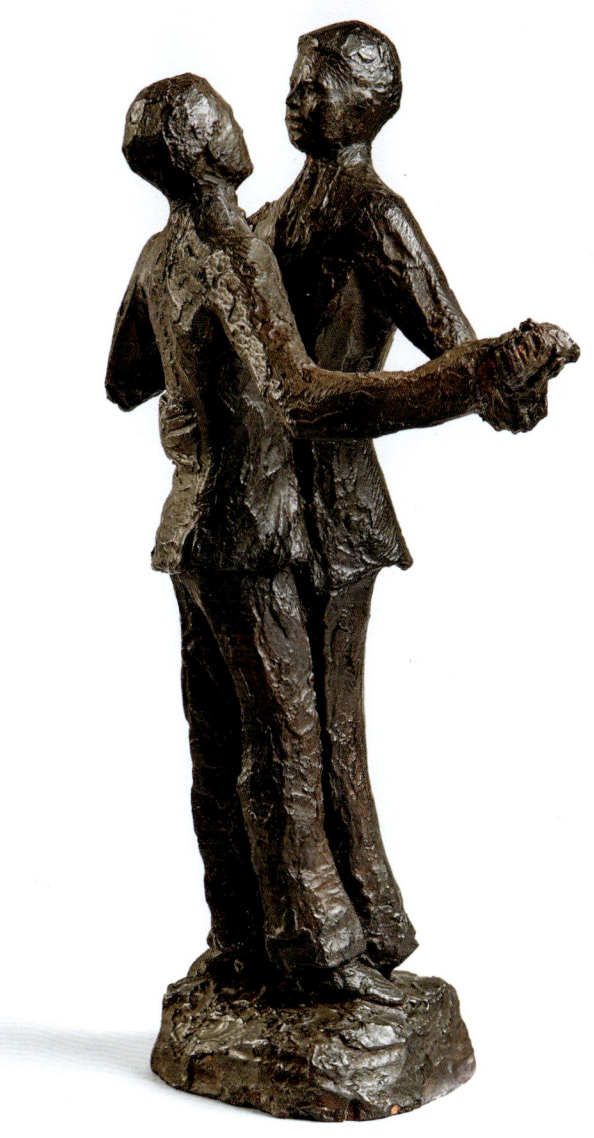

PLATE 45

Give Us Grace (Study 6:
African American Couple Dancing), 1991

Plaster, 16½ × 4½ × 4½ inches
The Philip and Muriel Berman Museum of Art at Ursinus College

PLATE 46

Give Us Grace (Study 7:
Male Couple Dancing), 1991

Plaster, 16¼ × 10¼ × 5⅛ inches
The Philip and Muriel Berman Museum of Art at Ursinus College

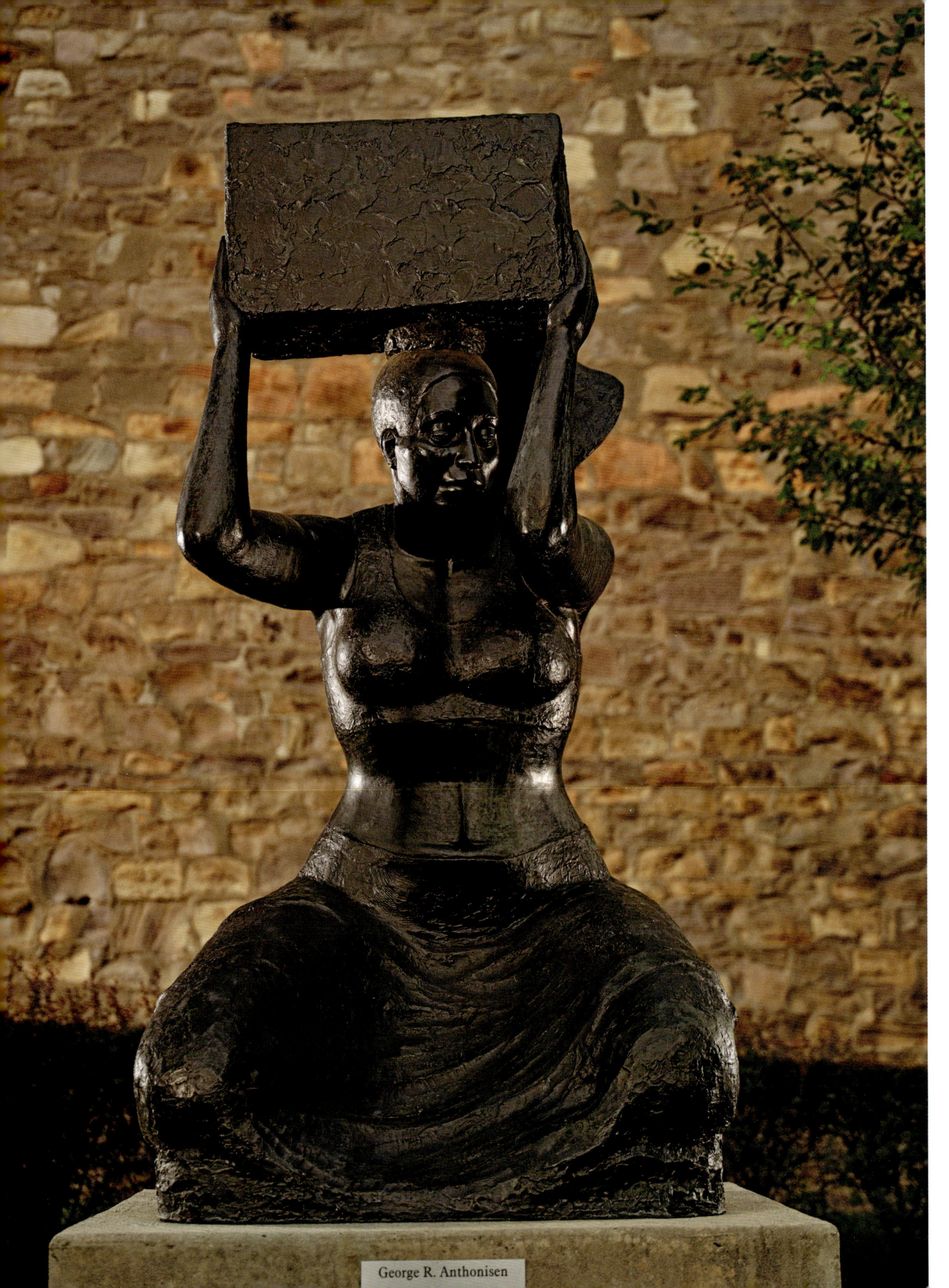

George R. Anthonisen

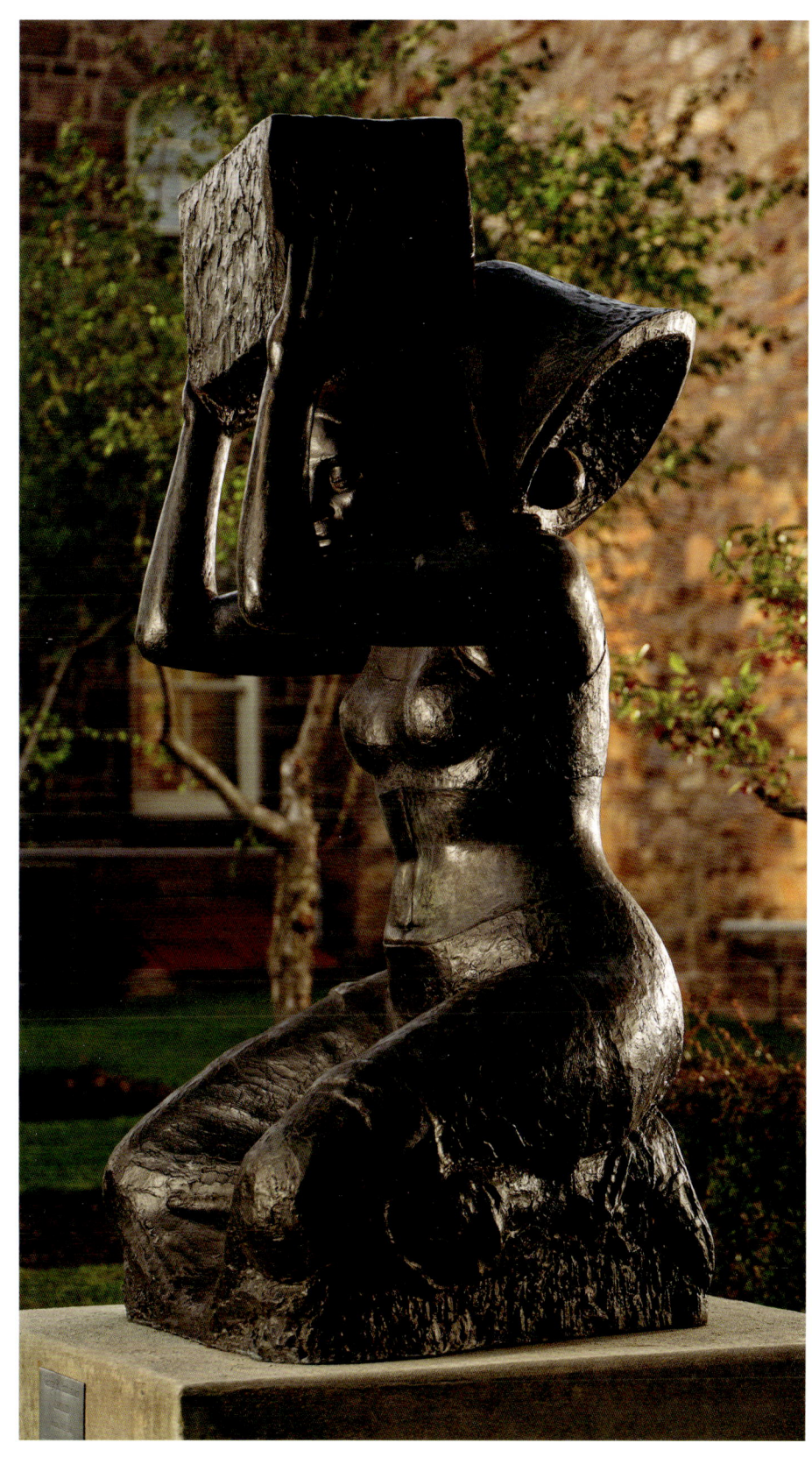

PLATES 47–48
Caryatid, 1994–2000
Bronze, 74 × 43 × 39 inches. Edition 1/5
James A. Michener Art Museum, Gift of George
and Ellen Anthonisen, 2016.13.2

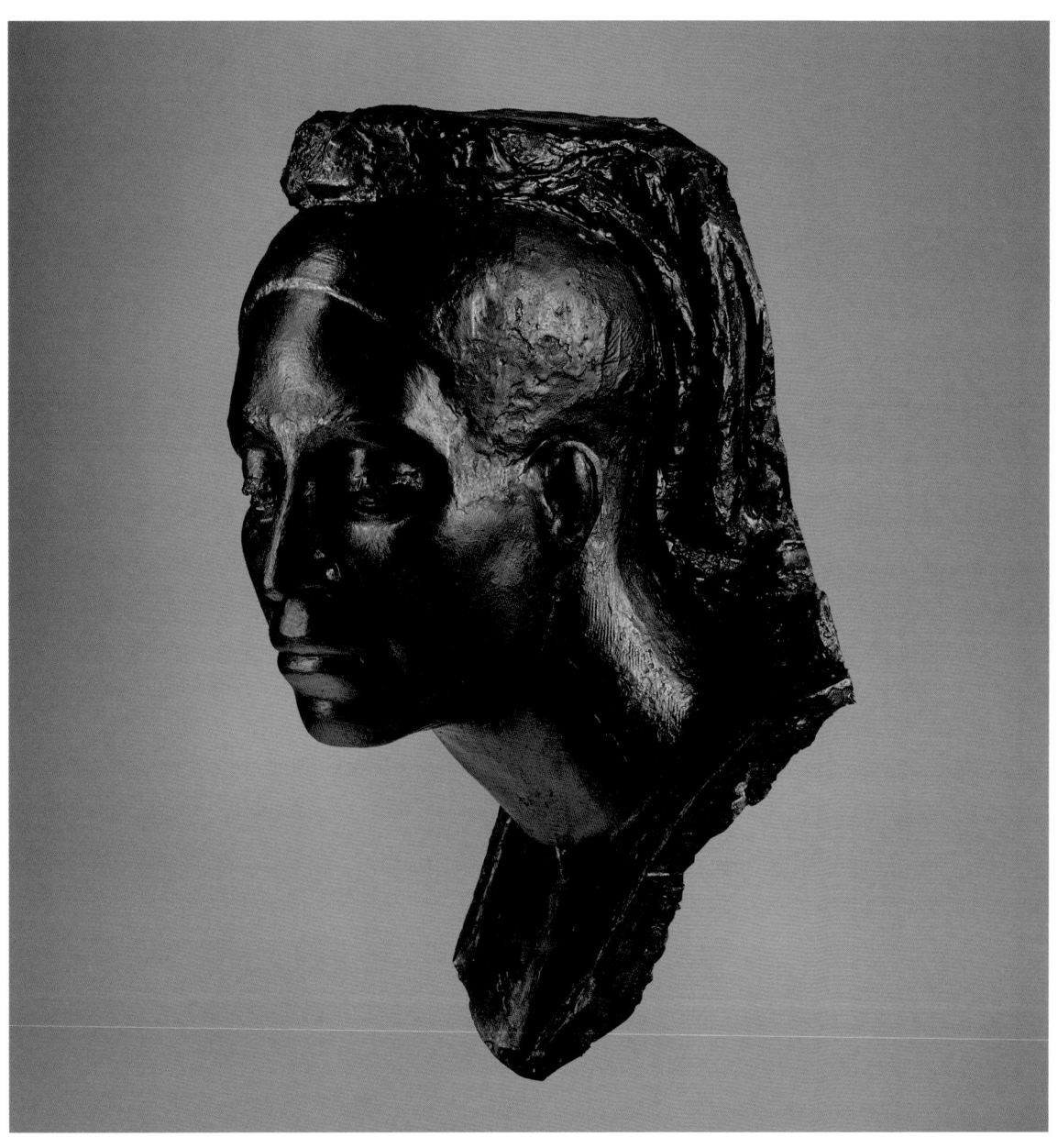

Transcendence (Caryatid Head), 1996–2022

Plaster, 24 × 14 × 14 inches
Collection of the artist

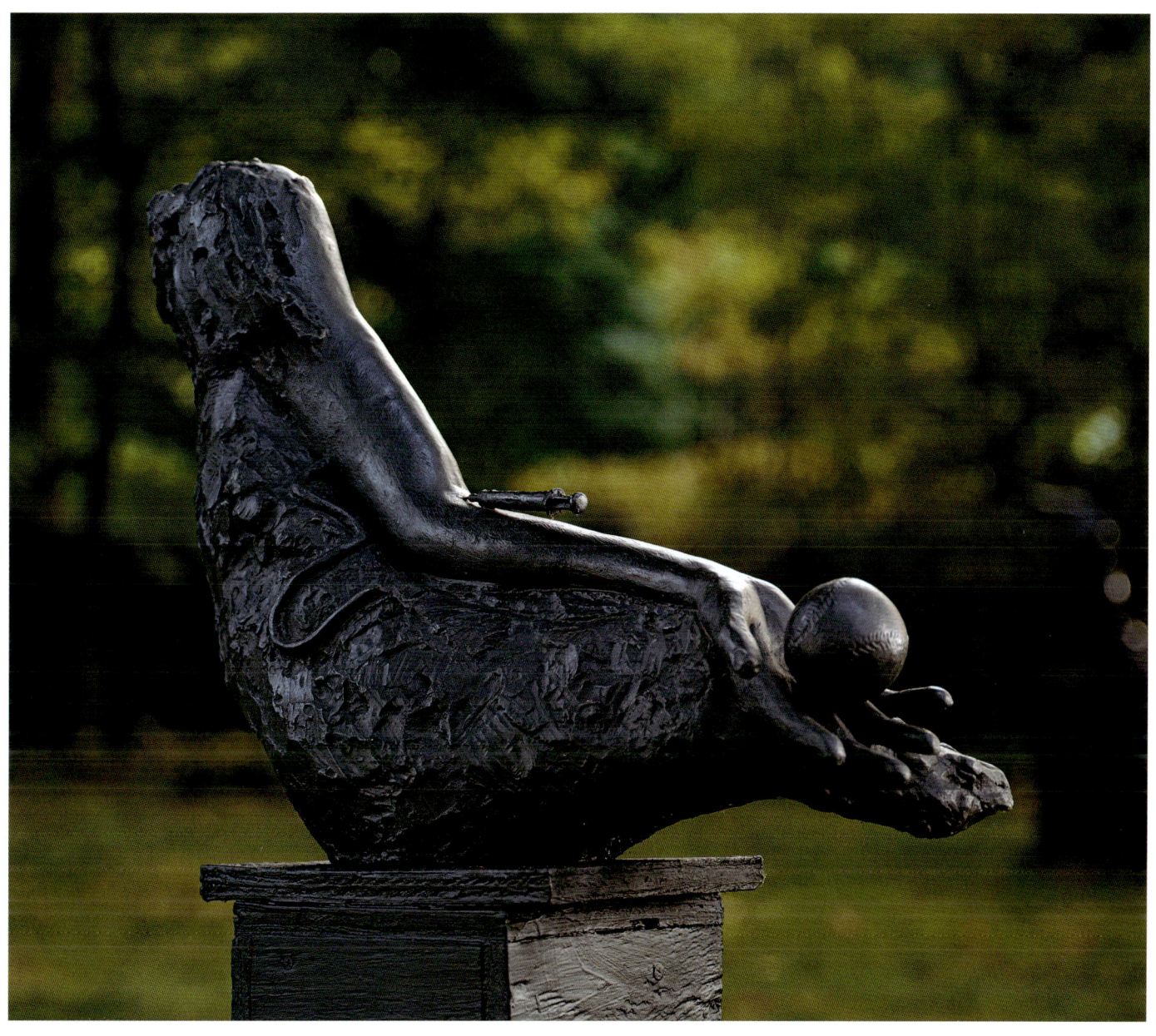

PLATE 50

Game Over, 1995–96

Bronze, 19 × 28 × 9 inches. Edition 1/9
The Philip and Muriel Berman Museum of Art at Ursinus College

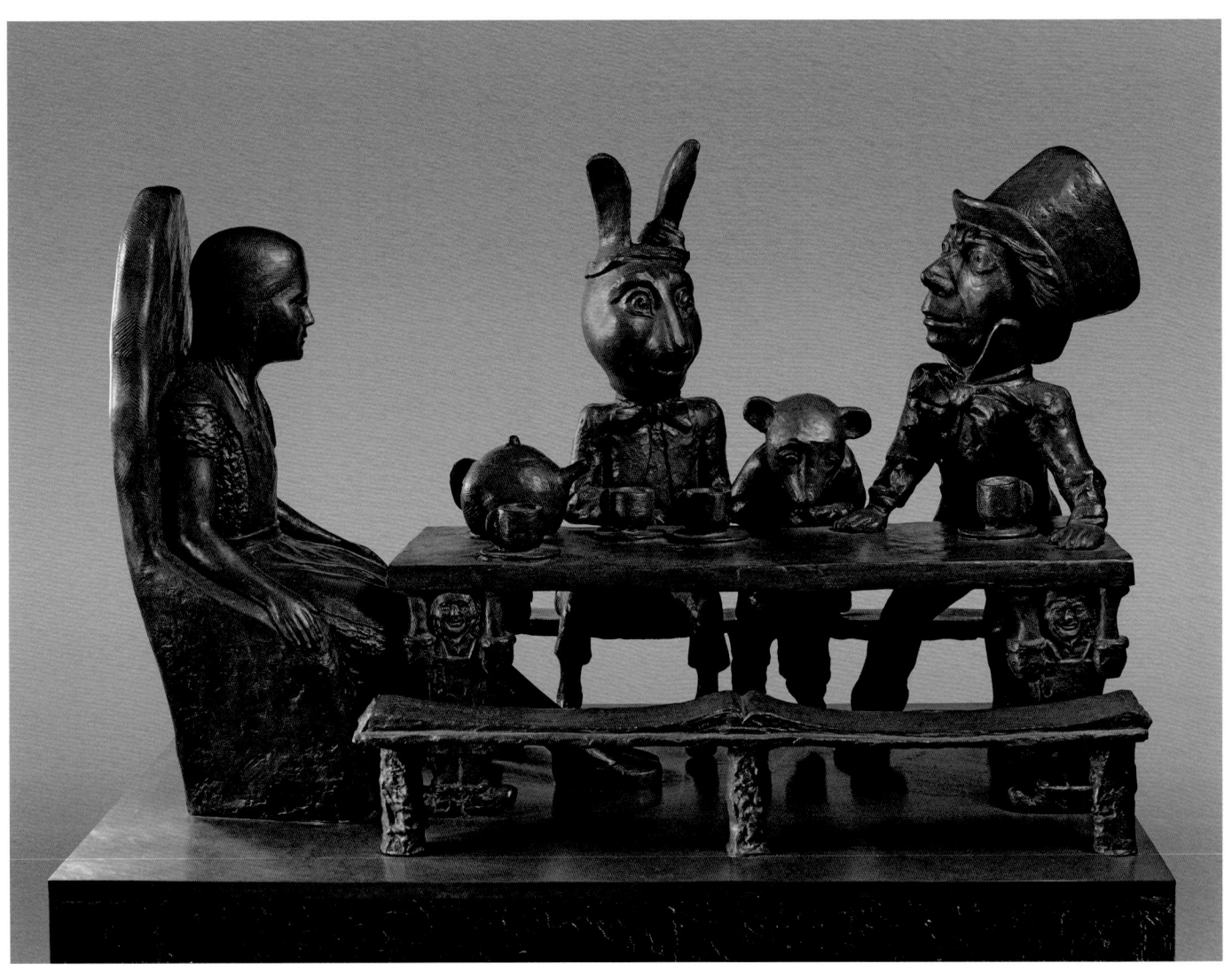

PLATE 51
Tea Party (maquette), 1996–97
Bronze, 20 × 32 × 19 inches. Edition 1/9
Collection of the artist

PLATE 52
Alice in Wonderland (maquette), 1997
Bronze, 12¾ × 6¾ × 6 inches. Edition 2/9
Collection of the artist

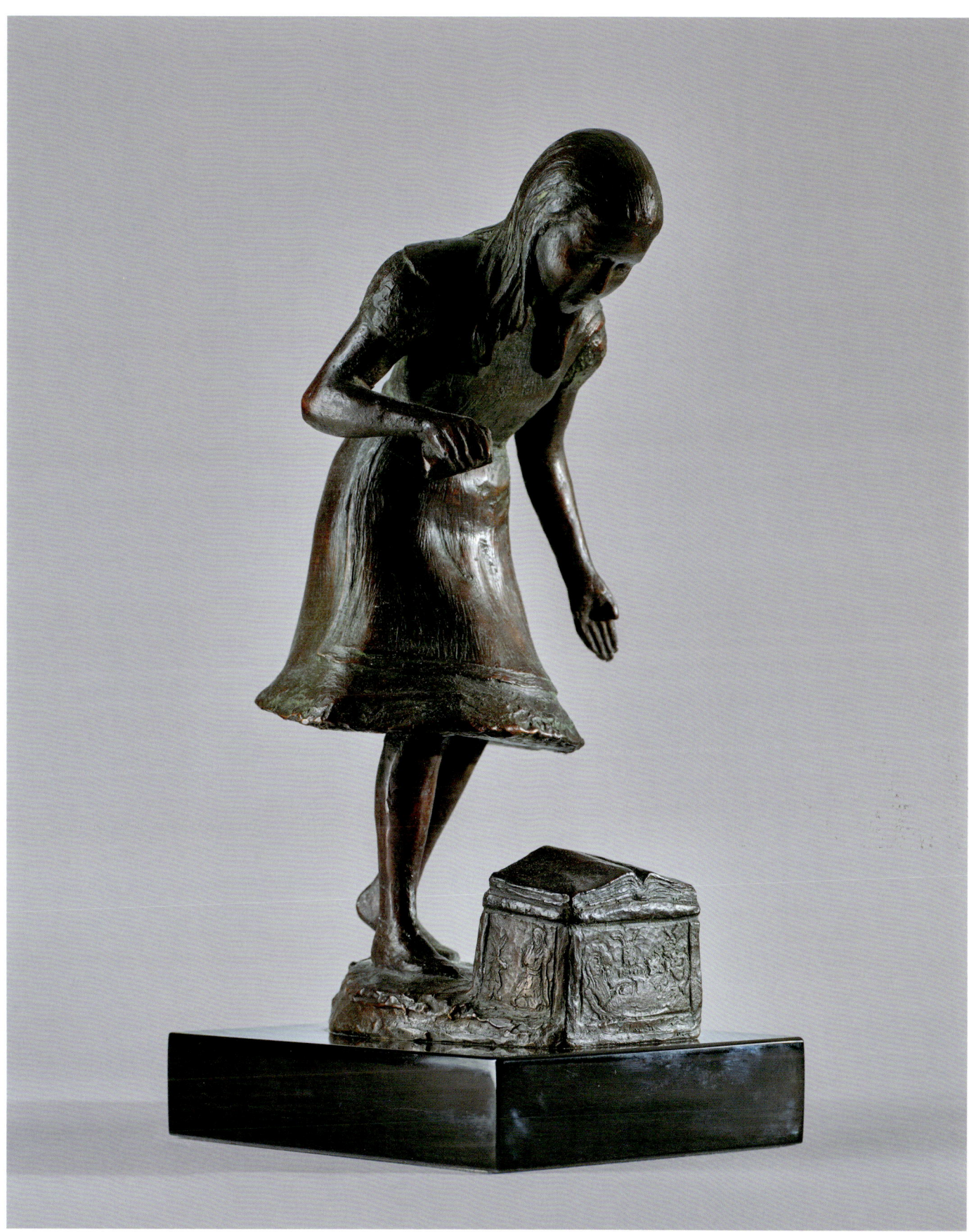

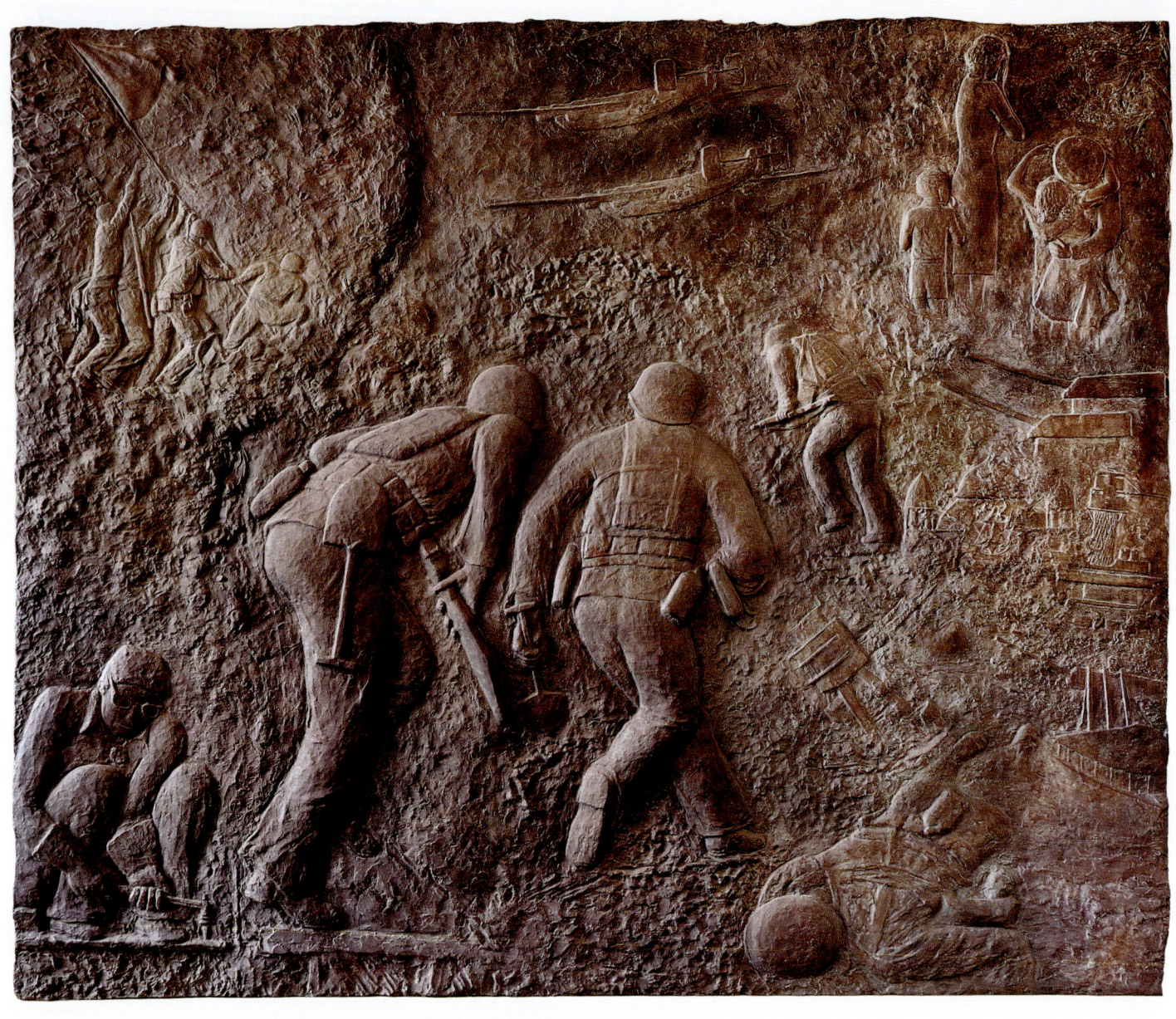

PLATES 53–54

Promise/Anthem, 1997–98

Bronze, 6½ feet × 8 feet × 4 inches. Edition 1/1
The Philip and Muriel Berman Museum of Art at Ursinus College

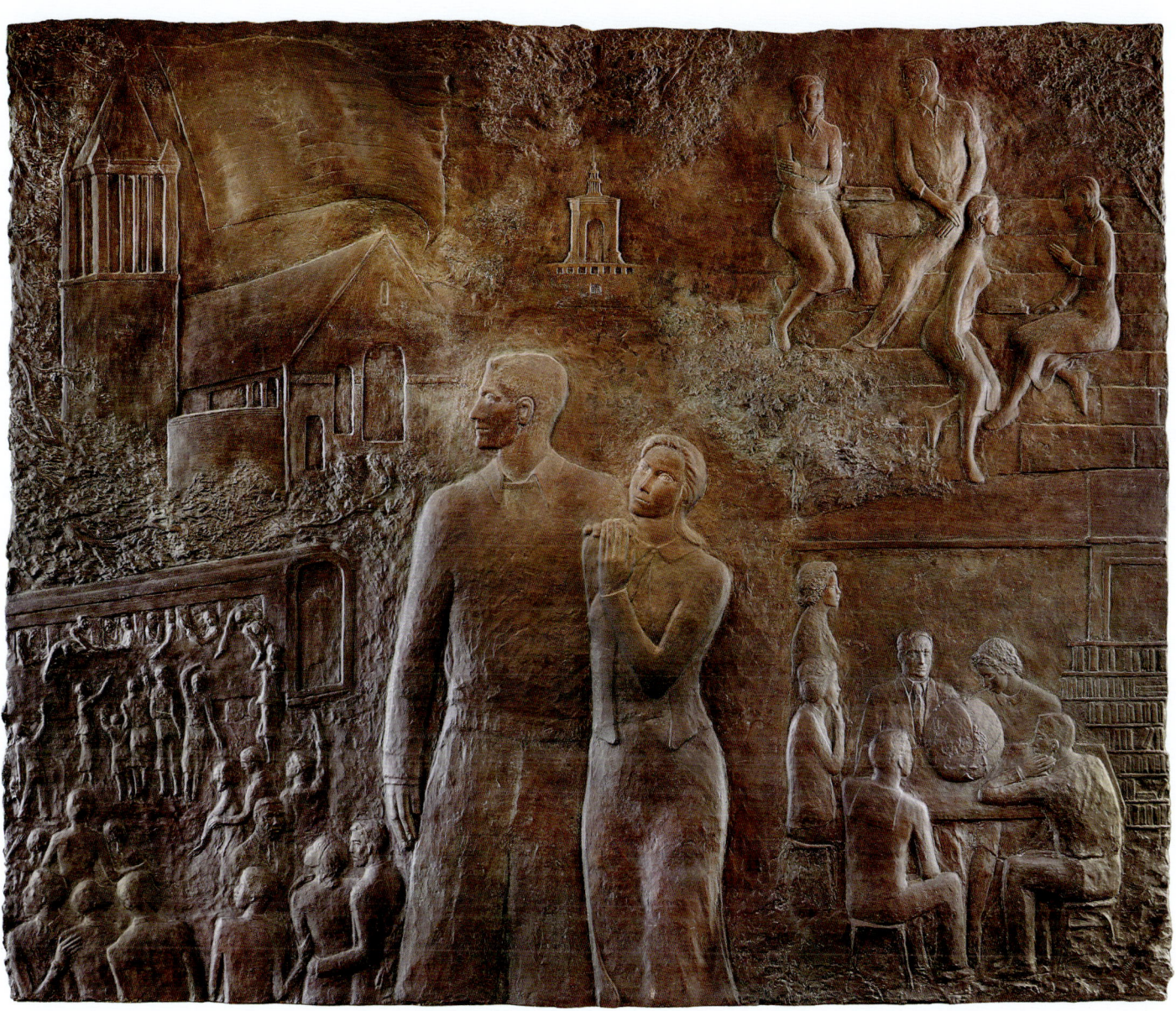

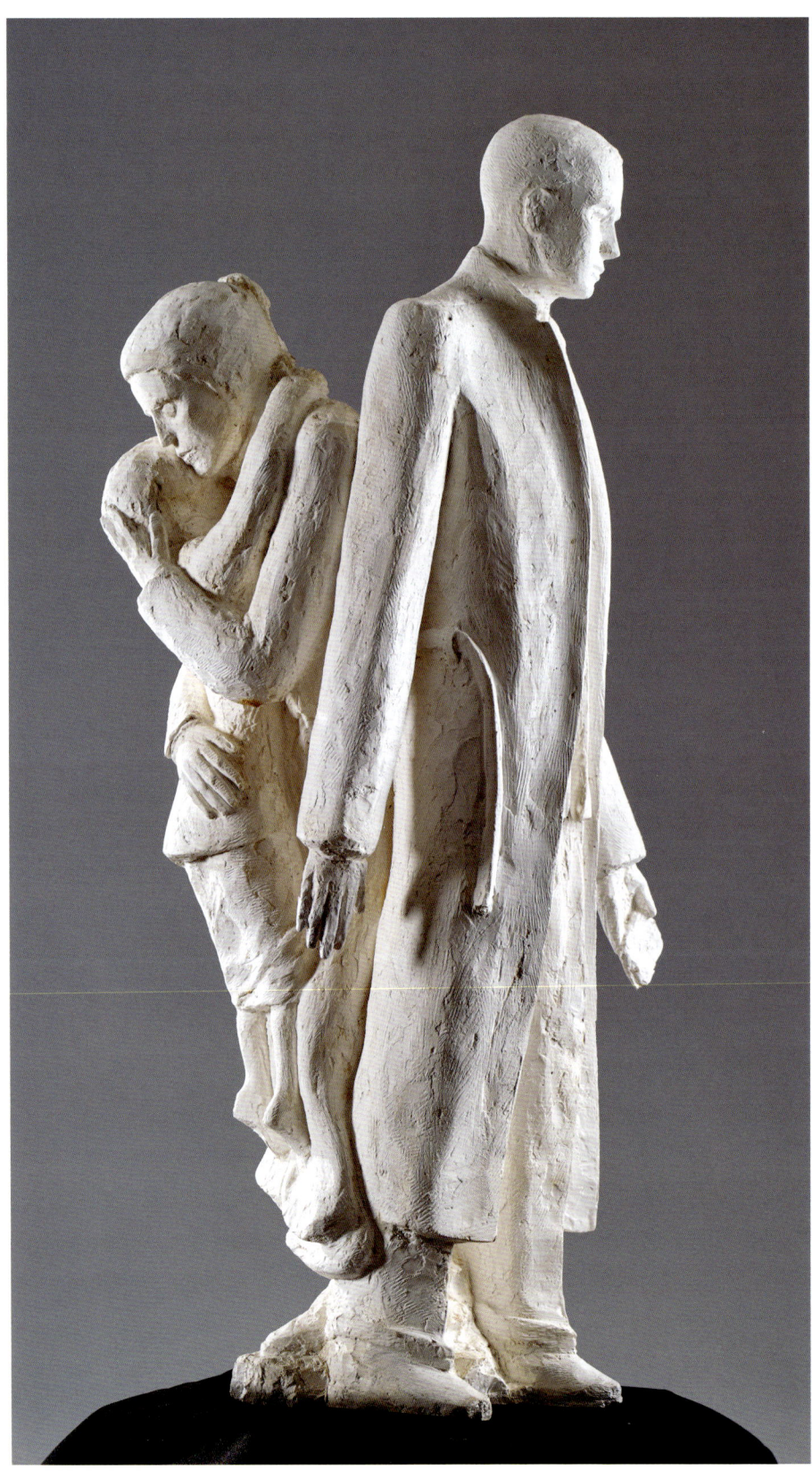

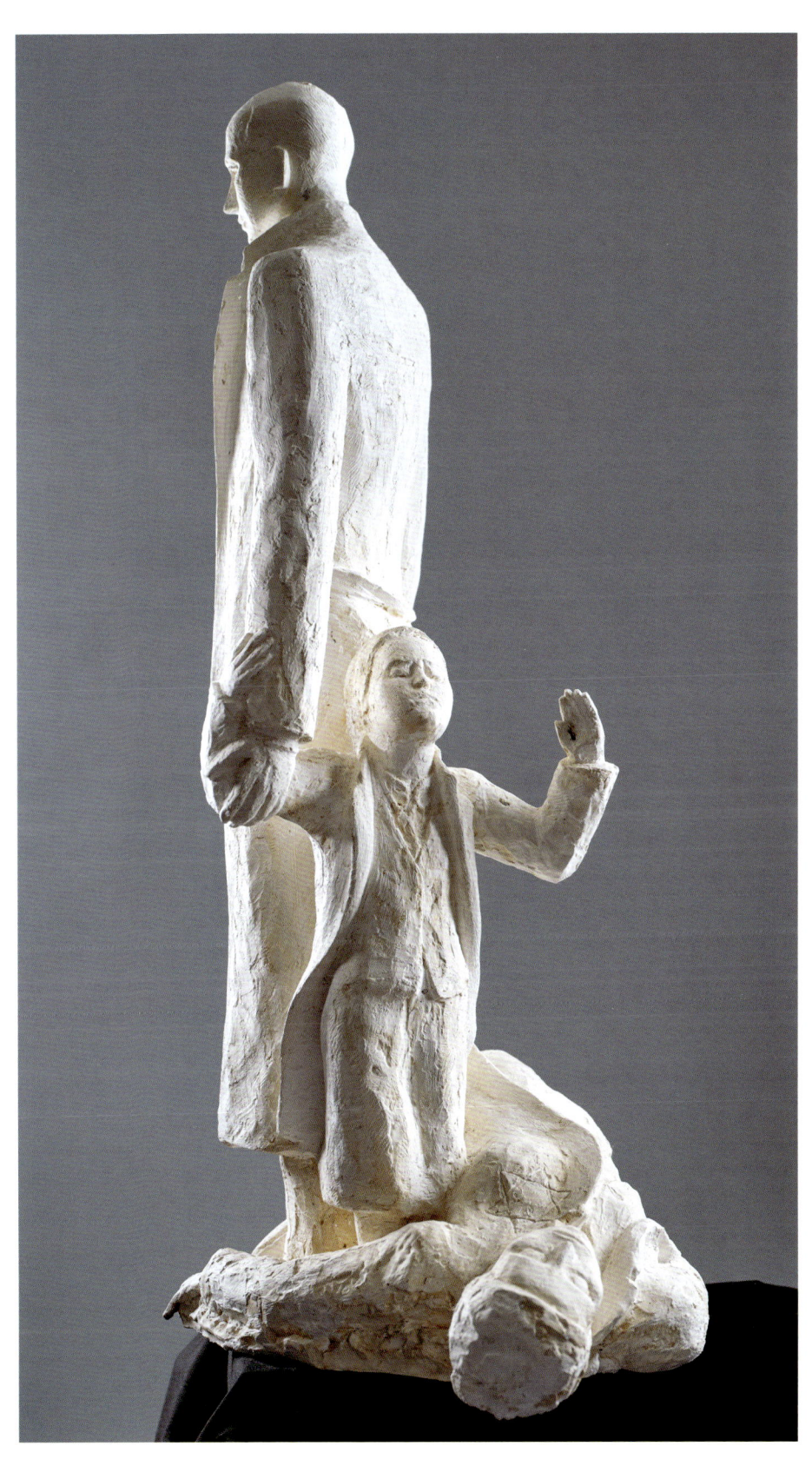

PLATE 56

Raoul Wallenberg II, 1998–2000

Plaster, 27 × 15 × 15 inches
Collection of the artist

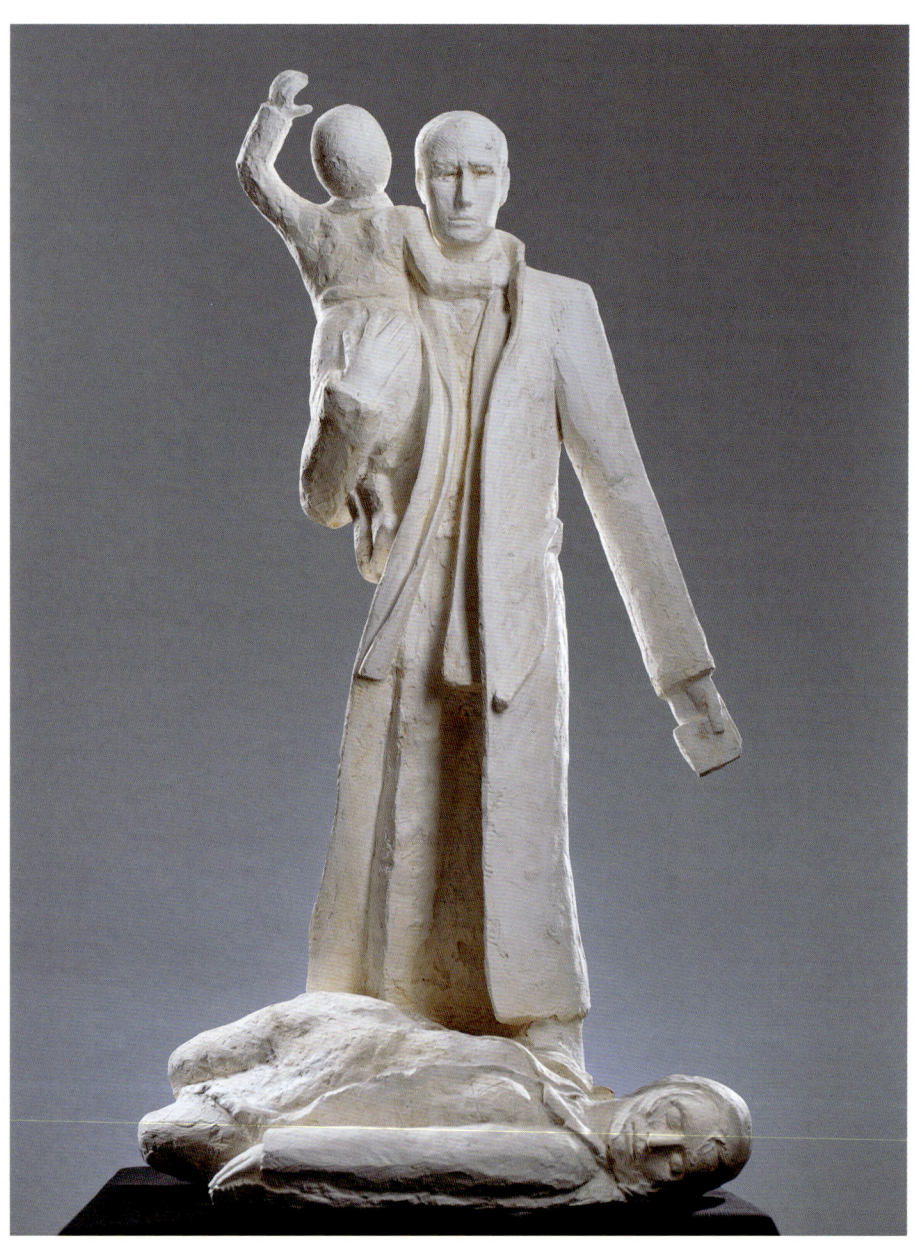

PLATE 57

Raoul Wallenberg III, 1998–2000

Plaster, 27 × 12 × 12 inches
Collection of the artist

PLATE 58

Dialogue, 2003–04

Bronze, 29 × 20 × 20 inches. Edition 1/9
Collection of Carol and Louis Della Penna

114   GEORGE R. ANTHONISEN: MEDITATIONS ON THE HUMAN CONDITION

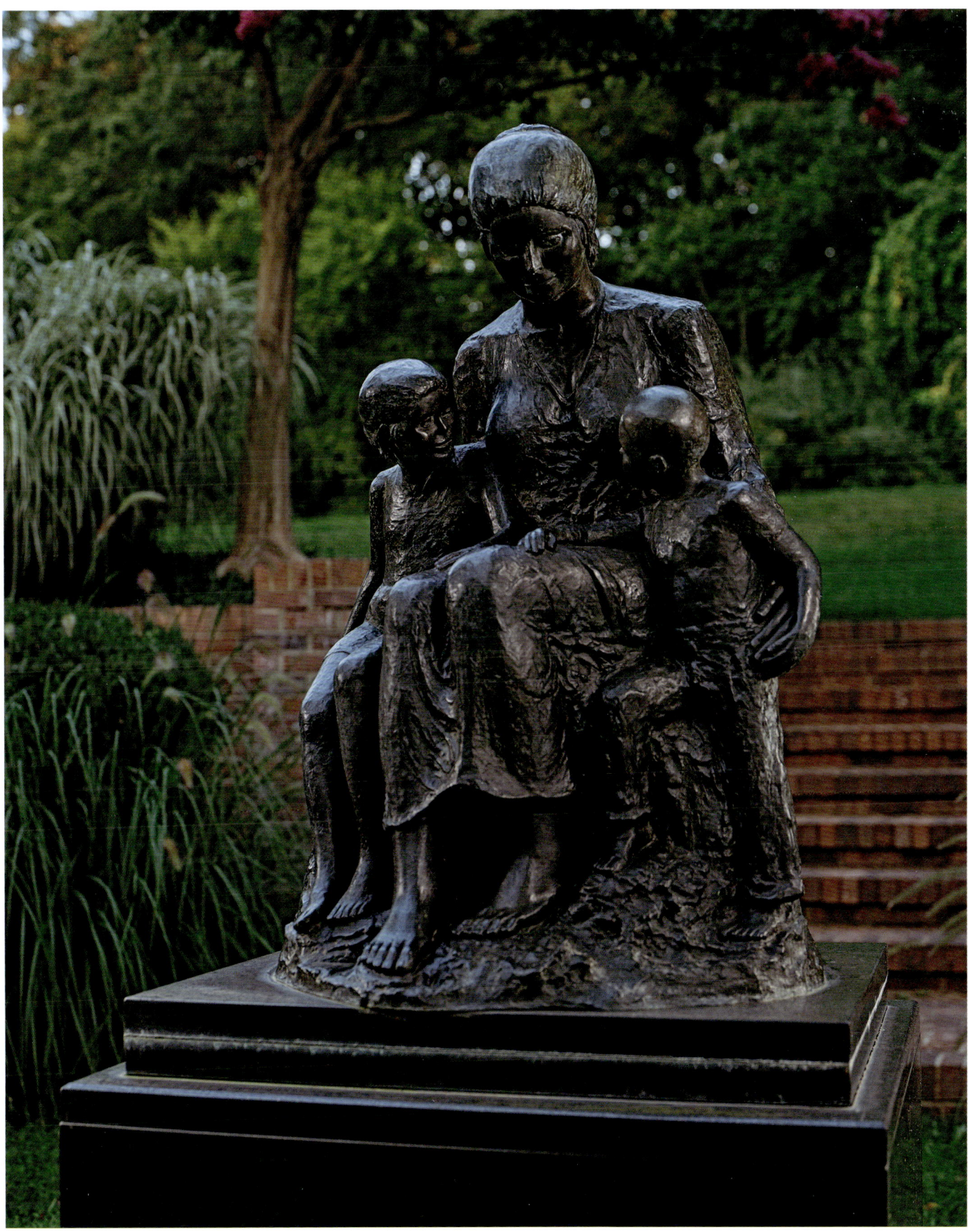

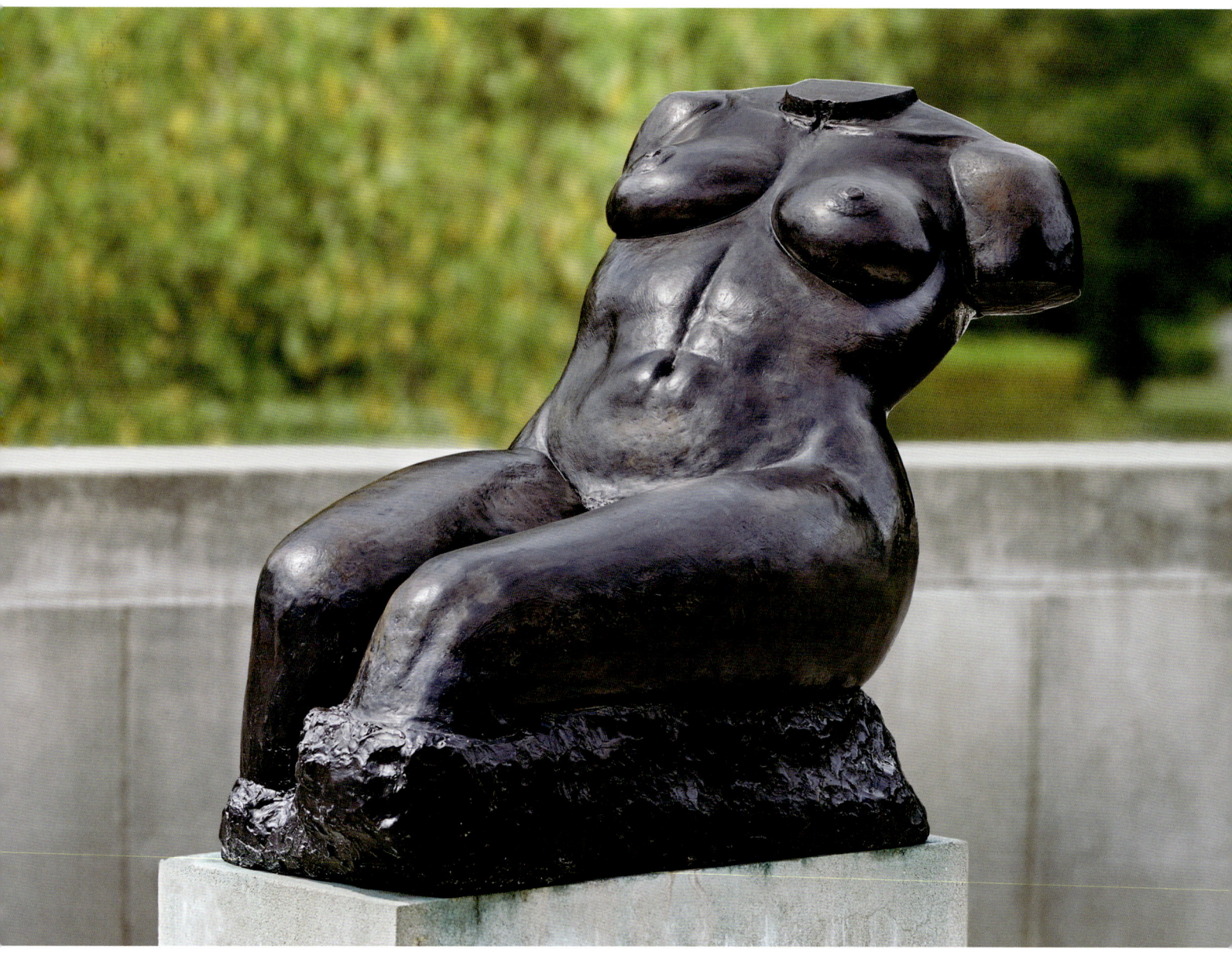

PLATE 59
Rising, 2004–06
Bronze, 29½ × 37½ × 15 inches. Edition 1/9
The Philip and Muriel Berman Museum of Art at Ursinus College

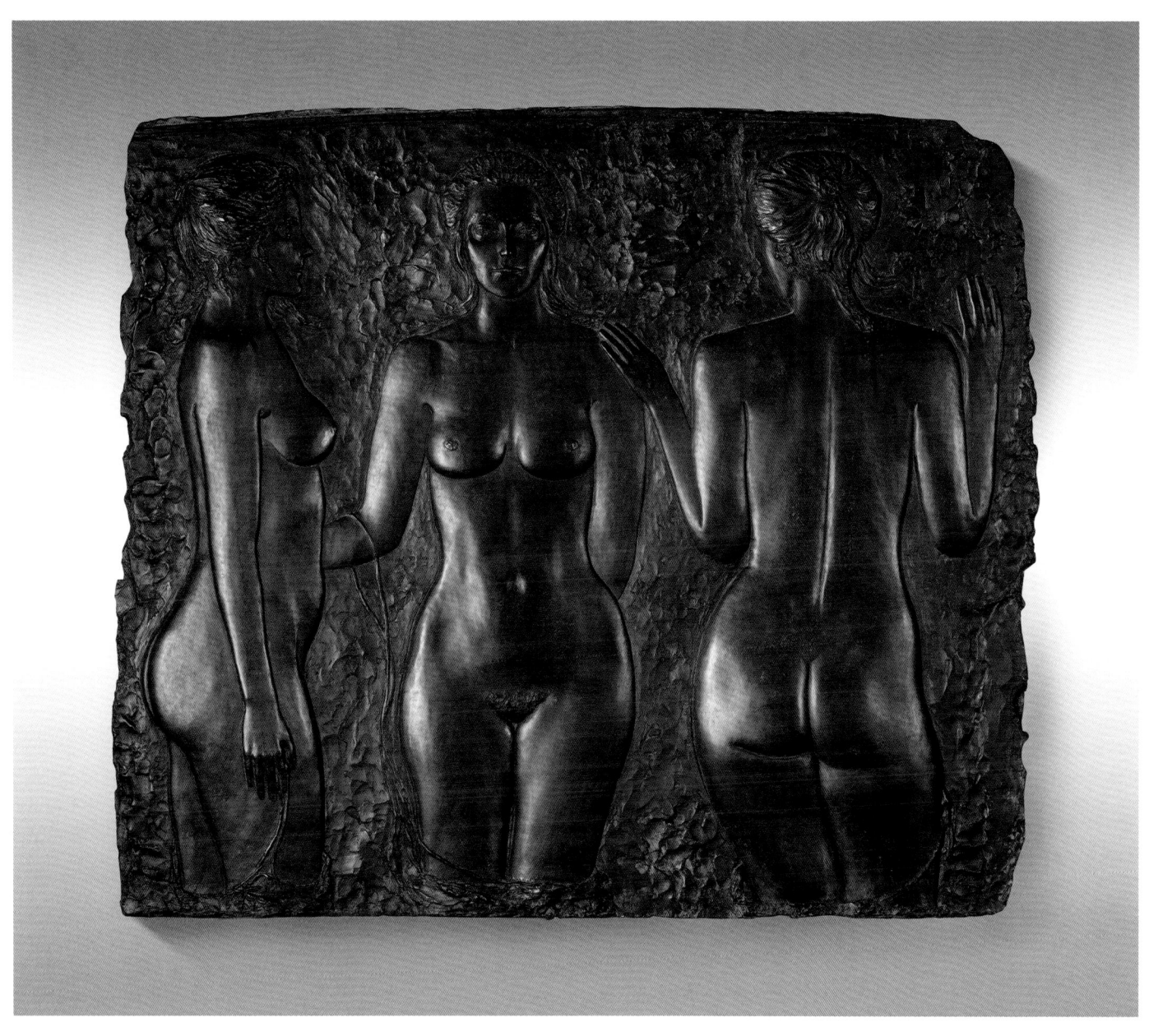

PLATE 60

Three Nudes (Graces), 2006–07

Bronze, 31⅜ × 36½ inches. Edition 1/9
Collection of the artist

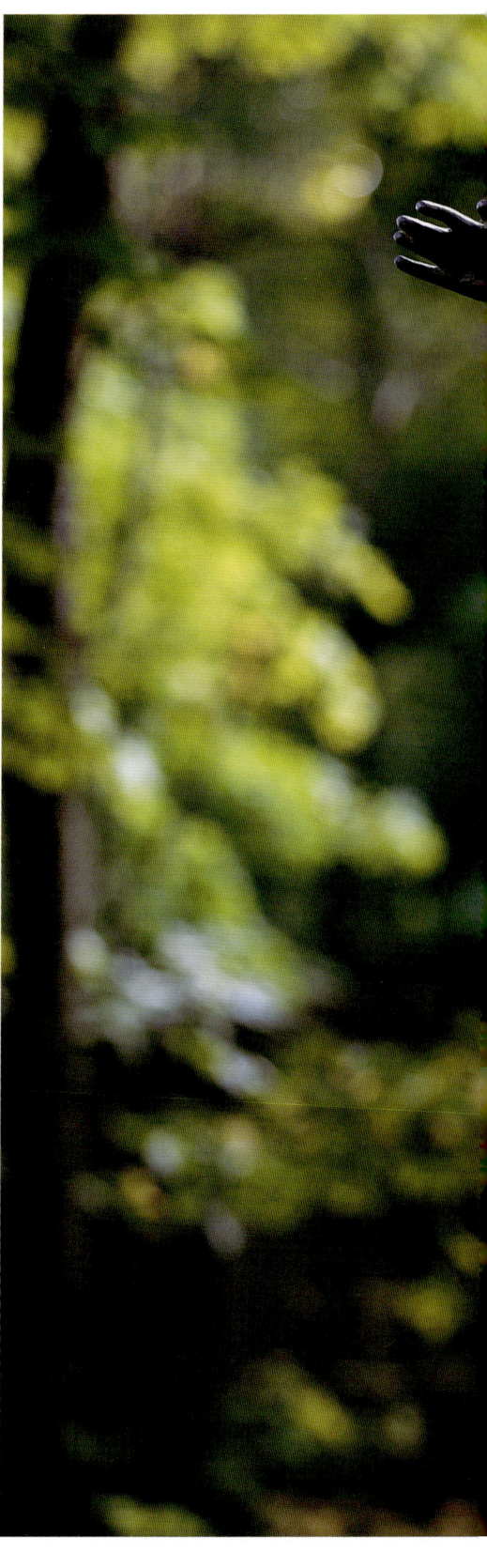

PLATE 61

Aspiration, 2007–08

Bronze, 35 × 30 × 29 inches. Edition 1/9
Collection of the artist

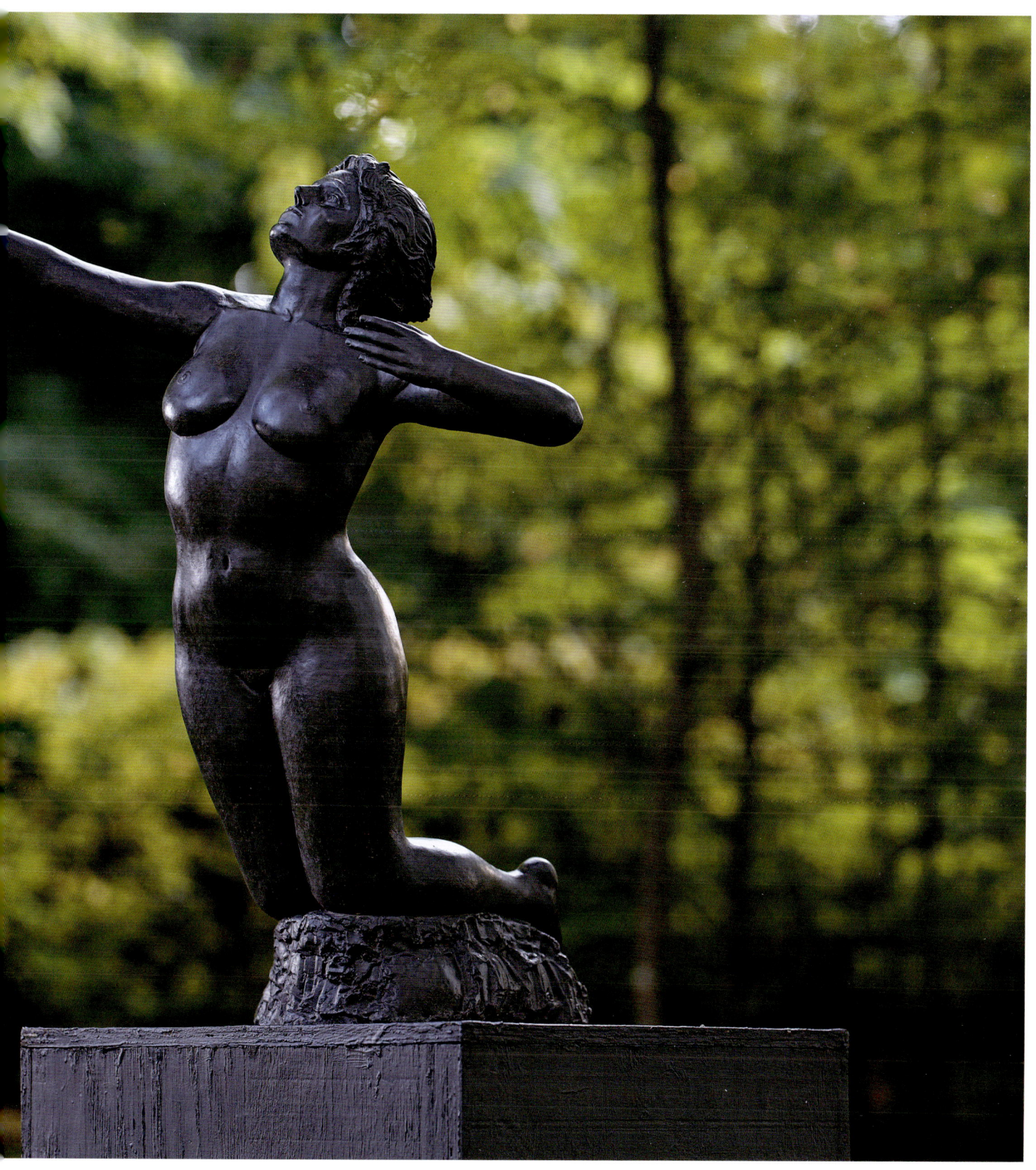

Serenity, 2010–11

Bronze, 13 × 15 × 10 inches. Edition 2/9
Collection of the artist

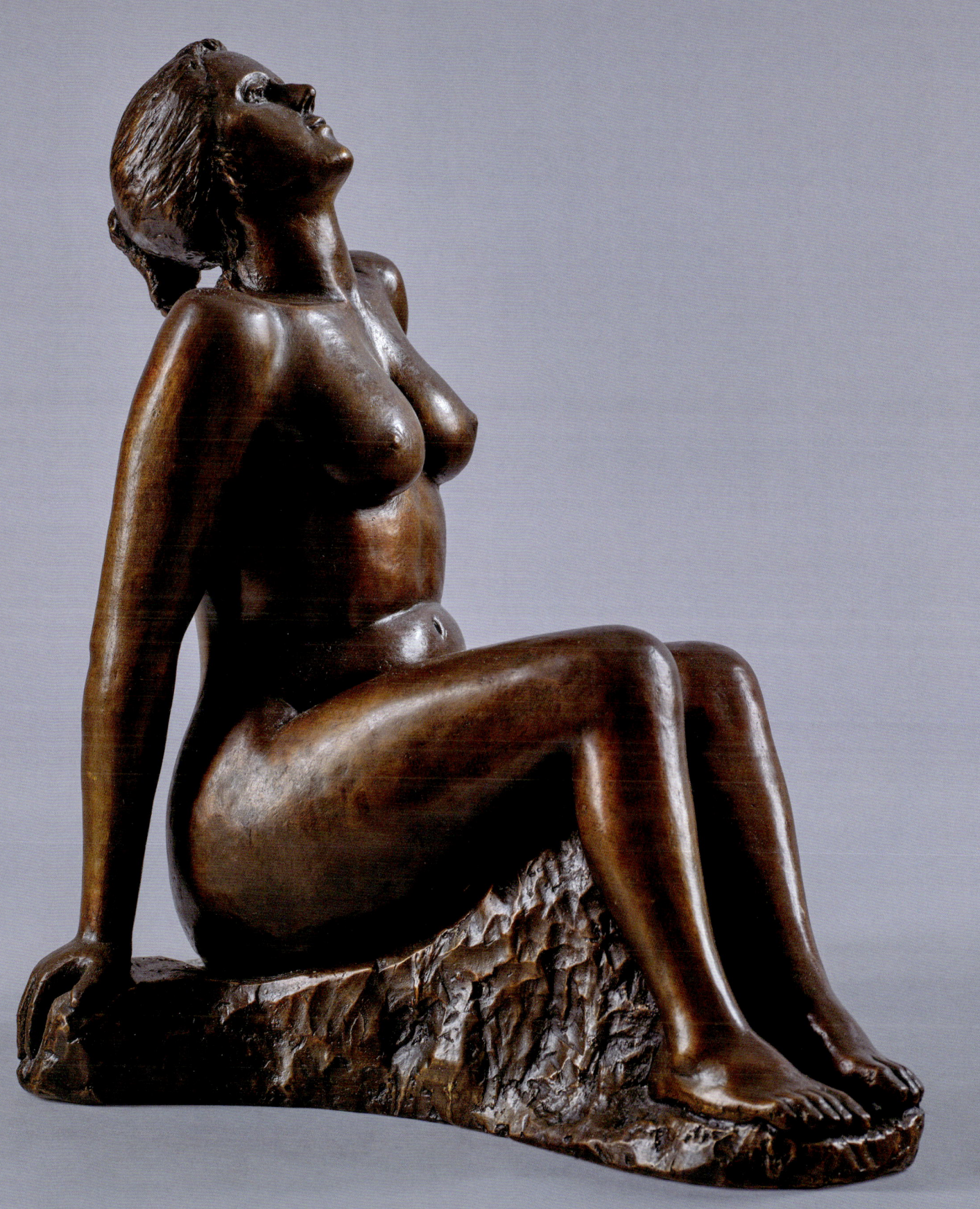

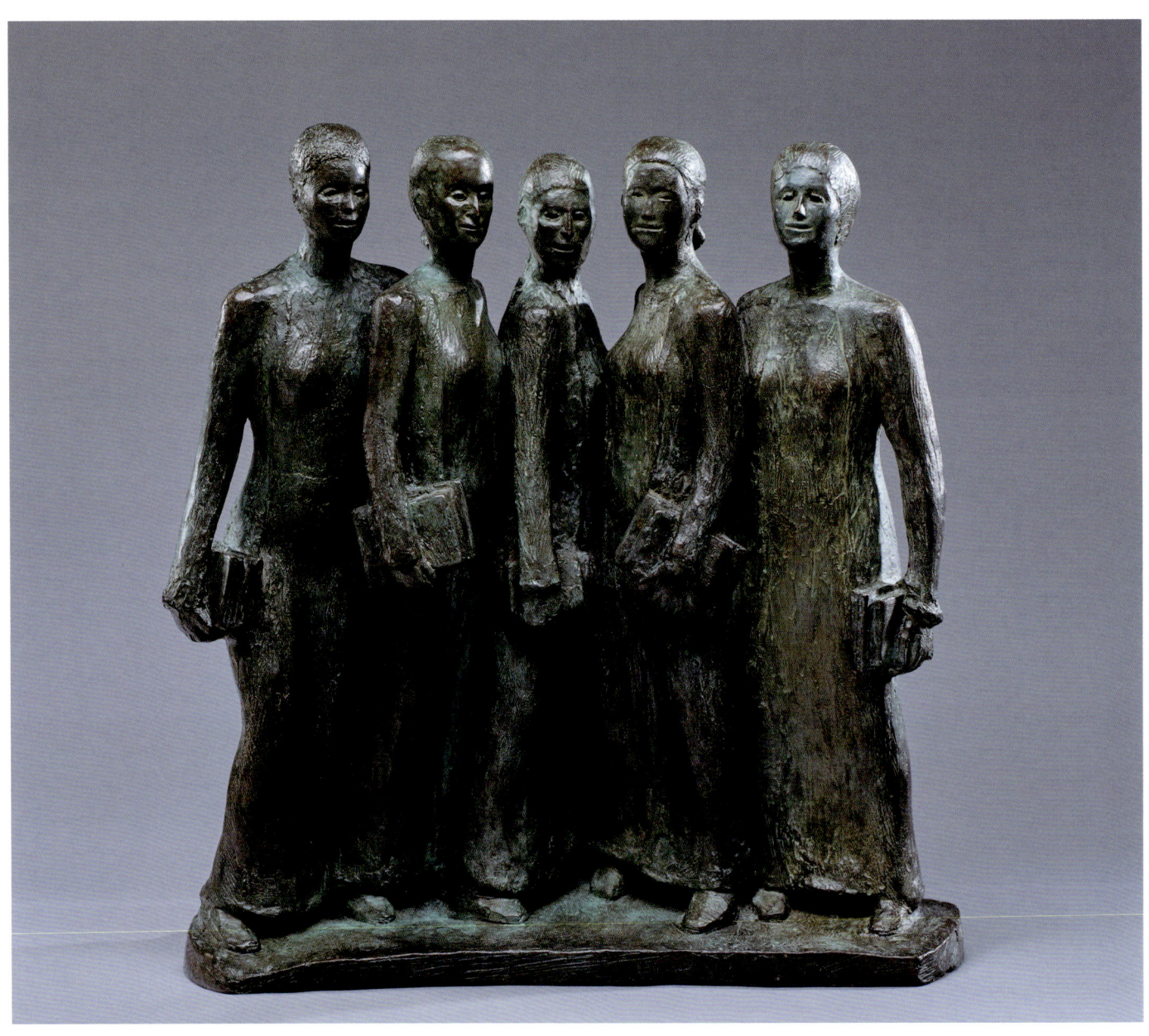

Five Women (front and back), 2010–12

Bronze, 15 × 14½ × 6 inches. Edition 3/9
Collection of the artist

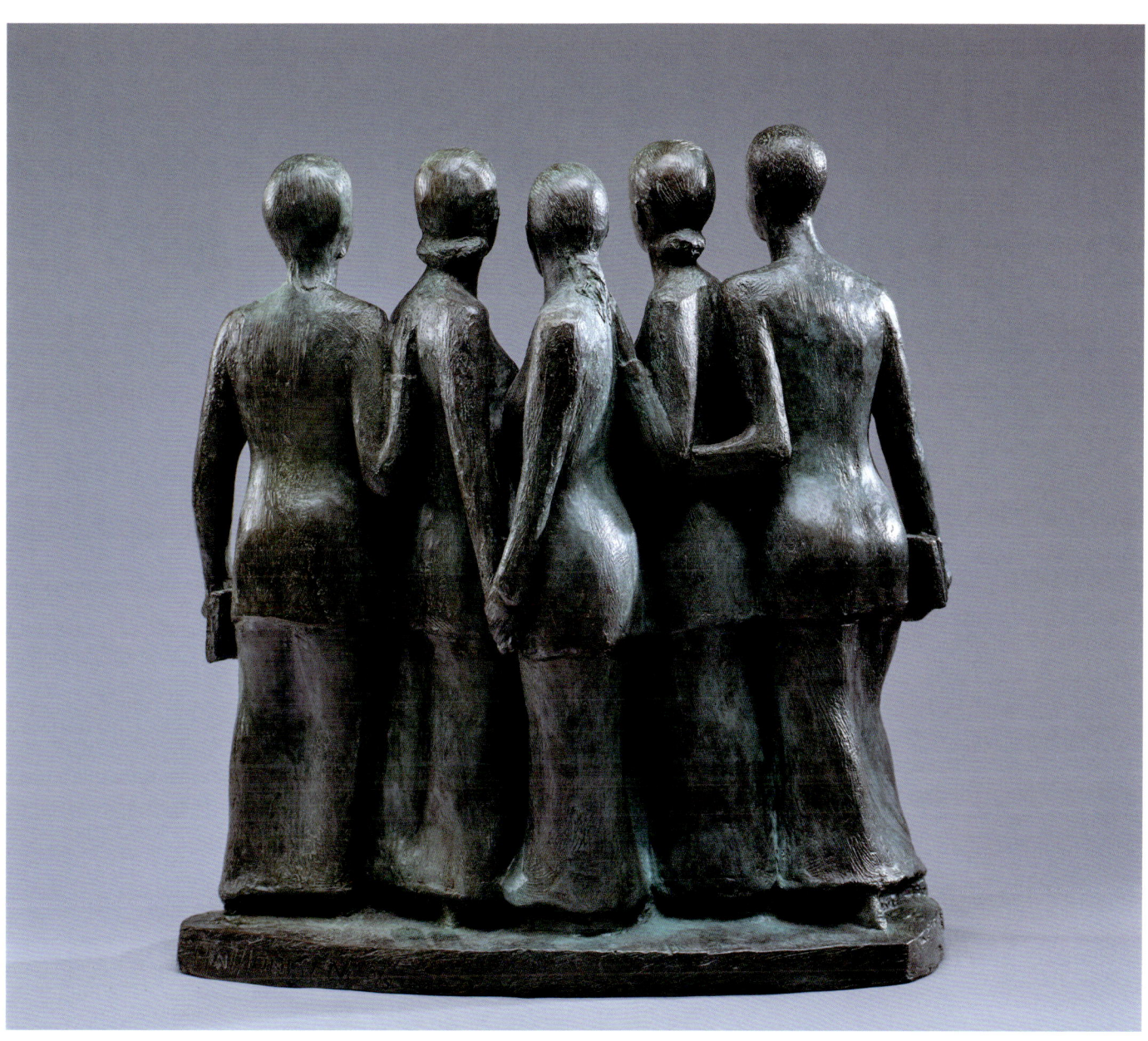

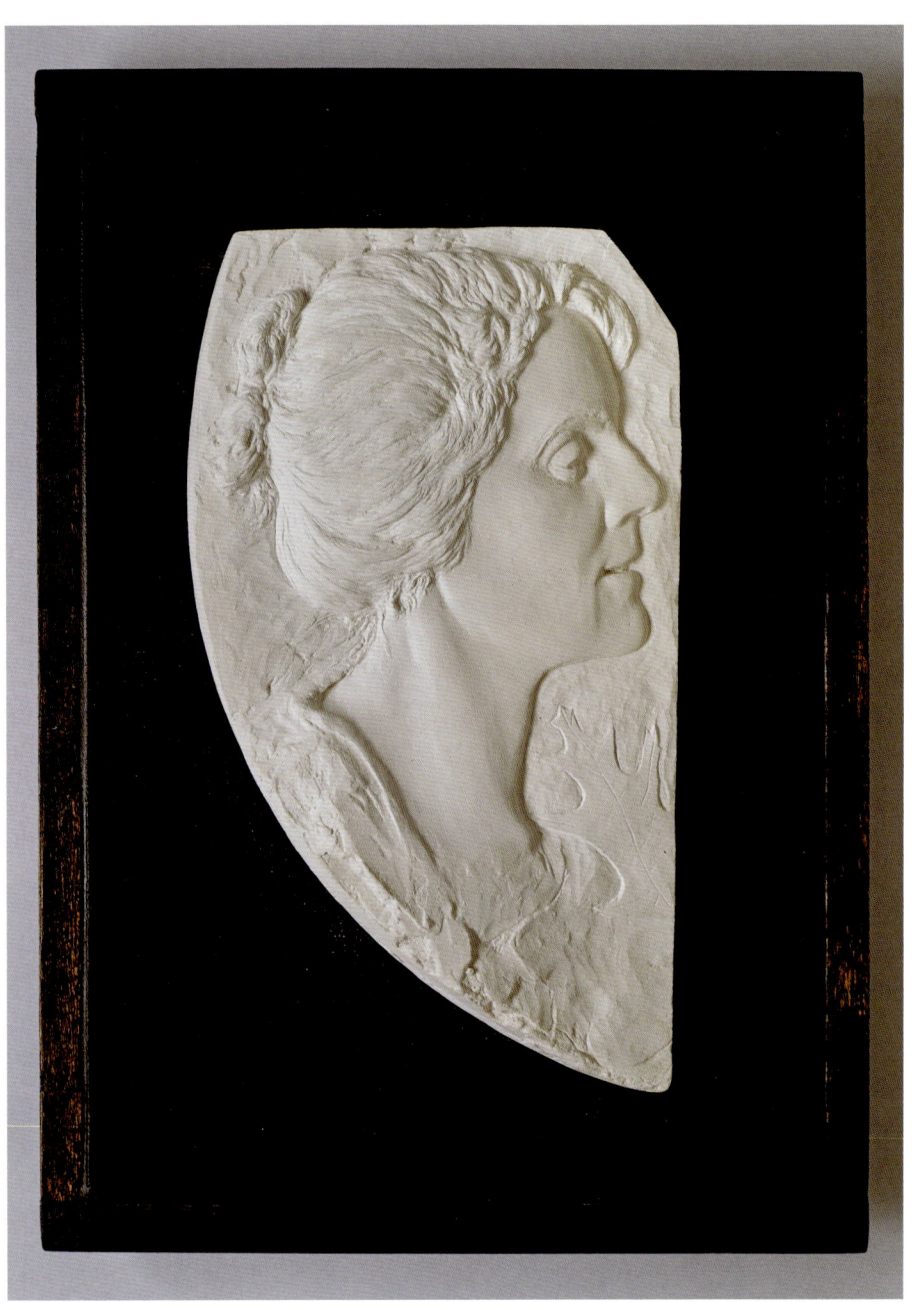

PLATE 65

Ellen, 2018–20

Plaster of paris, 8½ × 14 inches. Edition 1/5
Collection of the artist

PLATE 66

Conversation, 2017–20

Plaster, 17 × 15 × 11 inches
Collection of the artist

124   GEORGE R. ANTHONISEN: MEDITATIONS ON THE HUMAN CONDITION

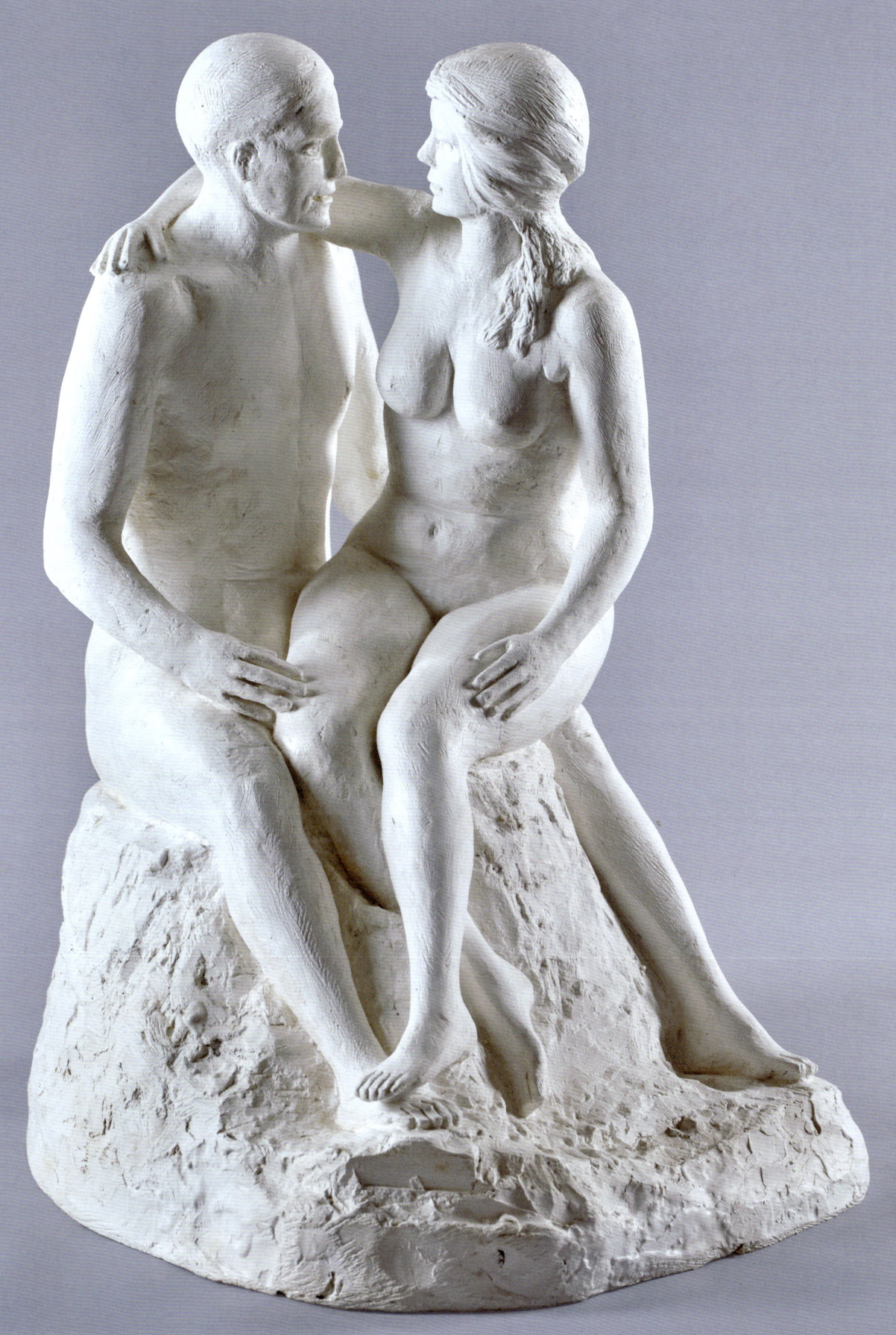

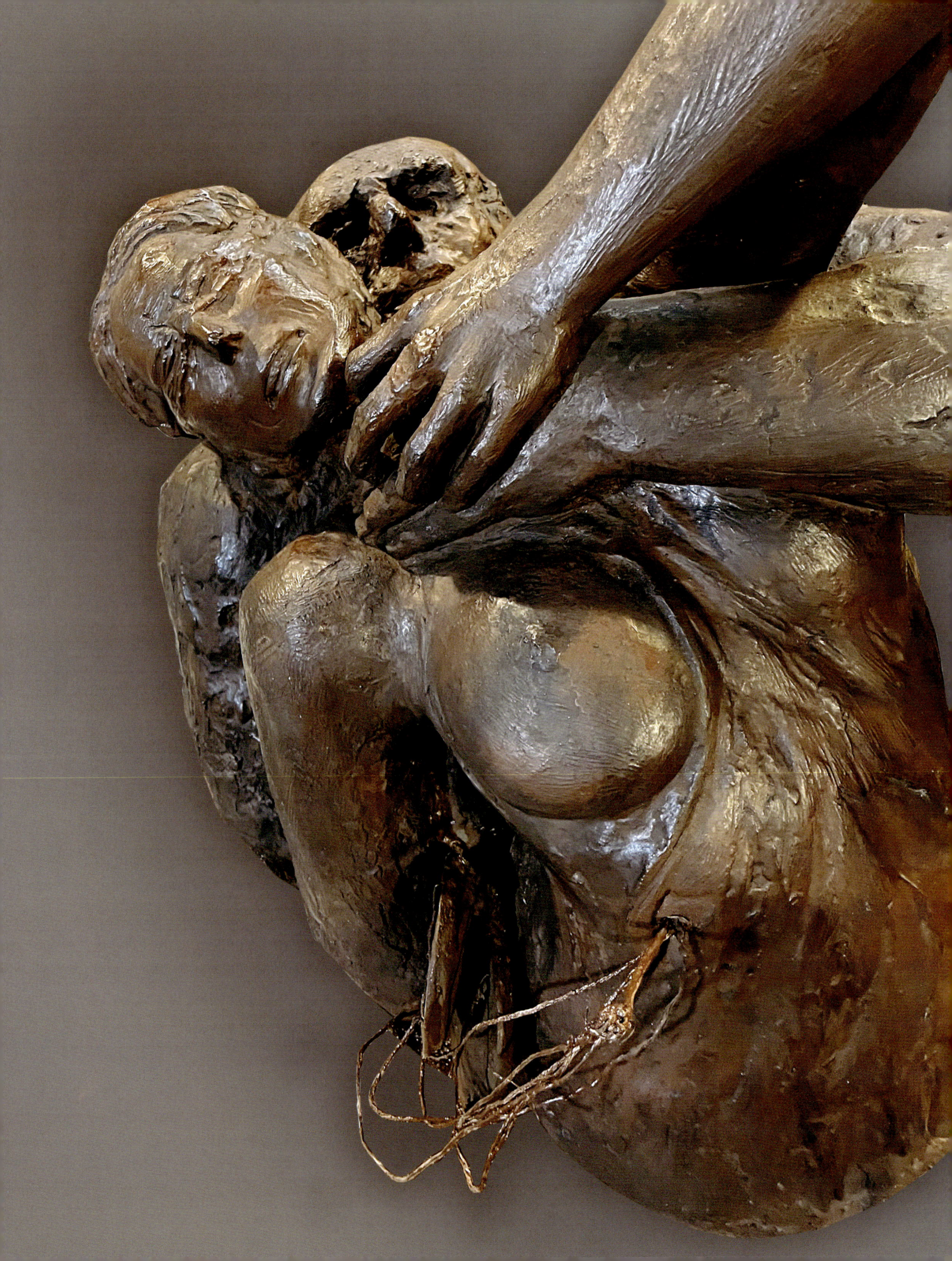

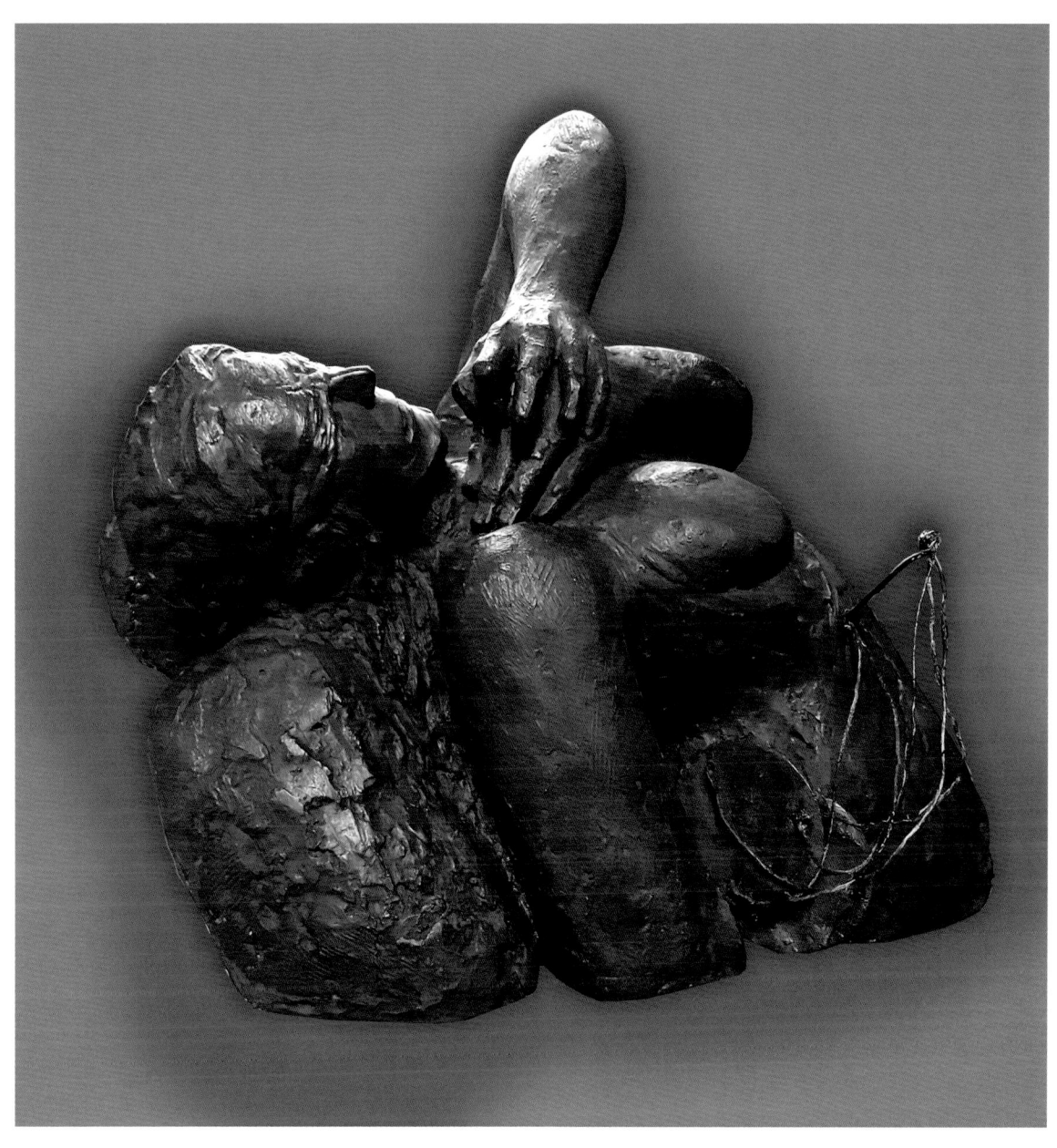

The Rape of Justice, 2020–21

Plaster, 20 × 22 × 22 inches
Collection of the artist

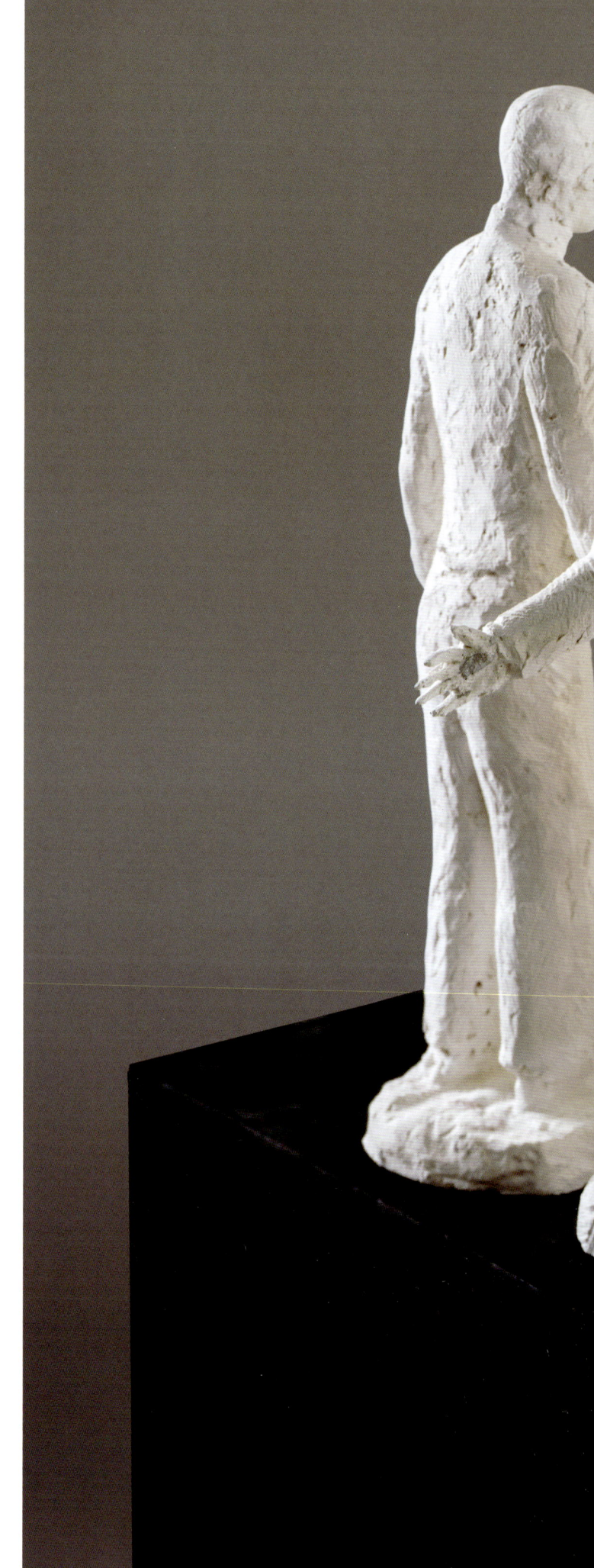

PLATE 69

The Choice, 2022–24

Plaster, 16 × 12½ × 12 inches
Collection of the artist

128

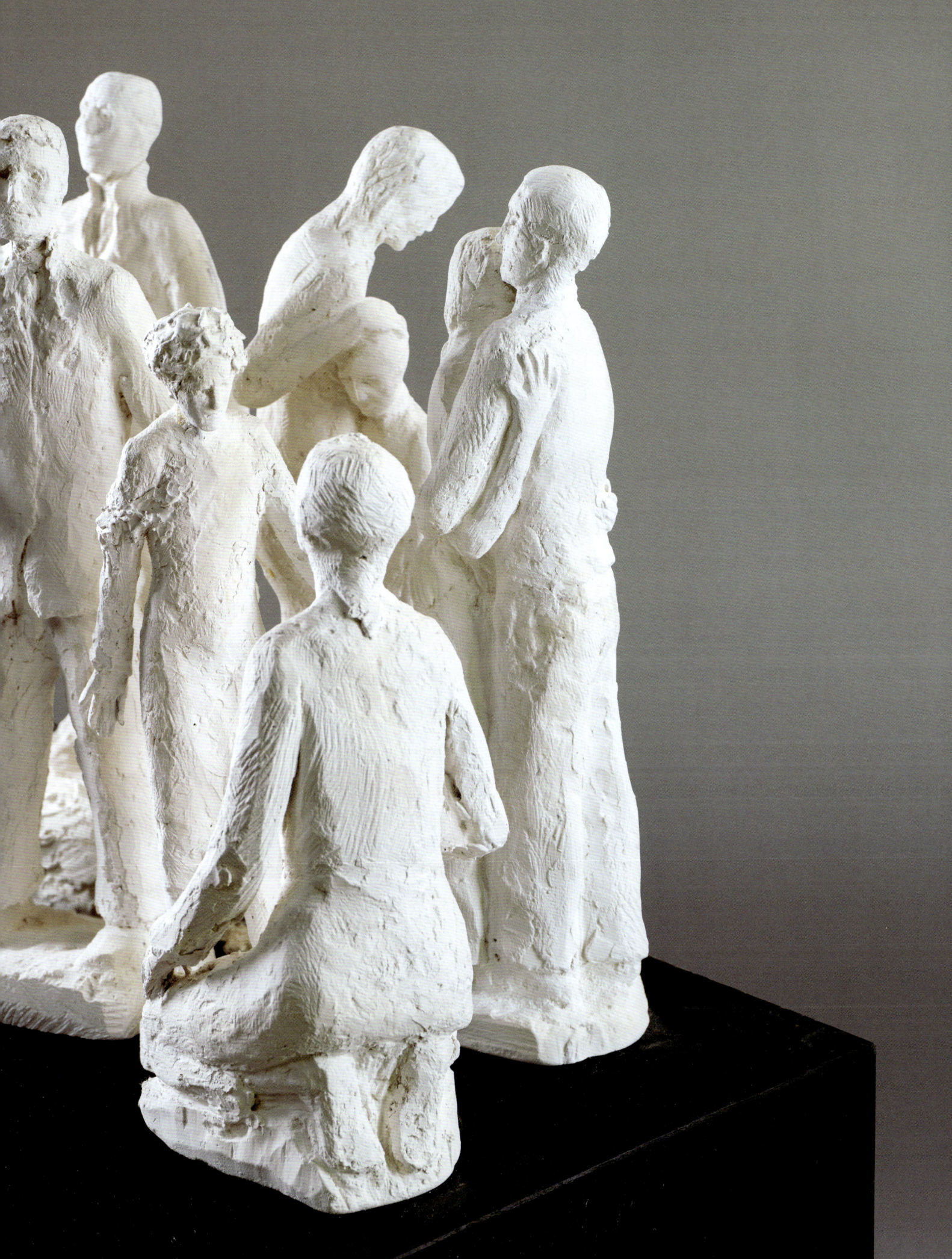

Frescoes

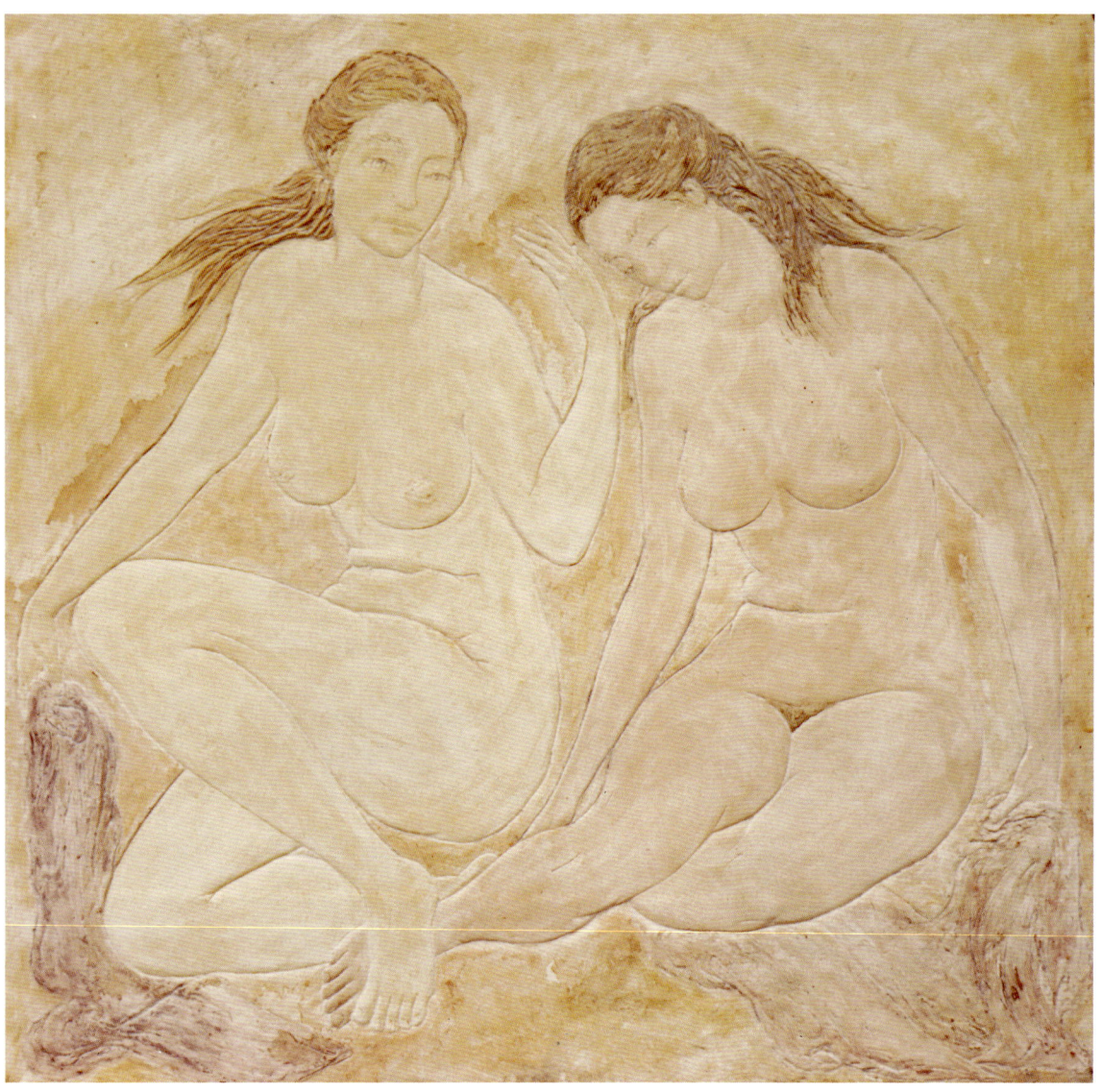

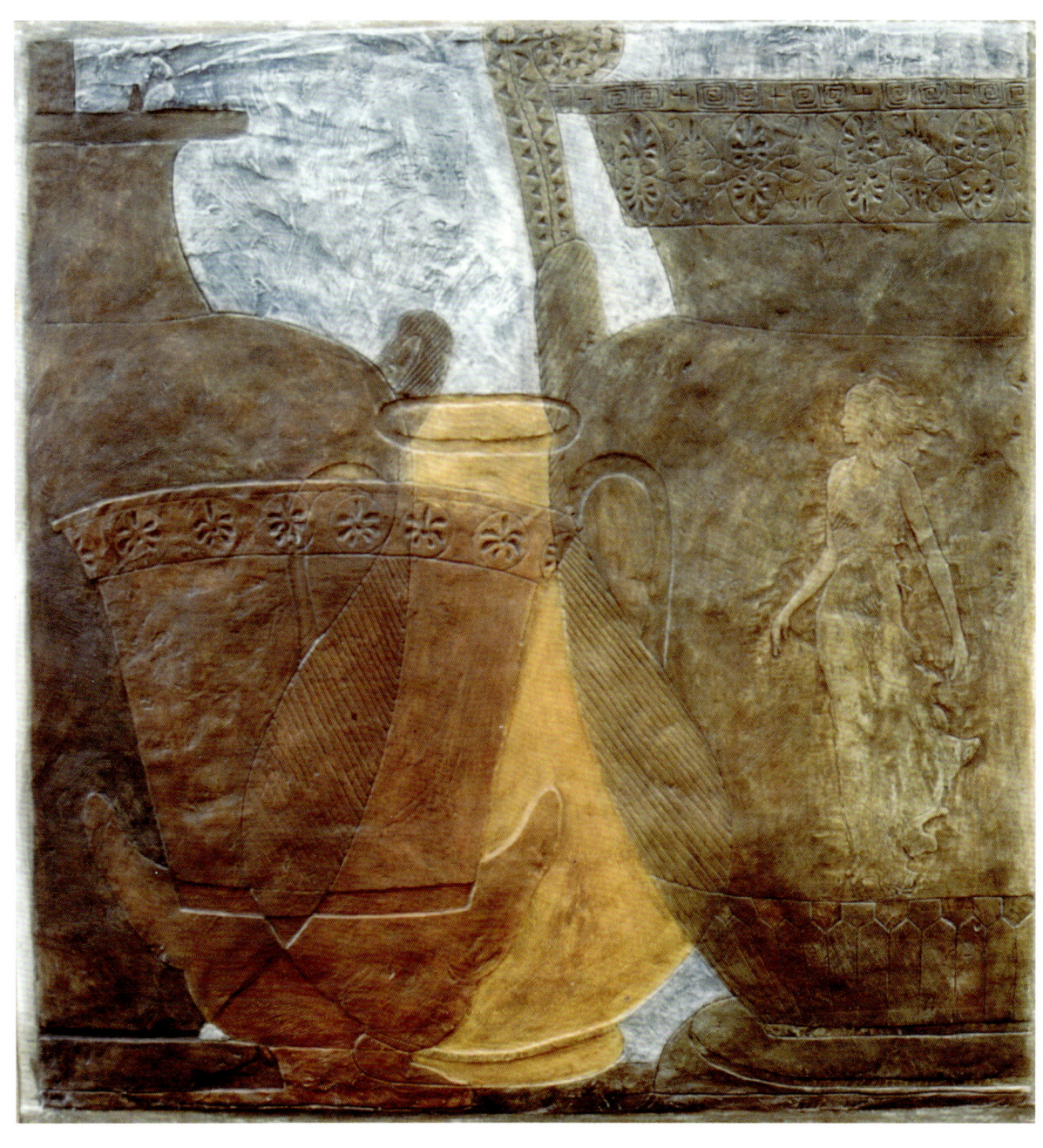

Leda and the Swan, 1985

Mineral colors, limewater, and casein on plaster, 38¾ × 37½ inches
Collection of Lois and David Schaffer, Great Neck, NY

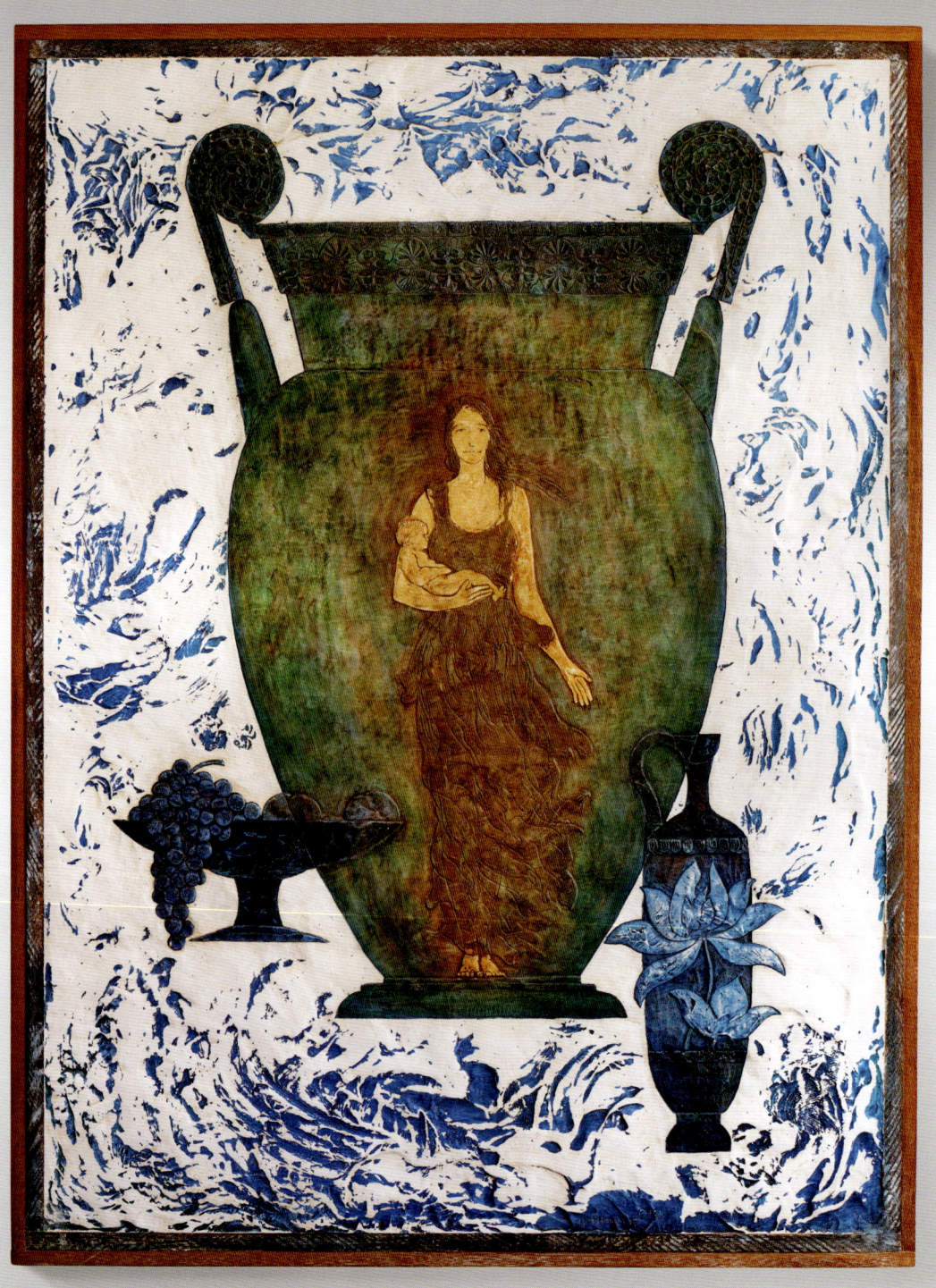

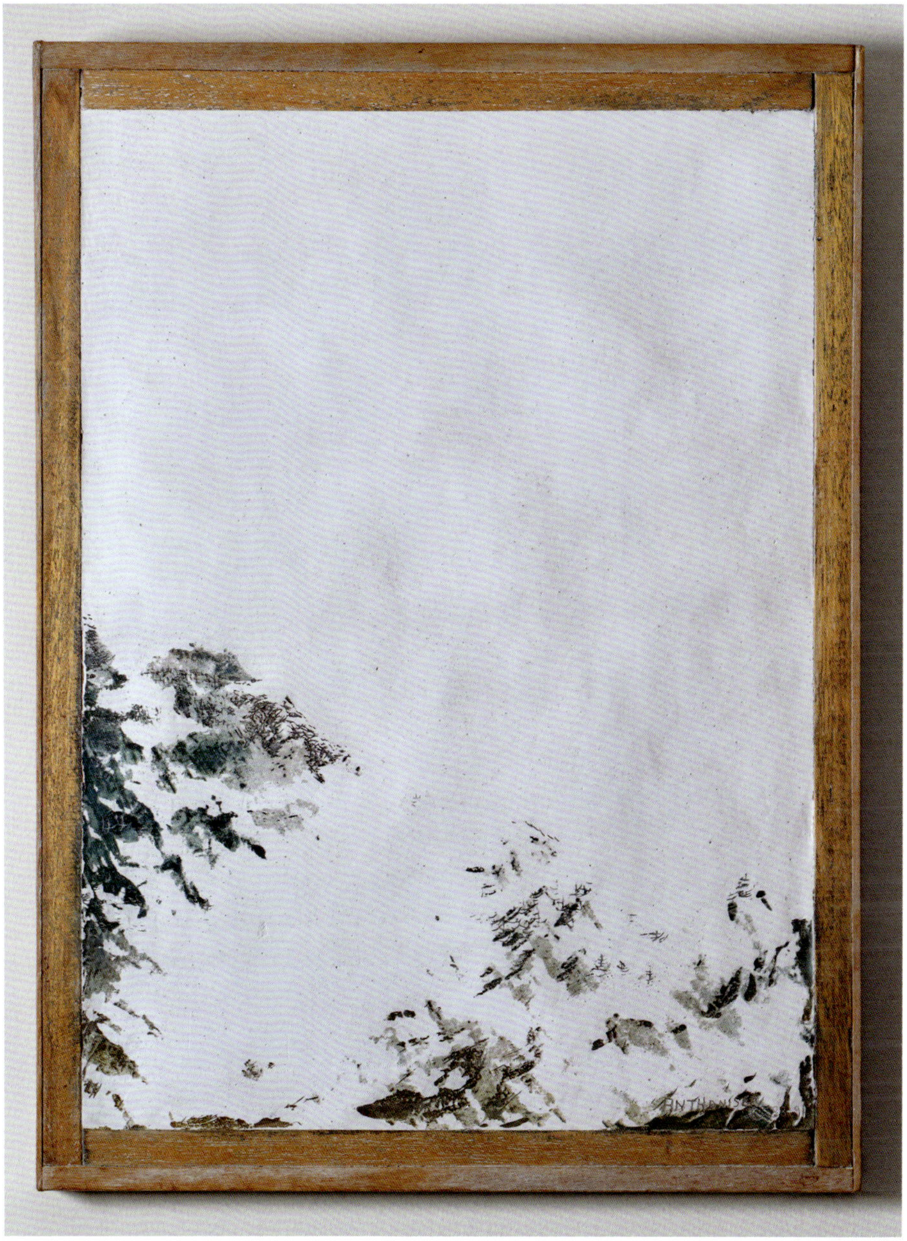

PLATE 72

Origins, 1987

Mineral colors, limewater, and casein
on plaster, 49¼ × 37¼ inches
Collection of the artist

PLATE 73

Snowstorm, 1988

Mineral colors, limewater, and casein
on plaster, 22¼ × 16½ inches
Collection of Susan Yacubian Klein

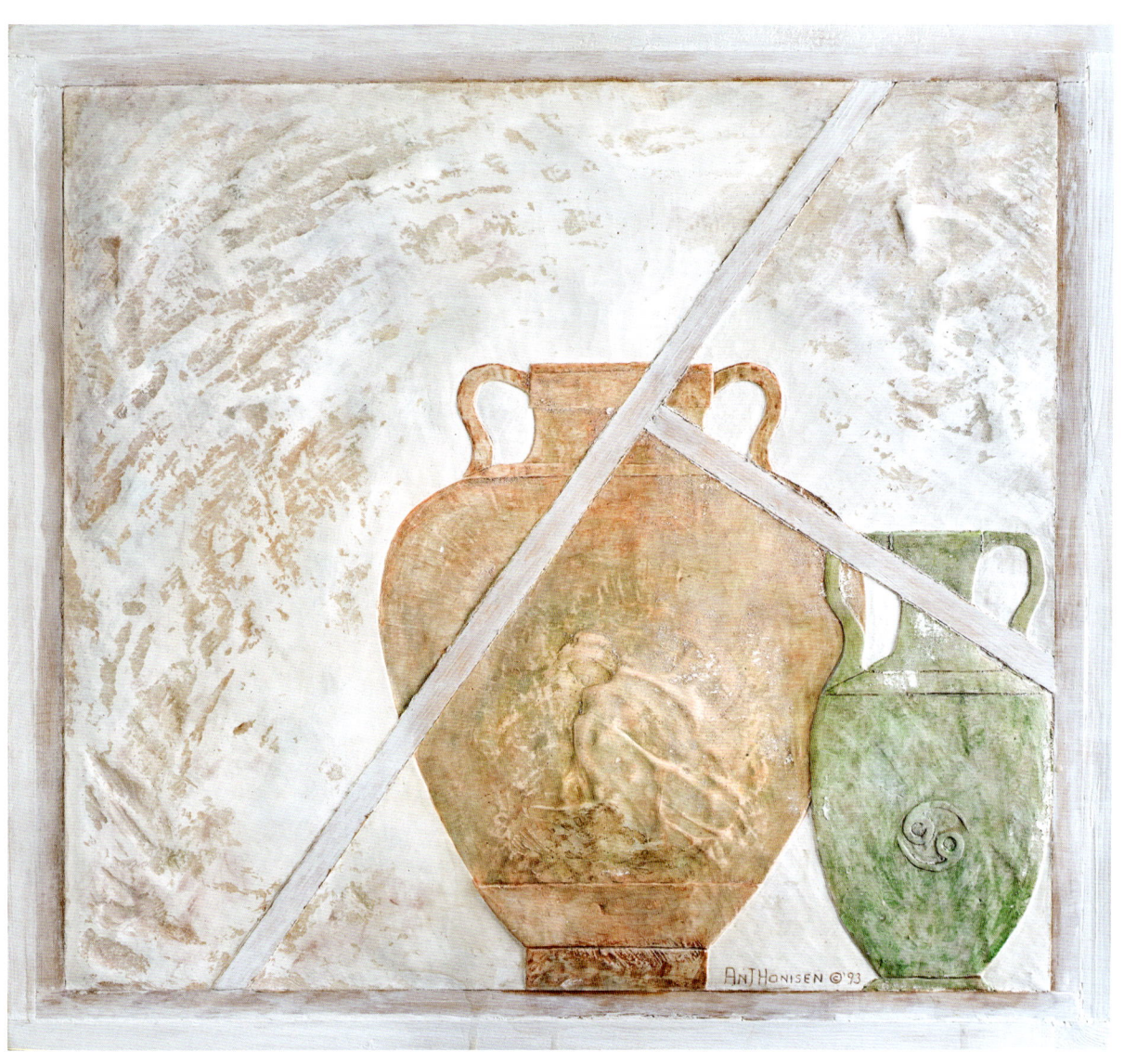

PLATE 74

Arrangement IV, 1993

Mineral colors, limewater, and casein on plaster, 23 × 25¼ inches
Private collection

GEORGE R. ANTHONISEN: MEDITATIONS ON THE HUMAN CONDITION

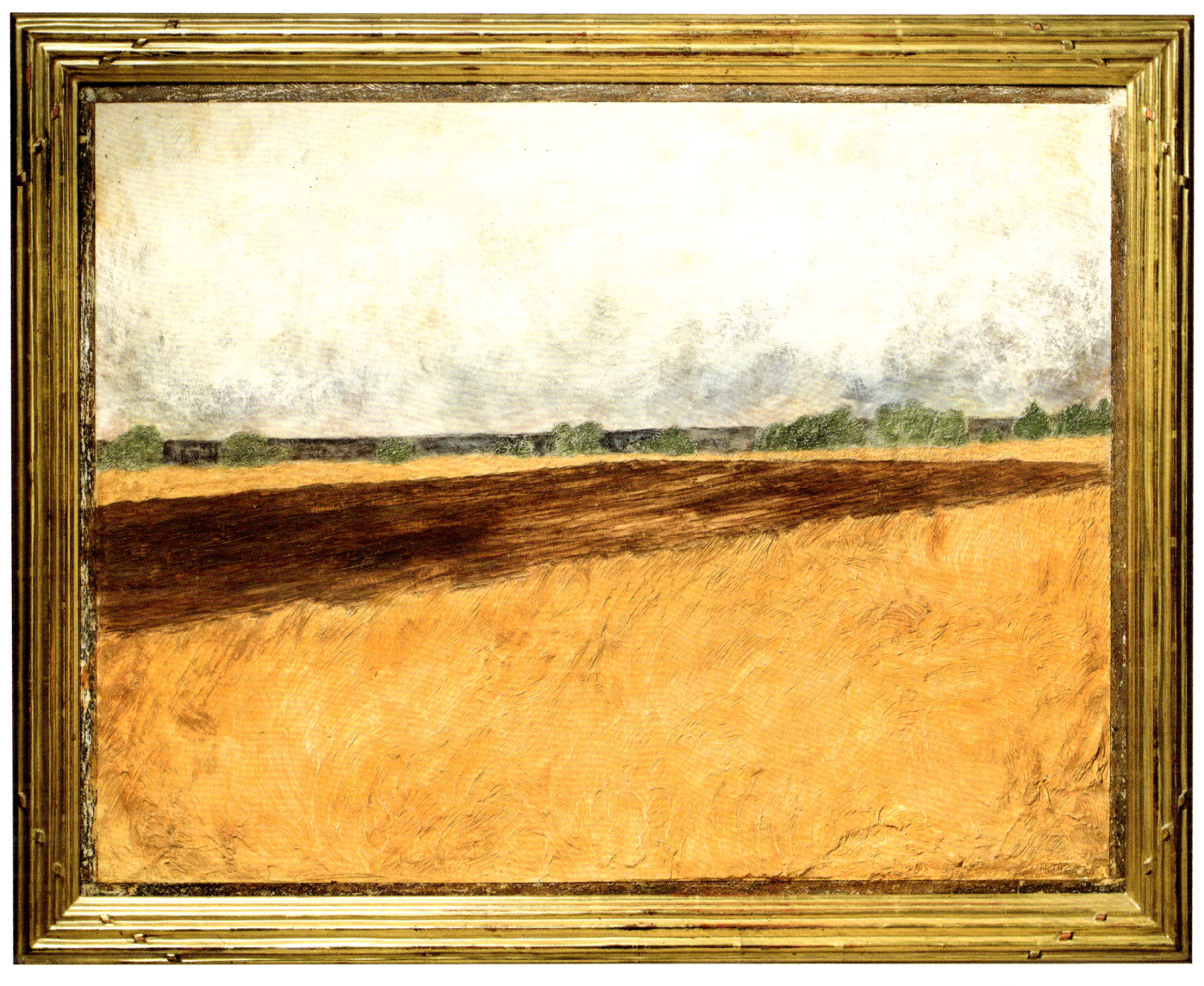

PLATE 75

Armitage Road, Solebury, 2000

Mineral colors, limewater, and casein on plaster, 24 × 32 inches
Collection of Ann and Daniel Bernstein

Drawings

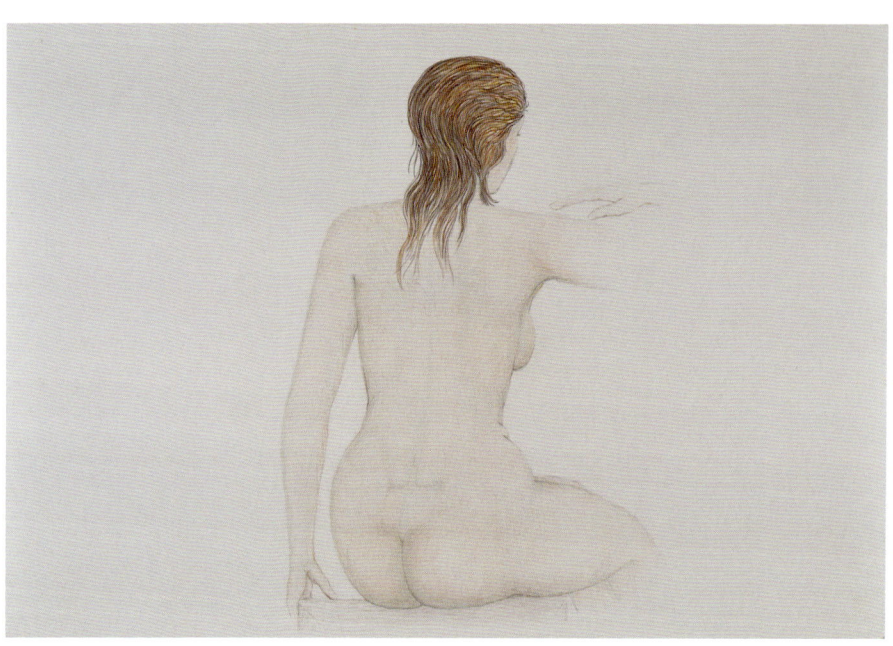

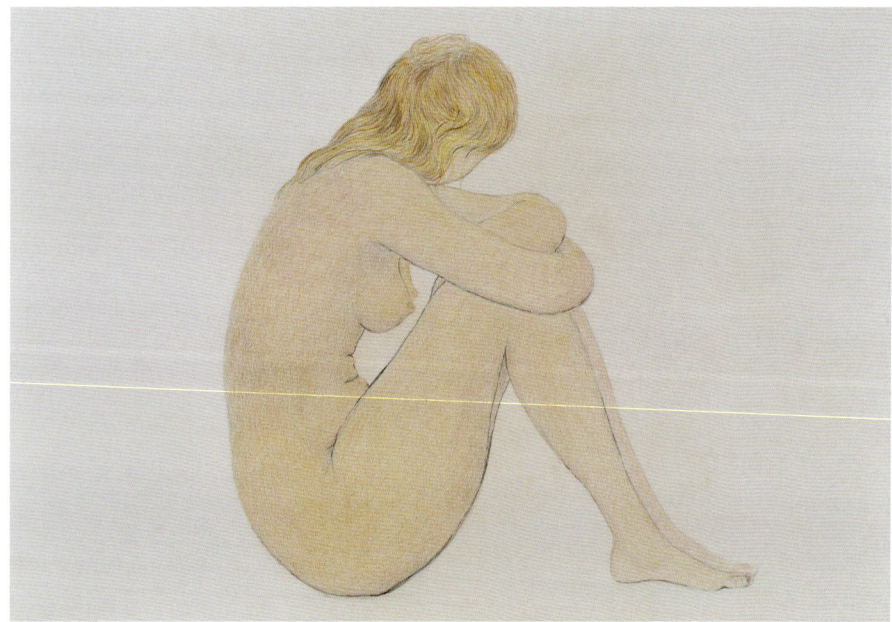

PLATE 76
Back of a Woman, 2014
Colored wax pencils on paper, 15 × 22 inches
Collection of the artist

PLATE 77
Seated Woman, 2013
Colored wax pencils on paper, 15 × 22 inches
Collection of the artist

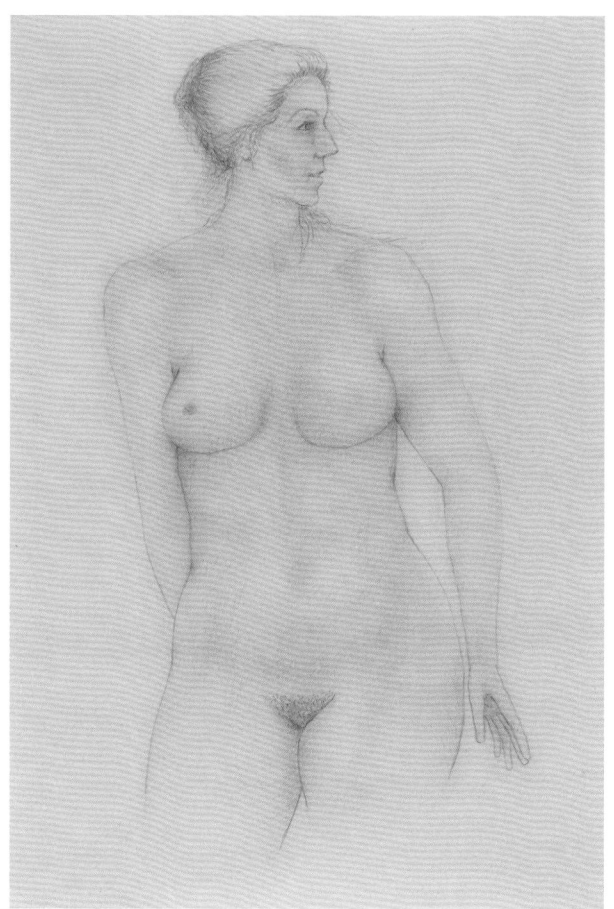

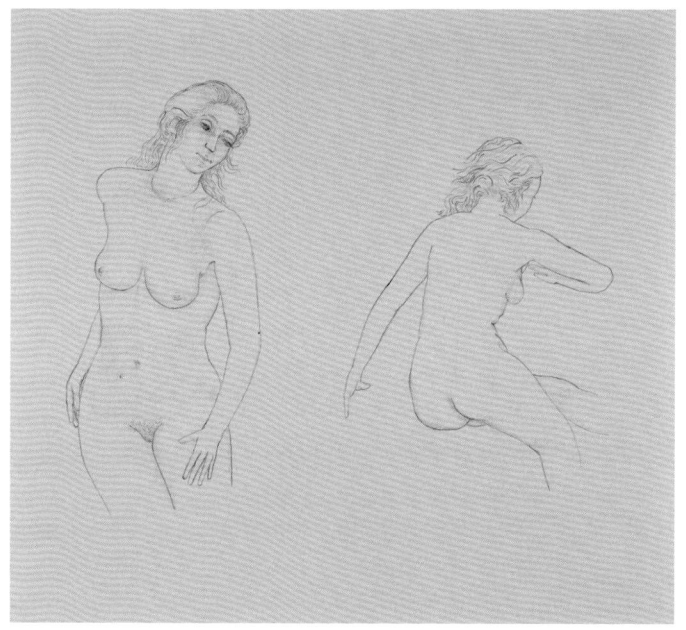

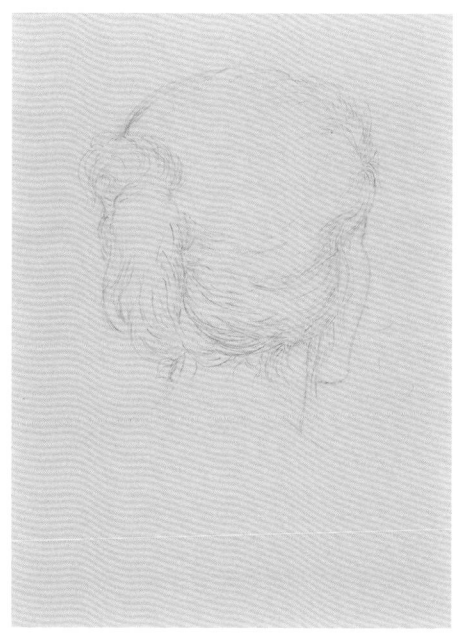

PLATE 78

Frontal Nude, 2017

Graphite on paper, 19 × 13 inches
Collection of the artist

PLATE 79

Two Figures in Motion, 2017

Graphite on paper, 15 × 7 inches
Collection of the artist

PLATE 80

Ellen, 2016

Graphite on paper, 11 × 8½ inches
Collection of the artist

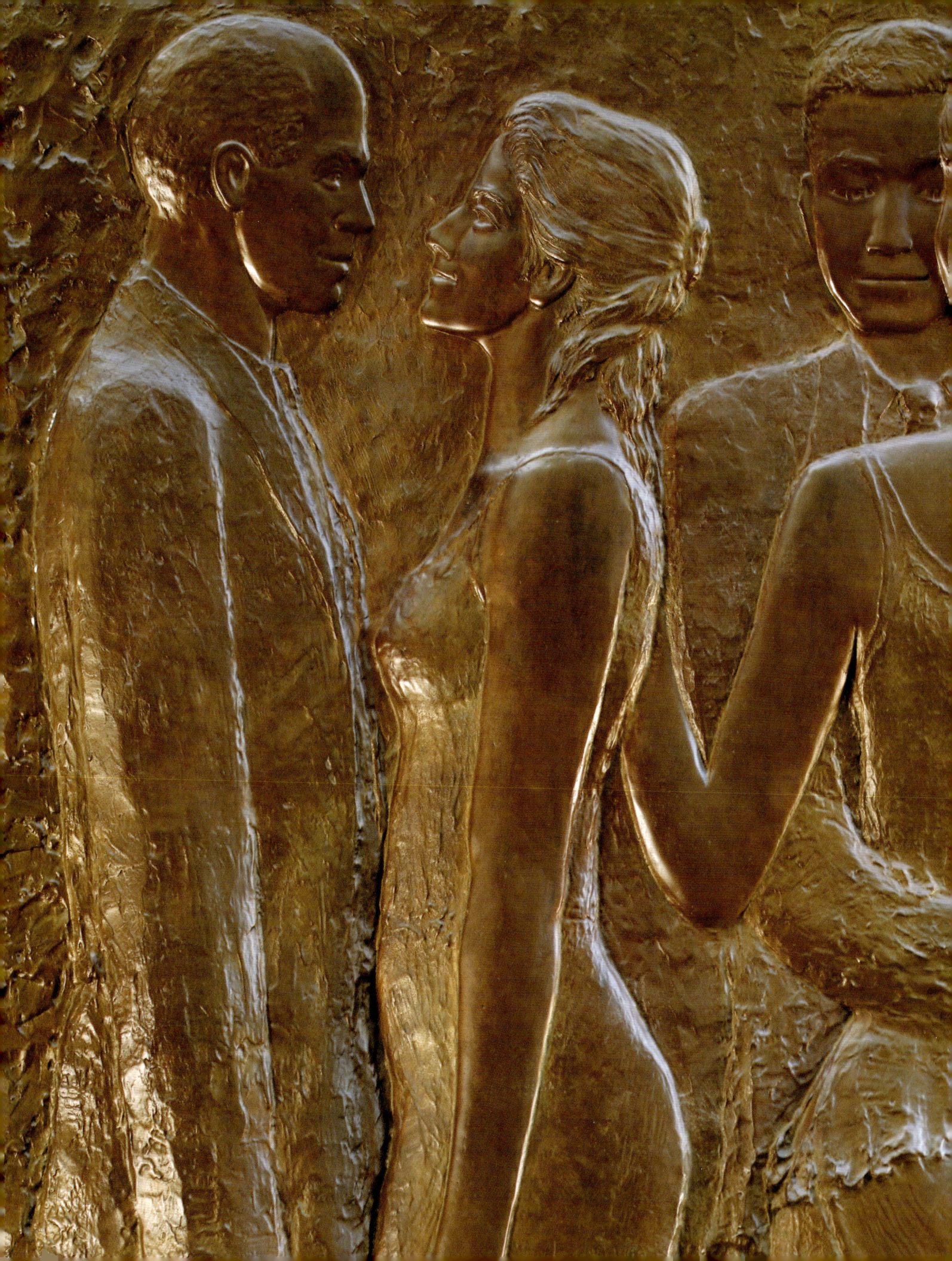

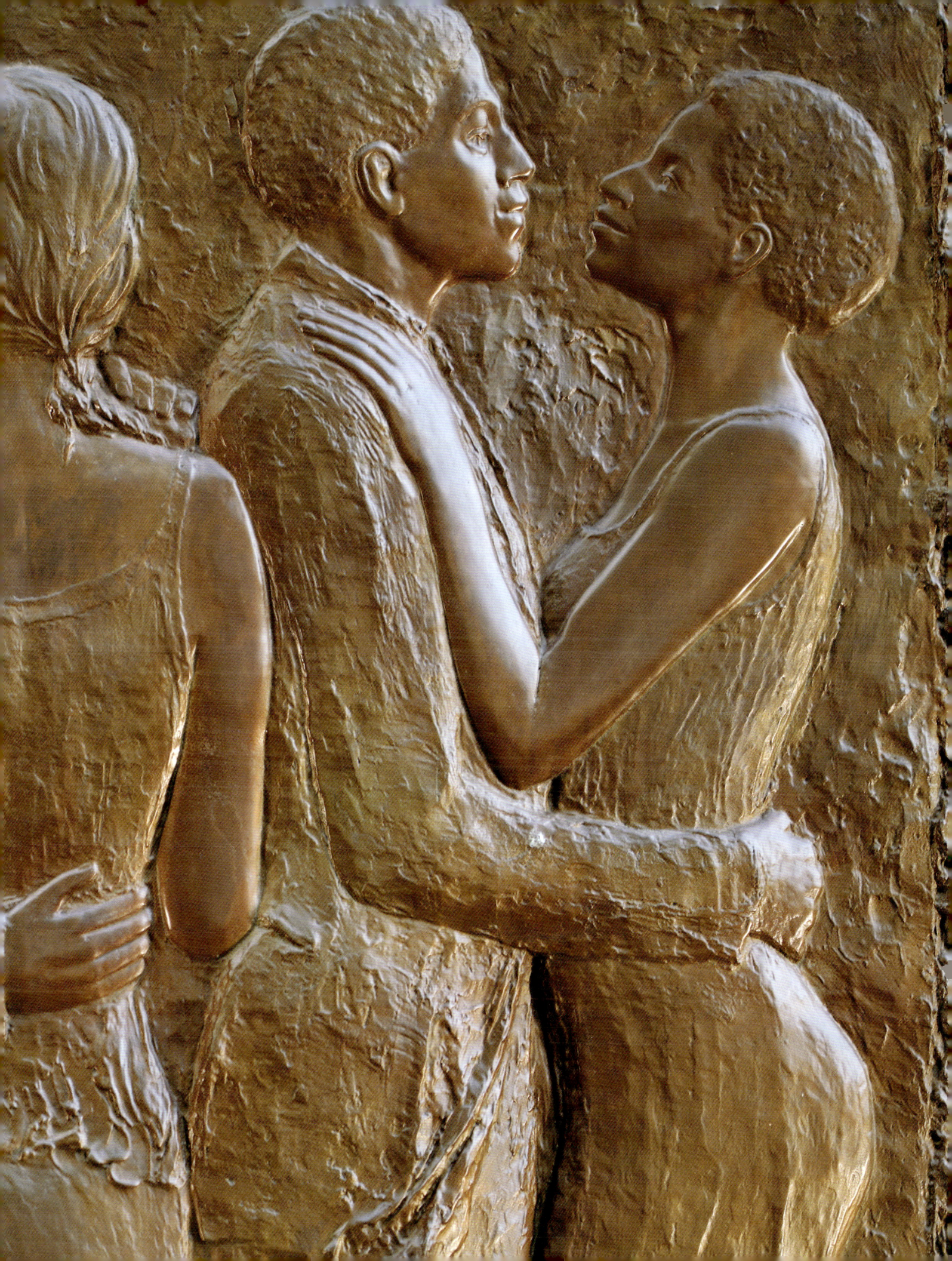

Chronology
and Exhibitions

Selected one-person and group shows are listed in bold-face type.

1936   Born George Rioch Anthonisen on July 31 in Boston, Massachusetts, the middle of three brothers, to Drs. Niels Landmark and Margaret Rioch Anthonisen. Niels, a psychoanalyst, emigrated from Norway in 1927, and Margaret Rioch, a child psychiatrist, emigrated from Canada the same year. They met at Johns Hopkins University, in Baltimore, Maryland.

1941   Niels Anthonisen takes a position at a psychiatric facility in Brattleboro, Vermont. George is diagnosed with dyslexia and is tutored by Elizabeth (Betty) Clark Gunther. The tutoring continues until he is twelve years old.

1946   Anthonisen family moves to Hanover, New Hampshire. George discovers the work of Mexican muralist José Clemente Orozco in the Baker Library at Dartmouth College.

1953   George enrolls at Sidwell Friends School in Washington, DC, to repeat his junior year.

1955   Graduates from Sidwell Friends School and enlists in the US Army, where he serves for two years. He is stationed in Hanau, Germany, and visits the Louvre, in Paris, for the first time.

1958   Enrolls at the University of Vermont.

1959   Professor Robert W. Cochran introduces Anthonisen to the world of ideas through English literature.

1960   During his third year at the University of Vermont, Anthonisen takes a class in sculpture taught by Paul Aschenbach, which he likens to a religious conversion.

1961–64   Graduates from the University of Vermont with a bachelor of arts in English and moves to New York City. With parents' financial help and emotional support, he studies at the National Academy of Design (1961–62) with Adolph Block, Paul Fjelde, and Douglas Gorsline and at the Art Students League (1962–64) with José de Creeft and John Hovannes.

1966   Marries Ellen Friedman.

Anthonisen, **Hopkins Center, Dartmouth College, Hanover, New Hampshire.** First solo exhibition.

Begins work on HEROIC TORSO.

1967   Undertakes study of anatomy through the dissection of cadavers at Dartmouth Medical School.

Receives a National Sculpture Society scholarship for further study at the National Academy of Design.

Begins teaching at Fairleigh Dickinson University, Rutherford, New Jersey.

Daughter Rachel is born.

Begins work on STANDING NUDE, modeling directly in plaster.

1968 *George Anthonisen Sculptures, Herbert Tobias Monotypes*, **Fairleigh Dickinson University, Rutherford, New Jersey.** Two-person show with Herbert Tobias.

Receives James Augustus Suydam Bronze Medal from the National Academy of Design.

Creates FAMILY GROUP, the artist's first public commission, for Mary Hitchcock Mental Health Center (now Dartmouth Hitchcock Medical Center, Lebanon, New Hampshire).

1969 *Recent Sculpture and Fresco: George R. Anthonisen*, **Center Art Gallery, New York** (Evelyn Marks, gallery owner and director).

Creates CAIN AND ABEL bas-relief, commissioned for MacNab Presbyterian Church, Hamilton, Ontario.

Completes HEROIC TORSO.

Begins studies for portrait of GEORGE GERSHWIN.

Leaves teaching position at Fairleigh Dickinson.

1970 Son Daniel is born.

Margaret Rioch Anthonisen dies.

1971 Moves to Solebury, Bucks County, Pennsylvania, on May 14.

Receives sculptor-in-residence fellowship from the US Department of the Interior at the Augustus Saint-Gaudens National Historical Park, Cornish, New Hampshire.

During the residency at Saint-Gaudens, creates THREE SOLDIERS, the first of five anti-war memorials, and RECLINING NUDE bas-relief.

Brother Theodore (Ted) Anthonisen, an art collector, commissions three bas-reliefs. For the next fifteen years, Ted continues to either commission or purchase work.

Explores ideas that will lead to DYNAMIC TORSO.

Exhibits small relief in the National Academy of Design annual exhibition.

1972 Meets Fred Clark, who goes on to purchase twelve works during the next seven years, exhibiting sculptures on a continuously rotating basis at the Fred Clark Museum in Carversville, Pennsylvania.

Starts forty-year association with Richard Polich and his foundry, Tallix.

Completes GEORGE GERSHWIN bronze portrait head.

1973 Elected member of the National Sculpture Society.

1974 *Recent Work: George R. Anthonisen, Paul Matthews*, **Stover Mill, Erwinna, Pennsylvania.** The artist's first show in Bucks County. Exhibits with painter Paul Matthews. The real estate section of the *New York Times* features both artists and their move to Bucks County.

GEORGE GERSHWIN presented to Carnegie Hall by Frances Gershwin Godowsky, Leontyne Price, and Carnegie Hall director Julius Bloom.

HINDMAN MEMORIAL/THE BOOK is commissioned and placed at Bush Hill United Presbyterian Church, Alexandria, Virginia.

Completes STANDING NUDE.

1975 STANDING NUDE purchased via the United Negro College Fund by an anonymous patron. Sculpture installed at Clark Atlanta University in the Trevor Arnett Library.

Begins work on MURDER: CAIN AND ABEL. Begins work on DYNAMIC TORSO.

1976 Wins national competition sponsored by the Alaska State Council on the Arts to create a seven-foot bronze figure of the late SENATOR ERNEST GRUENING for the US Capitol, Washington, DC.

Advances to fellow of the National Sculpture Society.

Creates DEATH AND STARVATION. Completes DYNAMIC TORSO. Completes MURDER: CAIN AND ABEL.

1977 Standing figure of SENATOR ERNEST GRUENING installed in the US Capitol Hall of Columns; later moved to Emancipation Hall, Capitol Visitor Center, Washington, DC. Portrait bust of the senator installed at the University of Alaska.

Teaches at the Fashion Institute of Technology for one semester, but leaves despite invitation to join the faculty.

1978 Creates AWAKENING for a sculpture competition for the front of the State House in Cheyenne, Wyoming, the first state to grant women the right to vote. Though rejected, it is featured on the front page of the *Cheyenne Times*.

1979 Creates SWORD AND PLOWSHARE, inspired by the 1978 Camp David Accords, in which Egyptian President Anwar Sadat and Israeli Premier Menachem Begin signed two frameworks for peace in the Middle East.

Starts research and sketches for I SET BEFORE YOU THIS DAY.

Recent Paintings and Sculpture by George R. Anthonisen, **Gentle Winds Gallery, Doylestown, Pennsylvania.** For the first time, Anthonisen exhibits frescoes along with sculpture.

George Anthonisen, **Moody Gallery, Pasadena, California.**

1980 Niels Landmark Anthonisen dies.

1981 *Limited Edition Bronze Sculpture*, **Bjorn Lindgren Gallery, New York.** Sixteen-inch maquette of I SET BEFORE YOU THIS DAY shown for the first time.

Anthonisen: Recent Sculpture, Paintings and Rubbings, **Bjorn Lindgren Gallery, New York.**

Begins CREATION.

1982 Begins PICASSO portrait. Completes CREATION.

1983 Father-in-law Sylvan F. Friedman dies.

Begins work on RUDOLF SERKIN.

1984 Competition sponsored by the Johnson Companies, Newtown, Pennsylvania, results in commissioning of the JOHNSON CARYATID, an award presented to the Bucks County Volunteer of the Year annually for ten years. This work is the prototype for the monumental CARYATID created in 1996.

Completes PICASSO. Completes RUDOLF SERKIN.

1985   DEATH AND STARVATION purchased by Japanese philanthropist Ryoichi Sasakawa for the World Health Organization in Geneva, Switzerland.

Artists Three, Rodman House, Bucks County Council for the Arts, Doylestown, Pennsylvania. With painter Paul Matthews and sculptor/etcher Charles Wells.

Receives Exemplary Achievement in the Arts Award from Bucks County Chamber of Commerce.

Changes concept for I SET BEFORE YOU THIS DAY; adds one more figure, making it a ten-figure composition.

1986   **Anthonisen, University of Scranton Art Gallery, Scranton, Pennsylvania.**

Begins work on VIOLINIST.

1987   Completes VIOLINIST.

Completes I SET BEFORE YOU THIS DAY. Art patron Richard C. Strain underwrites bronze casting of the work.

Through the efforts of Rabbi Jeffrey K. Salkin, Pastor Robert H. Linders, and Reverend Joseph C. Olczak, OSP, I SET BEFORE YOU THIS DAY is the focus of three interfaith services in Doylestown: it is shown in plaster at Temple Judea of Bucks County and St. Paul's Lutheran Church, and in bronze at the National Shrine of Our Lady of Czestochowa on the occasion of the thirty-ninth anniversary of *Kristallnacht*.

Celebration of the Figure: Selected Members of National Sculpture Society, Port of History Museum, Philadelphia, Pennsylvania.

Creates ANTIGONE maquette.

1988   **Contemporary Sculpture of the Region: Inaugural Exhibition of Twentieth-Century American Art, James A. Michener Art Museum, Doylestown, Pennsylvania.** DYNAMIC TORSO and I SET BEFORE YOU THIS DAY are among the featured sculptures.

Begins work on SUNNYSIDE UP and ANTIGONE.

Meets art representative Rosa Giletti, who connects him with Michael Schantz, former director of Woodmere Art Museum.

1989   **Anthonisen: Sculpture and Frescoes, Joy Berman Gallery, Philadelphia.**

I SET BEFORE YOU THIS DAY purchased by Bucks County residents Mark and Helene Hankin.

I Set Before You This Day and accompanying material exhibited in the Rotunda, Cannon House Office Building, US Capitol, Washington, DC.

Begins work on QUIESCENCE.

1990   Completes QUIESCENCE.

I SET BEFORE YOU THIS DAY presented by Helene and Mark Hankin to the James A. Michener Art Museum and installed on long-term loan.

Three frescoes installed at the Rittenhouse Hotel, Philadelphia.

1991   **Images of Courage and Compassion, Millersville University, Millersville, Pennsylvania.** Contemporary artists confront the genocide of European Jews.

Completes SUNNYSIDE UP and ANTIGONE.

Art patron Richard C. Strain commissions casts of ANTIGONE, CREATION, SUNNYSIDE UP, QUIESCENCE, and VIOLINIST.

Begins three-dimensional version of GIVE US GRACE, the first of three versions of the work.

Images from I SET BEFORE YOU THIS DAY used for dinner honoring Edgar M. Bronfman, recipient of the Recognition of Goodness Award, given by the Jewish Foundation for Christian Rescuers/Anti-Defamation League of B'nai B'rith.

1992   Meets art dealer and gallery owner Frank Bianco, who becomes the artist's sole representation in the Philadelphia area.

Completes three-dimensional version of GIVE US GRACE.

Anthonisen, **Woodmere Art Museum, Philadelphia, Pennsylvania.** First museum show, featuring seventy-five sculptures, frescoes, and rubbings. Anthonisen shows the three-dimensional version of GIVE US GRACE for the first time and decides it is unsuccessful.

Begins work on seventeen-inch CARYATID maquette.

Through Rosa Giletti, meets Lisa Tremper Barnes (now Lisa Tremper Hanover), director of the Philip and Muriel Berman Museum of Art at Ursinus College; exhibition of sculpture and fresco is scheduled for fall 1996.

1993   Creates twenty-eight-inch-high double-sided, curved bas-relief of GIVE US GRACE, the second version of the work.

Images of I SET BEFORE YOU THIS DAY are used for a ceremony organized by the Jewish Foundation for Christian Rescuers/Anti-Defamation League of B'nai B'rith. In addition to honoring the people of Denmark on the Fiftieth Anniversary of the Heroic Rescue of the Danish Jewish Community, the ceremony honors E. Robert Goodkind, Esq., recipient of the Recognition of Goodness Award.

The Second Century: Contemporary Works Exhibition, **National Sculpture Society, New York.**

1994   *George R. Anthonisen New Work: Fresco and Sculpture,* **Bianco Gallery, Buckingham, Pennsylvania.**

Anthonisen: Sculpture and Fresco, **Images Art Gallery, New York.**

Executes DAWN.

MEDITATION is commissioned, seven feet in height, for private garden.

Twenty-eight-inch bas-relief GIVE US GRACE is shown for first time in plaster.

Begins to enlarge GIVE US GRACE. Completes CARYATID maquette.

1995   Completes MEDITATION.

Gale Nurseries Presents Sculpture in Harmony, **Philadelphia Flower Show, Pennsylvania.** Five Anthonisen sculptures are included: DYNAMIC TORSO, CREATION, HEROIC TORSO, MEDITATION, SUNNYSIDE UP. Presentation wins Best in Show.

Begins GAME OVER.

1996 Completes third, enlarged version of GIVE US GRACE and casts it in plaster.

Enlarges CARYATID and casts it in plaster.

Completes GAME OVER. Begins work on TEA PARTY maquette.

The Compassionate Spirit: Sculpture and Fresco by George R. Anthonisen, **Philip and Muriel Berman Museum of Art at Ursinus College, Collegeville, Pennsylvania.** CARYATID and GIVE US GRACE are shown in plaster.

1997 Ursinus College War Years Classes of 1942–1949 and the US Navy V-12 and V-5 Units commission PROMISE/ANTHEM, a World War II memorial.

Through the War Years Committee, meets Henry W. Pfeiffer, who becomes a lifelong friend and patron.

Develops maquette for PROMISE/ANTHEM.

Begins enlarging PROMISE/ANTHEM, two bas-reliefs, each six and a half feet high by eight feet long. Begins work on bas-relief of JACKIE ROBINSON.

Caring: Humanity's Hope for Survival—Its Foundations in Biological, Cognitive and Spiritual Fact, **Samuel Dorsky Symposium on Public Monuments, Monuments Conservancy, Time & Life Building, Rockefeller Center, New York.** I SET BEFORE YOU THIS DAY and ANTIGONE are exhibited and discussed by a panel of distinguished scholars.

Receives commission to create ALICE IN WONDERLAND for Please Touch Museum, Philadelphia.

Patron Peter Skirkanich contributes funds to create a series of maquettes for ALICE IN WONDERLAND.

Completes ALICE IN WONDERLAND and TEA PARTY maquettes.

1998 *George R. Anthonisen: Sculpture and Fresco,* **Bianco Gallery, Buckingham, Pennsylvania.**

Completes enlargement of PROMISE/ANTHEM.

PROMISE/ANTHEM installed in the War Years Lobby, Wismer Campus Center, Ursinus College.

Please Touch Museum selects standing figure of ALICE IN WONDERLAND to enlarge.

Receives commission to create RAOUL WALLENBERG MEMORIAL from the Institute for Jewish-Christian Understanding, Muhlenberg College, Allentown, Pennsylvania. Begins work on seven clay maquettes.

1999 Three maquettes for RAOUL WALLENBERG MEMORIAL presented to executive committee, which selects one maquette to enlarge.

Reflections on the Human Condition: Nine Sculptures by George R. Anthonisen, **Center for Interfaith Relations, Festival of Faiths, Gardens of Louisville, Kentucky.**

2000 Patron Richard C. Strain underwrites bronze casting of CARYATID and GIVE US GRACE.

The Art Gene: Anthonisen, Dodge, Gowen, Osterman, **James A. Michener Art Museum, Doylestown, Pennsylvania.**

Untimely death of Frank Bianco.

Continuing the Bucks County Landscape Tradition: 26 Artists Share Their Perspective of the

New Century, **Bianco Gallery, Buckingham, Pennsylvania, and Salmagundi Club, New York.**

2001   *The Garden of Eden*, **Memphis Botanic Garden Foundation, Tennessee.** Presented by Sculptureworks, Inc.

2002   ALICE IN WONDERLAND installed at Please Touch Museum.

Begins ON WINGS ASCENDING, a stainless steel and bronze memorial to 9/11.

Creates DIALOGUE maquette.

Four years after commission, receives notice that RAOUL WALLENBERG MEMORIAL will not occur.

Sherrie Bianco closes Bianco Gallery. Lauren Travis invites Anthonisen to join Travis Gallery, New Hope, Pennsylvania.

2003   Enters ON WINGS ASCENDING II MEMORIAL, created in conjunction with Gale Nurseries, in nationwide competition for the World Trade Center site.

Artists of the River Towns, **Philadelphia Sketch Club, Pennsylvania.** Receives honorary membership.

Begins full-size DIALOGUE. Completes bas-relief of JACKIE ROBINSON and casts it in bronze.

2004   Completes DIALOGUE. Begins GENERATIONS and RISING.

Meets art representative Peter Aaronson.

2005   Mother-in-law Maxine K. Friedman dies.

Completes GENERATIONS. Begins bas-reliefs WEDDING I and WEDDING II.

Sculpture Along Bear Creek, **Sculptureworks, Inc., Keller, Texas.**

Aaronson communicates with Gary Haller, headmaster at Jonathan Edwards College, Yale University, to explore possibility of an exhibition.

2006   Completes RISING, WEDDING I, and WEDDING II. Begins bas-relief THREE NUDES.

The Sculpture of George R. Anthonisen, **Jonathan Edwards College, Yale University, New Haven, Connecticut.** Eighteen sculptures are exhibited.

2007   Begins ASPIRATION. Completes THREE NUDES.

Life in Bronze: The Sculpture of George Anthonisen, **the Cooley Gallery, Old Lyme, Connecticut.**

Anthonisens gift selected bronze sculptures, frescoes, maquettes, and works in plaster to the Philip and Muriel Berman Museum of Art at Ursinus College.

2008   Completes ASPIRATION.

2009   Receives commission to create bas-relief honoring HENRY W. PFEIFFER and the founders of the Berman Art Museum at Ursinus College.

Receives honorary degree, doctor of humane letters, from Ursinus College.

2010   Completes HENRY W. PFEIFFER bas-relief. Begins FIVE WOMEN and SERENITY.

Seven bronze sculptures by Anthonisen are installed on the Philip and Muriel Berman Foundation Sculpture Terrace at the Berman Museum of Art at Ursinus College as part of the museum's permanent collection.

2011   Begins PRAYER. Completes SERENITY.

2012   Completes FIVE WOMEN. Works on a series of small bas-reliefs.

       RUDOLF SERKIN bas-relief presented and installed in Curtis Institute of Music, Philadelphia.

2013   Begins bas-relief portrait of RACHEL.

2014   Completes PRAYER and RACHEL. Begins relief of ELLEN.

2015   Destroys relief of ELLEN but reworks and keeps fragment. Begins large circular relief, works on it for most of the year, but destroys it and reworks fragments.

       The Rodin Legacy, **James A. Michener Art Museum, Doylestown, Pennsylvania.** An exhibition of fifty-two works by Auguste Rodin from the Cantor Collection, augmented by a small show of sculpture and drawings by contemporary American artists.

       When I Was Here, **Augustus Saint-Gaudens National Historical Park, Cornish, New Hampshire.** A retrospective exhibition of the Sculptor-in-Residence program, the oldest artist residency in the National Park Service, on the fiftieth anniversary of the park.

2016   Begins BOTTOMS UP.

       Invited to participate in Senior Artists Initiative, resulting in a videotaped oral history interview with the artist.

2017   Completes BOTTOMS UP. Begins CONVERSATION.

       Anthonisens gift CARYATID and GIVE US GRACE to the James A. Michener Art Museum.

2018   Begins work on THE SEEKER. Works on fragment portrait of ELLEN. Begins bas-relief of LISA TREMPER HANOVER. Begins bas-reliefs TRIO I and TRIO II.

2019   Completes bas-relief of LISA TREMPER HANOVER.

2020   Completes ELLEN, THE SEEKER, CONVERSATION, TRIO I, and TRIO II. Begins bas-relief portrait DANIEL III and THE RAPE OF JUSTICE.

       JACKIE ROBINSON bas-relief gifted by its owner to Jackie Robinson Museum, New York.

       Bucks County Artists: A Cross Section, **Hicks Art Center, Bucks County Community College, Newtown, Pennsylvania.**

2021   Completes THE RAPE OF JUSTICE and bas-relief portrait of DANIEL III. Begins portrait of son-in-law MICHAEL ANTHONY GATES.

       Theodore (Ted) Anthonisen dies.

       Named fellow emeritus of National Sculpture Society, along with fellow sculptor Bruno Lucchesi.

2022   Reworks head of *Caryatid*, titled TRANSCENDENCE. Completes bas-relief of MICHAEL ANTHONY GATES. Begins bas-relief of RICHARD WEIL.

       Receives commission to create reduction of *I Set Before You This Day*, titled THE CHOICE.

2024   Completes THE CHOICE.

       George R. Anthonisen: Meditations on the Human Condition, **James A. Michener Art Museum, Doylestown, Pennsylvania.**

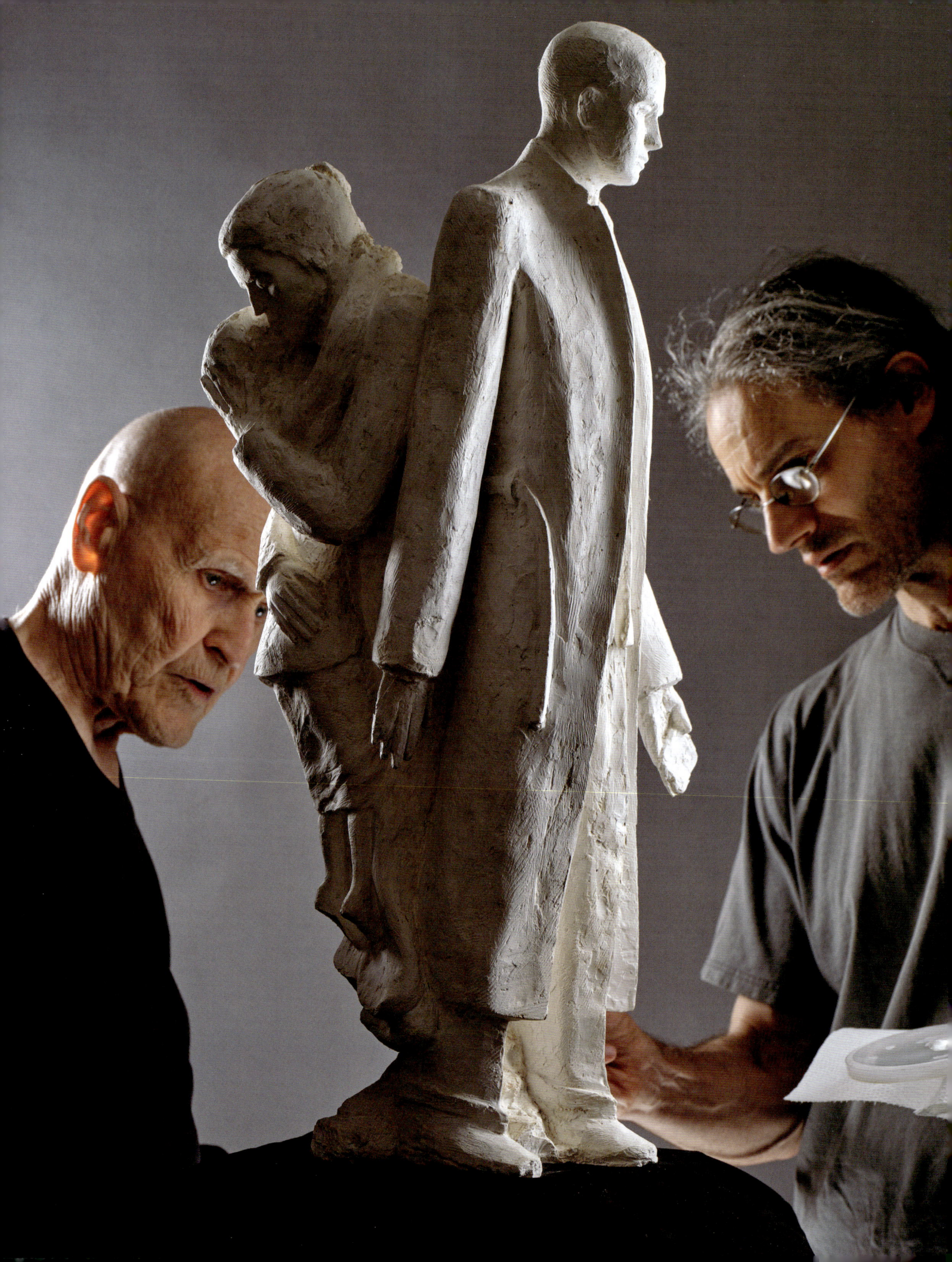

Contributor Biographies

Clarisse Fava-Piz, PhD, is assistant curator of European and American art before 1900 at the Denver Art Museum. She holds a PhD from the University of Pittsburgh and is a specialist of nineteenth- and early twentieth-century sculpture in Europe and the Americas. She previously worked at the Musée du Louvre, the National Gallery of Art, and the Getty Research Institute, among other institutions. Most recently, she was the 2021–23 Mellon Curatorial Fellow at the Meadows Museum at Southern Methodist University, where she curated the exhibition *In the Shadow of Dictatorship: Creating the Museum of Spanish Abstract Art* (2023) in partnership with the Fundación Juan March in Madrid. She was the primary editor of its accompanying catalogue. Her research and curatorial projects have been supported by the Smithsonian American Art Museum, the Terra Foundation for American Art, the Casa de Velázquez, and the Center for Curatorial Leadership.

Lisa Tremper Hanover initiated physical, programmatic, and operational transformations for the organizations in her charge in her forty years as a museum professional. In her broader role as a senior leader in the cultural field, she has had a positive impact on art and history museums, humanities organizations, and other nonprofit entities. Hanover was named director and chief executive officer of the James A. Michener Art Museum (2012–17) after a successful tenure as director of the Philip and Muriel Berman Museum of Art at Ursinus College (1987–2012). She later served as the interim director of operations for the Berman Museum of Art (2020–21). Hanover has been an active peer reviewer for the American Alliance of Museums (AAM) excellence programs for eighteen years. She currently serves the cultural field as a consultant specializing in organizational reviews, strategic planning, collection assessments, and preparing institutions for AAM accreditation. Hanover is an enthusiastic and knowledgeable public speaker. In addition to presenting at numerous regional and national conferences, she has juried over one hundred art exhibitions and public art commissions.

Laura Turner Igoe, PhD, is Gerry and Marguerite Lenfest Chief Curator at the James A. Michener Art Museum, in Doylestown, Pennsylvania. She previously held curatorial and research positions at the Philadelphia Museum of Art, the Princeton University Art Museum, the Harvard Art Museums, and the Barnes Foundation. A co-editor of *A Greene Country Towne: Philadelphia's Ecology in the Cultural Imagination* (Penn State University Press, 2016), she has contributed essays to the journals *American Art*, *Panorama*, and *Commonplace* and the exhibition catalogue *Nature's Nation: American Art and Environment* (Princeton University Press, 2018). At the Michener, she curated *Impressionism to Modernism: The Lenfest Collection of American Art* (2019) and *Rising Tides: Contemporary Art and the Ecology of Water* (2020), and she co-curated *Through the Lens: Modern Photography in the Delaware Valley* (2021), *Daring Design: The Impact of Three Women on Wharton Esherick's Craft* (2021–22), and *Never Broken: Visualizing Lenape Histories* (2023–24).

George R. Anthonisen and Daniel Anthonisen
touching up *Raoul Wallenberg I* (1998–99), 2023.

149

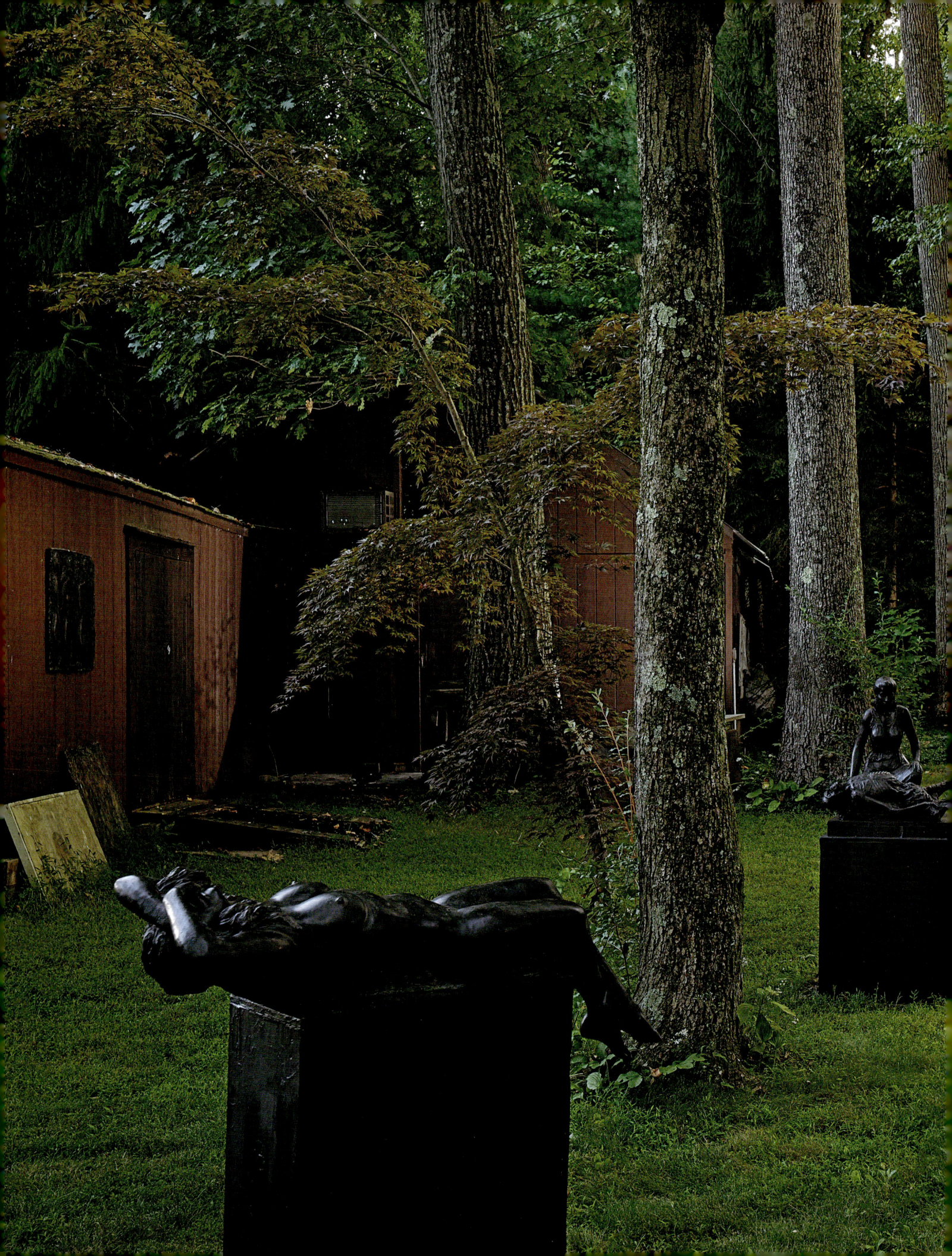

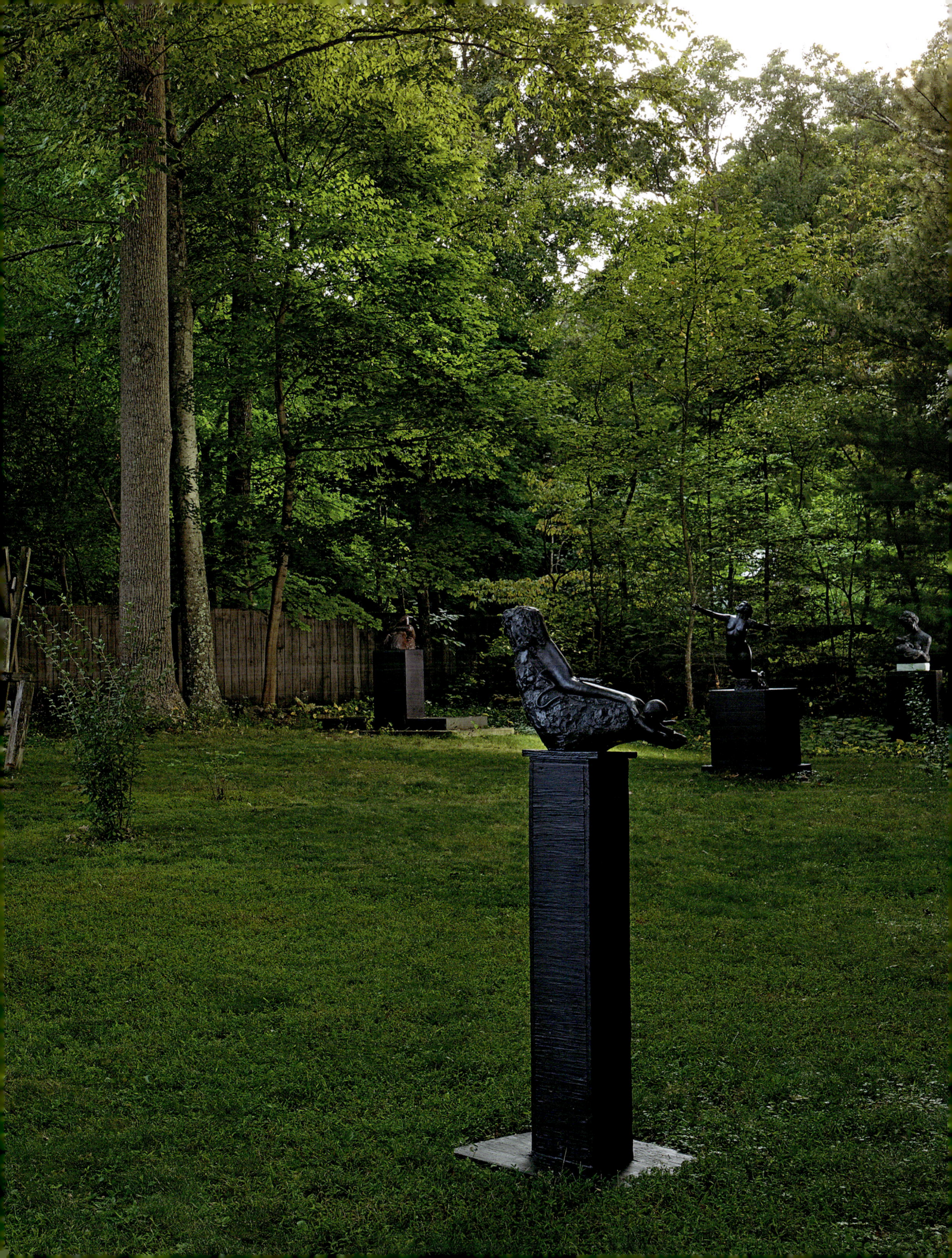

This book is published in conjunction with the exhibition *George Anthonisen: Meditations on the Human Condition*, presented at the James A. Michener Art Museum, Doylestown, Pennsylvania, from April 20 through October 13, 2024.

Funding for this catalogue was generously provided by Cherry and Eddie Robinson.

Support for the exhibition was generously provided by Carol and Louis Della Penna, the Byers Family, Ann and Daniel Bernstein, Kathy and Ted Fernberger, and the Estate of Henry W. Pfeiffer.

Library of Congress Control Number: 2023949064
ISBN 978-1-879636-18-7

Published by the James A. Michener Art Museum
www.michenerartmuseum.org

Distributed by the University of Pennsylvania Press
www.pennpress.org

Produced by Marquand Books, Seattle
www.marquandbooks.com

Edited by Kristin Kearns
Designed by Thomas Eykemans
Typeset in Adobe Jenson Pro by Maggie Lee
Proofread by Ted Gilley
Color management by I/O Color, Seattle
Printed and bound in China by Artron Art Group

Note: For dimensions, height precedes width precedes depth.

Front and back cover: Plates 21–22.
Page 2: Detail of Plate 47.
Page 4: Detail of Plate 43.
Page 52: George R. Anthonisen (b. 1936), *Serenity* (back), 2010–11. Bronze, 13 × 15 × 10 inches. Edition 2/9. Collection of the artist.
Pages 56–57: George R. Anthonisen (b. 1936), *Aspiration*, 2007–08. Bronze, 35 × 30 × 29 inches. Edition 1/9. Collection of the artist.
Pages 138–39: Detail of Plate 42.
Pages 150–51: The Anthonisens' backyard sculpture installation, 2023.

Photography Credits

Page 6: Photo by Carla M. Klouda. Page 15: Photo by Robin Johnstone. Pages 8, 52, 56–57, 148, 150–51: Photos by Christian Giannelli.

Challenges, Triumphs, and Resilience: A Biography of George R. Anthonisen

Figures 1, 3, 8: Photos by Christian Giannelli. Figure 2: Photo courtesy of the *Doylestown Intelligencer*. Figures 5, 16: Photos by John Hoenstine. Figure 7: Photo courtesy of Scala / Art Resource, NY. Figure 9: Photo by Francis King. Figure 10: Image copyright © The Metropolitan Museum of Art. Image source: Art Resource, NY. Figure 11: Photo by Michael E. Myers. Figures 12–14: Photo by Charles W. Haney. Figure 17: Photo by Stephen Barth.

A Birth in Bronze: *Creation* in Context

Figures 1, 4–5: Photos by Christian Giannelli. Figures 2–3: Photo by Charles W. Haney. Figure 6: Digital Image © The Museum of Modern Art / Licensed by SCALA / Art Resource, NY. © 2023 Estate of Pablo Picasso / Artists Rights Society (ARS), New York. Figures 7–8: Image copyright © The Metropolitan Museum of Art. Image source: Art Resource, NY. Figure 9: Photo courtesy of Scala / Art Resource, NY. Figure 10: Photo © Tate. © Jeff Koons. Figure 11: Reproduced with permission © ESO.

In Conversation with George R. Anthonisen

Figures 1, 4: Photos by Christian Giannelli. Figures 2–3, 6, 9–10: Image copyright © The Metropolitan Museum of Art. Image source: Art Resource, NY. Figure 7: Photo by Michael E. Myers. Figure 8: Photo by John Filo via Getty Images. Figure 11: Photo © 2023 Artists Rights Society (ARS), New York. Figure 12: bpk Bildagentur / Skulpturensammlung / Staatliche Kunstsammlungen/Dresden/Germany / Photo by Hans-Peter Klut / Art Resource, NY.

Plates

Plates 1, 8–9, 16–19, 31, 41, 44–46, 53–54, 59: Photos by Michael E. Myers. Plate 2: Photo by Charles W. Haney. Plates 25–28, 70–71: Photos by Stephen Barth. Plates 3–7, 11–15, 20–24, 29–30, 32–40, 42–43, 47–52, 55–58, 60–66, 69, 72–80: Photos by Christian Giannelli. Plates 67–68: Photos by Ellen Anthonisen.